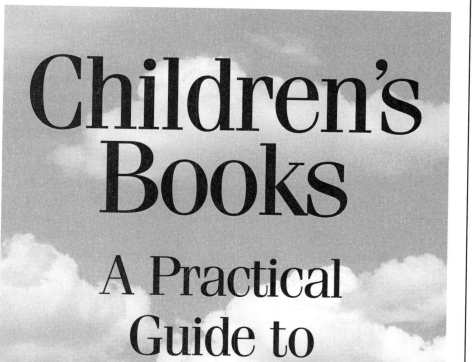

Children's Books

A Practical Guide to Selection

Phyllis J. Van Orden

Sunny Strong

Neal-Schuman Publishers, Inc.
New York   London

Published by Neal-Schuman Publishers, Inc.
100 William St., Suite 2004
New York, NY 10038

Printed and bound in the United States of America.

The paper used in this publication meets the minimum requirements of American National Standard for Information Sciences—Permanence of Paper for Printed Library Materials, ANSI Z39.48-1992.∞

ISBN–13: 978-1-55570-584-8
ISBN–10: 1-55570-584-7

Library of Congress Cataloging-in-Publication Data

Van Orden, Phyllis J.
  Children's books : a practical guide to selection / Phyllis J. Van Orden, Sunny Strong.
    p. cm.
  Includes bibliographical references and index.
  ISBN 978-1-55570-584-8 (alk. paper)
  1. Children's libraries—Book selection. 2. Children—Books and reading—United States. 3. Children's literature—Bibliography. I. Strong, Sunny. II. Title.
  Z718.1.V335 2007
  025.2'187625—dc22
                                                        2007007642

Table of Contents

APPENDICES: Selection Support Tools

List of Figures

List of Color Plates

*Indicates double-page spread

All color plates are used by permission.

List of Stoplights, Spotlights, and Boxes

LIST OF BOXES

Preface

How do you buy the right books for the children in your school or community? How do you avoid adding any more "shelf sitters" to your collection? How do you tackle the task of consistently selecting quality, relevant titles? *Children's Books: A Practical Guide to Selection* presents a two-fold approach to the process. First, this handbook offers thorough, comprehensive, annotated lists of recommended titles; second, it details key strategies for *how* to choose materials by utilizing easy-to-learn criteria and effective principles.

We, the authors, through our many years of experience in school libraries, public libraries, and education of children's and school librarians, have discovered that selecting quality children's books is both a skill and an art. We planned and wrote *Children's Books: A Practical Guide to Selection* for novice librarians and seasoned professionals alike.

The information can be used equally well by individuals or by a group making selection decisions (such as for opening-day collections or major purchase decisions). We planned the questions-to-consider criteria as a way to spark debate, discuss individual volumes, or compare titles on the same subject. Evaluating the merits of a book and balancing that information with your institution's needs will help make final choices both creative and reasoned. Recognizing that school and public libraries have different missions and thus different collection development goals, we have peppered all the chapters with a feature called "Spotlights" and "Stoplights." They are direct calls of advice, notices, and warnings geared specifically to address the concerns of these two overlapping yet distinct audiences.

ORGANIZATION

Children's Books: A Practical Guide to Selection begins with a broad perspective on evaluation and then moves to more specific elements of selection decisions.

Part I, "Selecting Books for Children," explores the general criteria that apply to all materials and identifies basic selection resources.

- "The Selection Process," in the first chapter, introduces the process and explores ways in which children, selectors, and books can interrelate.
- Chapter 2, "General Criteria for the Selection Process," describes standards for evaluating all genres.
- Chapter 3, "Selecting a Diverse Range of Works," looks at the titles that feature a wide range of characters and the human condition, translations, and international and multicultural literature.
- Chapter 4, "Using Selection Tools Effectively," describes the major guides (print and electronic) and reviewing media.

The general background information in these four chapters lays the foundation to the next chapters, which concern particular interests.

Part II, "Special Selection Criteria for Specific Genres," shows how each type possesses unique characteristics that require different standards.

- Chapter 5, "Picture Books," examines illustrated works. The chapter defines artistic elements, describes composition and medium, and gives criteria for illustrations and wordless books.
- Chapter 6 surveys "Fiction."
- Chapter 7, "Fiction Genres," covers picture storybooks, historical fiction, fantasy, mysteries, animal stories, and sports stories.
- Chapter 8, "Folk Literature," gives selection criteria for folktales, fables, myths, legends, tall tales, and fairy tales.
- Chapter 9, "Rhymes and Poetry," describes Mother Goose, narrative poems, and lyric poems.

Part III, "Special Selection Criteria for Specific Subjects," looks at the other important books in the selection process.

- Chapter 10, "Information and Reference Books," addresses general standards for information books and reference works. Noting the ever-increasing dependence on electronic reference materials over paper, this chapter highlights print references which are still useful.
- Chapter 11, "Additional Subjects," shows how to apply the appropriate criteria to alphabet books, concept books, biographies, how-to-do-it books, mathematics, music, science and technology, social studies, and visual arts. Where appropriate, the questions reflect curriculum standards adopted by various professional organizations.

Each chapter opens with an introduction to the subject, and is followed by explanations of the terms associated with it, criteria on which to base evaluation, and questions that hone selection skills.

The listings of author, illustrator, and titles offer our recommendations of notable titles to consider.

You can glean additional information with:

- Resources featuring other books and Web sites to aid selection
- Spotlights, stoplights, boxes, and figures
- Appendices including a glossary (terms are highlighted in bold in the text), print and electronic resources, organizations, and sample policy statements

THE PURPOSE

All passionate librarians know the selection process is much more than just picking out books to purchase from an ever-increasing number of titles. We wrote *Children's Books: A Practical Guide to Selection* to show you *how* to choose using both universal and specific evaluation tools while holding on to a firm grasp of the unique collection mission of your individual institution. Our goal is simple. We want you to select the best variety of titles so you can offer the right book to the right child at the right time.

Acknowledgments

We gratefully acknowledge our appreciation to the publishers and individuals who granted permission for us to use their illustrations: Uri Shulevitz; Harcourt, Inc.; HarperCollins Publishers; Houghton Mifflin; William Morrow and Company, Inc.; and Penguin Group (USA) Inc.

Phyllis:

To Pat Pawelak-Kort, another note of appreciation for your help and support with the "behind-the-scenes" aspects of preparing a manuscript. To Pat Thurston, thanks for the support and assistance.

One of the fun and stimulating experiences is to discuss books with friends, such as Sunny, Adele Fasick, and Mary Anderson. From each of these individuals and many others, my insight into children's literature has been expanded and enriched. May our readers equally enjoy their discussions.

Sunny:

To my husband, Michael, and to Phyllis, for their steadfast encouragement.

PART I

SELECTING BOOKS FOR CHILDREN

Chapter 1

The Selection Process

CHOOSING BOOKS FOR CHILDREN

"Children deserve nothing but the best," is the mantra of Shankar, in full, Keshav Shankar Pillai (Codell, 2003: 209). The relationship among children, books, and selectors is the focus of this book. Each child is different; what is best for one child may not be the best for the next. We'll be exploring how the adult selector tries to meet this challenge.

Selecting books is a satisfying responsibility, one that calls for your knowledge of children: their growth and development, their interests and learning styles, their literature, their motivation and skills in reading both fiction and factual writing. Whether you are selecting a book to borrow or to purchase for an individual child, for the classroom, or for a library collection, you need to evaluate each title by applying appropriate criteria to make selections within your budget and to ensure the title will find anticipated users and meet their needs.

Box 1.1: Collection Development

For librarians, selection of individual titles is done within the context of *Collection Development*. This term encompasses the broad, overall, interacting processes of knowing the community: external environment and internal or the goals and objectives of one's institutional setting; assessment of needs; acquisition; knowledge of the internal and external collection (sources available in print, audiovisual, and electronic forms); establishment of policies, procedures, and criteria; maintenance: inventory, housing, circulation, weeding; dealing with fiscal

---

> and access issues: budgets, licensing, resource sharing, intellectual freedom; and evaluation of the collection. Appendix 4 provides examples of selection policy statements and identifies resources for the development of policies.

In addition to reading expert opinion about quality literature, listen to children. Ask what they like about a favorite book. Their answers will guide you as you decide which titles to select.

Be prepared to adjust your selection as new factors influence children's lives. As Eliza Dresang writes in *Radical Change*

> **Evaluation of books for children in the digital world may require thinking of literature in a different way** (Dresang, 1999: 254; original in bold).
>
> "Reading" [quotes in the original] no longer means interacting with words on the page alone. In an increasingly graphic environment, words and pictures are merging (Dresang, 1999: 65).

Selection is a lifelong learning experience. You'll learn about the limitations of your own interests, biases, preferences, and blind spots and, most importantly, how to put those personal traits aside and make professional decisions. This self-awareness will help you identify areas in which you will want to seek the opinion of others.

Figure 1.1: Relationship of Child, Book, and Selector		
Child	**Book**	**Selector**
The child is a person with growth/development needs such as social, emotional, moral, psychological, physical, and chronological. A child has interests and a specific gender.	A book contains the what of vocabulary, comprehension, phonetics, and appreciation and the why of inspiration, relaxation, information, learning, self-awareness, and identifying with others, vicarious experiences, literary preferences, visual preferences and heritage	The selector holds the responsibility to match the child with the right book. Knowledge of children, books. How to compare, evaluate, select, apply criteria, use resources, use opportunities for reading, sharing books

REVIEWING THE PRESELECTING PROCESSES

Before beginning the selection process, you need to know how to choose for the child by knowing:

- The range of quality in children's books
- The child or children's interests, developmental levels, reading abilities, and learning needs
- That a child's size, age, and grade alone do not determine reading level
- Whether the book is a "read alone" or a "read aloud" book
- What level of materials the child can handle

You also need to know how to choose for your institution by knowing:

- The current collection
- The current demographics and other characteristics of the community being served
- Your own biases to avoid rejecting items outside your personal beliefs, practices, and reading preferences
- Not to prejudge books by their candor, their subject matter, or their viewpoint
- The reality of budget constraints

Spotlight 1.1:   Selecting for Public Libraries

Know the library's mission and goals. In addition to understanding your budget for purchases, be familiar with all policies affecting selection.

   Read voraciously and study your collection so you know what is needed. Talk with children and take time to forward their requests to the appropriate selectors. Read community bulletin boards and local newspapers. Patronize businesses near the library so you understand the community and monitor its changes. Interact with local schools and other child-serving agencies. This aids your selection and also informs your programming and displays.

Spotlight 1.2: Selecting for School Libraries	

School library media specialists' selection decisions are guided by knowledge of the:

- district and school's philosophy, goals, policies, and procedures
- curriculum, teaching styles, and learning styles
- extracurricular activities sponsored by the school
- characteristics and needs of the children (physical, psychological, intellectual, informational, recreational, cultural, native language)
- program of the school library media center
- needs of the school's staff

EXAMINING SELECTING PROCESSES

The selection process involves:

- applying selection criteria that relate to literary and artistic elements
- applying criteria that relate to each book's intellectual content
- applying criteria that relate to the unique characteristics of the genre or subdivision that the book represents
- comparing a single book with others of the same subject or genre
- anticipating who will use a book, how they will use it, and why they might use it

ASSESSING SELECTING PROCEDURES

The selection procedures include understanding how to:

- consult and evaluate selection guides and reviewing media
- spend within the constraints of the budget
- provide full information about the specific title (usually provided on the **verso** [back] of the title page or at the end of the book); author, editor, reteller, compiler; titles; edition; place of publication; publisher; date of publication; **ISBN** (International Standard Book Number); and source
- document unmet needs to support future budget requests

Spotlight 1.3:   Who Does the Selecting?

Spotlight on Public Libraries

Experienced librarians will tell you many different answers and they may all be true! Some common configurations:

- Jobber selects small discretionary budget for local items.
- One person selects for the library system or independent library.
- A selection team formed of branch staff and management selects.
- Subject experts purchase in their specialty area.

Spotlight on School Libraries

You may encounter a variety of patterns for the handling of selection procedures:

- Each building level person may be responsible for the final selection decision for that building.
- The building level person may be chair of a selection committee composed of teachers and staff members who approve the selections.
- An approved selection list may be created at the district level for the majority of purchases with a limited amount of funds set aside for unique purchases (those not on the approved list).
- One jobber may be designated to handle the purchases for the district or the individual school.
- Some districts or regional educational units have examination collections, where one can look at new materials.
- Opportunities to discuss possible purchase ideas with other school library media specialists can be found in local professional associations, such as a citywide or county-level group. This organization may include public librarians and those from private institutions.

ESTABLISHING CRITERIA AND FOLLOWING GUIDELINES

This book identifies questions you will ask yourself when making selection decisions. There are criteria that apply to all books and others that apply to specific genres. As you evaluate books, you will find some criteria are more important than others for a specific title. Your knowledge of what is available, the needs and interests of the children using these books, and the needs of adults working with them can help you weigh the importance of any one criterion.

Our attention centers on the selection of **trade books** (general ones), those designed for library and home use, rather than **textbooks**, which are designed for instruction in a classroom. In trade books, the author generally uses a narrative (fiction, storybooks) or expository approach (nonfiction or factual books). More recent authors may use a nonlinear approach to the presentation.

Figure 1.2: Comparison of Traditional and Changing Characteristics of Writing		
Narrative	**Expository**	**Changes**
Story containing characters, plot, theme, and setting	Explains or sets forth information, reports events, actions, and behaviors	Text is nonlinear and nonsequential
Seeks to entertain	Seeks to inform	
Uses illustrations to extend text meaning	Uses illustrations to clarify or explain	A word's design or placement may represent sounds; words tell the story by their size, color, and position
	Written in present tense	Color may take place of words
Written in first person	Written in third person	
Uses dialogue	Organized by comparison/ contrast, cause-effect, and problem solving	Text may be super-imposed on a picture
Uses prose paragraph style		
Variety of writing styles	Uses information-giving words	Pictures, maps, or graphs play a dominant role
Concrete concepts related to experience	Uses headings and titles	Ending may be unresolved
Reader gets meaning from events and characters	Uses technical vocabulary that is not repeated	
	Terse writing style	
	Abstract concepts	
Reader suspends disbelief	Reader assumes information is accurate	Reader interacts with text and images
Plot holds reader's attention	Reader attends to organization of information	Reader depends on instinct
Reader may read material quickly	Reader uses flexible, slower reading rate	Reader's eye darts to visuals. Each reader attacks materials individually

CONSIDERING GENRE GUIDELINES

Genre refers to a type of literature sharing common characteristics. Literary elements (character, plot, setting, theme, point of view, style, and tone) function differently from one genre to the next. A specific element may be more significant in a particular genre than in others, but the distinction may be blurred. For example, when children seek information, the distinction between fiction and nonfiction may be unclear. Many fictional works provide information. Some nonfiction books are a blend of narrative and factual (exploratory) writing.

Figure 1.3:	Characteristics of Literary Elements in Various Genres				
Genre	**Character**	**Theme**	**Setting**	**Plot**	**Point of View**
Realistic	Characters reflect everyday life	Has a theme	Real and believable	Uses any kind of realistic conflict	Told from a particular point of view
Historical Fiction	Act, speak, and have values of time period	Relates to a historical period	Authentic	Focuses on time of stress or change	Told from a particular point of view
Fantasy	Characters believe in their experience/ may not be human	Conveys a universal truth	Imagery but believable	Uses conflict between good and evil or present and future	Narrator who influences the reader's acceptance of the story
Folklore	Flat and stock characters	Theme: moral with universal appeal	Backdrop	May be between people and animals	No time to go into characters' thoughts and feelings
Poetry	Regular or imaginary	Theme: universally understood message			Narrator
Biography	Real people	Theme of Universal Truth	Authentic	Believable problem or goal	Point of view or narrator
Informational	May explain or demonstrate behavior	Central issue or problem	Authentic and provides information		Point of view or narrator
Note: Style and tone depend on the author in all genres.					

BOX 1.2:   Using Award Books as Guides: The Newbery Award

One way to learn the range of "effective and able writers" is to read some of the Newbery Award and Honor books as a point of comparison with other titles. The Newbery Award is presented "annually to the author of the most distinguished contribution to American literature for children published in the United States during the preceding year" (Association for Library Service to Children, 2006) and administrated by the Association for Library Service to Children (ALSC), a division of the American Library Association. An important factor in this award is the following definition of *distinguished:*

- marked by eminence and distinction: noted for significant achievement
- marked by excellence in quality
- individually distinct (Association for Library Service to Children, 2006)

The committee considers:

- interpretation of theme or concept
- presentation of information including accuracy, clarity, and organization
- development of plot
- delineation of characters
- delineation of setting
- appropriateness of style
  (American Library Association, 2006)

BOX 1.3:   John Newbery

John Newbery, British publisher in 1744 of the first book designed to amuse children, *A Little Pretty Pocket-Book.* In 1765, he published the first novel written for children, *The Renowned History of Little Goody Two Shoes, Otherwise Called Mrs. Margery Two Shoes.*

The audience for the titles considered by the committee is composed of children up to and including age 14. The announcement is made during the midwinter meeting of the American Library Association, is available at the ALSC Web site, and is published in the spring issue of *Children & Libraries* and the February issue of *School Library Journal.* Figure 1.4 is a list of the Newbery Award books for the past 11 years.

			Figure 1.4: Newbery Award Recipients, 1997–2007

Title	Author	Publisher	Date of Publication/ Award
The View from Saturday	E. L. Konigsburg	Jean Karl/ Atheneum	1996/1997
Out of the Dust	Karen Hesse	Scholastic	1997/1998
Holes	Louis Sachar	Farrar, Straus & Giroux	1998/1999
Bud, Not Buddy	Christopher Paul Curtis	Delacorte	1999/2000
A Year Down Under	Richard Peck	Dial	2000/2001
A Single Shard	Linda Sue Park	Clarion	2001/2002
Crispin: The Cross of Lead	Avi	Hyperion	2002/2003
The Tale of Despereaux: Being the Story of a Mouse, a Princess, Some Soup, and a Spool of Thread	Kate DiCamillo	Candlewick Press	2003/2004
Kira-Kira	Cynthia Kodahata	Atheneum	2004/2005
Criss Cross	Lynne Rae Perkins	Greenwillow	2005/2006
The Higher Power of Lucky	Susan Patron	Simon & Schuster	2006/2007

Source: American Library Association. "Newbery Medal & Honor Books, 1922–Present." Chicago: ALA. (February 7, 2007) Available: www.ala.org/alsc/awardsscholarships/literaryawds/newberymedal/newberyhonors/newberymedal.htm

---

Spotlight 1.4:   Acquiring the Newbery Award-Winning Titles

Spotlight on School Libraries

The Newbery Award is prestigious. For school library media specialists, its prestige raises the question whether every library should have a copy of each winner. The answer is yes if you think the title will add to your collection and be used, and no if you think the title will be of limited use. One reason for taking the "no" position on specific titles is that the books considered for the award are written for people up to and including age 14. You may find that some of the plots, character developments, and themes are complex and beyond the comprehension level of the children you are considering. If you question the appropriateness of a title, borrow a copy and use it with a few children. You may be surprised at their reaction and their willingness to be challenged even though you may consider the book too mature.

SUMMARY

Children rely on adult selectors to provide a variety of books so that they can explore and learn. Being a selector is a gratifying experience that demands knowledge of books, people, and your situation. The responsibility calls for decision making based on the consideration of appropriate criteria. Learning which criteria should have the greatest weight in any given situation is part of a lifelong learning experience. Focusing on a child's needs, interests, and abilities should keep you grounded.

Chapter 2 identifies questions you will ask as you make selection decisions.

REFERENCES

American Library Association. "Newbery Medal & Honor Books, 1922–Present." Chicago, IL: ALA. (February 7, 2007) Available: www.ala.org/ala/alsc/awardsscholarships/literaryawds/newberymedal/newberyhonors/newberymedal.htm

American Library Association. "Newbery Terms & Criteria." Chicago, IL: ALA. (August 9, 2006) Available: www.ala.org/alsc/newbery_terms.html

Codell, Esme Raji. 2003. *How to Get Your Child to Love Reading*. Chapel Hill, NC: Algonquin Books of Chapel Hill.

Dresang, Eliza T. 1999. *Radical Change: Books for Youth in a Digital Age*. New York: H. W. Wilson.

Lukens, Rebecca J. 2002. *A Critical Handbook of Children's Literature*. 7th ed. Boston, MA: Allyn & Bacon.

Moss, Barbara. 2003. *Exploring the Literature of Fact: Children's Nonfiction Trade Books in the Elementary Classroom.* New York: Guilford Press.

RESOURCES

Association for Library Service to Children. 2006. *The Newbery and Caldecott Awards: A Guide to the Medal and Honor Books, 2006 Edition.* Chicago, IL: American Library Association. Annual.

Includes Sue McCleaf Nespeca's essay "Sharing Picture Books with Children to Promote Art Appreciation." Provides annotations for each of the books. Identifies media used in Caldecott books.

Horn Book and Association for Library Service to Children. 2001. *The Newbery & Caldecott Medal Books: 1986–2000.* Chicago, IL: American Library Association.

Opens with essays on the medal winners, followed by reviews from *Horn Book* and *Booklist* with the medalists' acceptance speeches.

Chapter 2

General Criteria for the Selection Process

LEARNING TO ASK THE RIGHT QUESTIONS

Selecting books for children to use at home, in their classroom, or in their school or public library involves more than an "I-like-this" approach. When purchasing a book for yourself, probably your first question is, Do I like it? or Does it meet my information needs? Your second may be, Can I afford it? Selecting a book for children, whether for purchase or to borrow from a collection, is more complex. This chapter identifies general guidelines to help you evaluate books. These guidelines, or criteria, serve as an aid in the selection process. There are many reasons for choosing a specific title, and knowing why you select a title is important.

The first step is to consider the book as communication. Will it be popular? Does it have literary appeal? These descriptions may not apply to the same title. Observe children's use of books to discover what is popular.

The questions posed in this chapter will help you develop your ability to judge quality in books.

Here are some general questions:

- Who will use the book?
- In what ways will they use it?
- Will this book appeal to children?
- Is this title or a similar work available to these children? Do they need access to both?
- Does this book offer new content or a new approach to the subject?

Selection decisions often are subjective. The purpose of establishing criteria is to guide selection decisions in an objective fashion. Applying the same criteria regularly leads to consistent decision making. You evaluate a book's content, physical form, and potential value to the users. This chapter focuses on general criteria related to the idea of the book (its intellectual content) and the book as a physical item. Later chapters will discuss multicultural aspects, international books, and criteria for specific genres and subjects.

The need for specific information or for a particular type of book may be more important than other criteria. As a selector, you will face conflicting needs. Members of the group for whom you are selecting books will have different needs or interests. Some will prefer one type of literature, others another.

Before you make your final selection, think about the following questions: What are the strengths of this book? What are its weaknesses? How does it compare with other books?

You want to avoid spending money on a shelf sitter. Here's some practical advice:

- Not all "good" books meet all the criteria.
- One can learn from one's mistakes.
- Most of us have selected at least a few shelf sitters. Try to figure out what prompted you to buy those books and avoid those actions in the future.
- Read and evaluate as many books as possible so you have points of comparison.
- Observe who uses which titles.
- Read or listen to what others say about a title and see if you agree with them.
- Be prepared to make hard decisions. Trying to meet a wide range of needs when faced with limited financial resources is not an easy task.
- Do not feel alone in the process. You can ask others to help. There are many resources, as you will discover throughout this book, including children's literature discussion Web sites, classroom teachers as subject experts, children's and school librarians as children's literature specialists, and the children themselves. Seek their opinions.
- Have fun as you learn about children's books!

QUESTIONING THE INTELLECTUAL CONTENT

What is the idea, the intellectual content, of the book? To judge the intellectual content, you need to apply specific criteria: (1) authority, (2) appropriateness of content to users, (3) scope, (4) accuracy of information, and (5) treatment. You also will be judging the book's organization, literary quality, and special features. All these factors will be weighed along with the number of books available on the subject, the reputation of the author and illustrator, and possible uses of the title. Translations and books in series raise more questions for you to consider and are presented in other chapters.

Is It Authoritative?

The term **authority** refers to the qualifications of the people who created the book. Questions to consider:

- What are the author's or illustrator's credentials?
- Has this individual written or illustrated similar works?
- How knowledgeable is this person about this subject or type of literature?
- Does the author acknowledge specialists who contributed to or checked the information in the book?
- Is there an author's note about the creation of the book or the source of the folktale?

You can look for information about authors and illustrators on the book jackets, in the preface of the book, in reference works such as *Something about the Author: Facts and Pictures about Authors and Illustrators of Books for Young People* (Gale Research, 1971—), or in their Web sites. Sometimes reviews include information about the author or illustrator. Other suggestions and examples are identified in "Resources" at the end of this chapter and in Appendix 2, "Complete Resources."

Is It Appropriate?

The content is appropriate if the reader understands the concepts, facts, and fantasies. Questions to consider:

- Is the presentation appropriate for the reader's social and emotional development?
- Is the sense of humor one the reader will understand?
- Will the content be of interest to a child?

No one title will be appropriate for every child. Individual titles may appeal equally well to children at different developmental levels. As you talk with children, you will learn which books are appropriate or of interest to each of them.

Is It Accurate?

Information should be **accurate**. Questions to consider:

- Does the author distinguish opinions from fact?
- Does the author present unbiased opinions?
- Does the author credit the source of photographs?
- Is there an author's note? Does it identify the sources of information used to write the book?
- Is there an acknowledgment section crediting content consultants?
- Is the information up-to-date?

This last question is particularly important for books about science, technology, and political boundaries. Unfortunately, a recent publication date or copyright date does not ensure that this information is correct.

To check the accuracy of information, you can compare the information in the book with a variety of sources, including subject-oriented magazines and newspapers or Web sites of specialists (individuals or organizations). You also can consult subject specialists (teachers, school personnel, or parents who have an interest in the subject).

What Is the Scope?

Scope refers to the author's goal or the purpose of the book and the breadth and depth of coverage. Questions to consider:

- What is the purpose of the book?
- Does the purpose meet a known need?
- Does the author state the limitations of the book?
- Does the book present information with an introductory style, in detail, or in a technical manner?

Look for the statement of purpose in the introduction or preface of the book. Examine the table of contents and the index entries to determine the depth of coverage.

How Is the Treatment?

Treatment refers to how the author presents the material. The style of presentation should be appropriate for the subject and the potential use of the book. Words describing treatment include *instructional, authoritative, inadequate, superficial, concise, humorous, emotional, objective, entertaining, moralizing* (or *didactic*), *stimulating,* or *dull.* Questions to consider:

- Does the book appeal to and catch the attention of the reader?
- How does the book involve the reader?
- Does the book hold the reader's attention?
- Does it encourage problem solving by identifying issues or presenting more than one point of view?
- Does the book encourage creativity by suggesting open-ended activities?
- Does it stimulate readers to explore the subject further?
- Does it identify additional sources of information on the subject?
- Does the book deal with concepts the child can understand? If the concepts might be new to the reader, does the text explain them in terms the child will understand?
- Does the author use appropriate vocabulary?
- Does the text explain new terms? If the new terms are explained in a glossary or in footnotes, will this distract the child and affect the usefulness of the book?
- What role do visual materials (pictures, graphs, and charts) play in presenting the information? Are they an integral part of telling the story of the text? Do the visual materials provide information not found in the text? Are the visuals for decorative purposes, adding to the aesthetic appeal of the book but not providing additional information? Are charts simple and self-explanatory?
- Do the author and illustrator avoid stereotypes dealing with race, sex, and age?
- Does the book reflect our multicultural society?
- Will an adult need to help the child use the book? For safety reasons, children may need an adult to help them use books about science experiments, cookbooks, craft books, and how-to sports books.

Spotlight 2.1:   Selecting Information Books for Public and School Libraries

---

Spotlight on Public Libraries

Students, whether homeschooled or in classrooms, depend on the public library for a wide selection of information books. The reading level and formats should be as varied as the subjects to appeal to different types of learning styles.

Look for books on indoor and outdoor hobbies, sports, and arts to appeal to many different children. In fact, the books you choose may well provide introductory information to adults as well. Surprise the public with leisure time materials on activities they have yet to explore. Public libraries can be Idea Factories!

Spotlight on School Libraries

The emphasis given in the curriculum and by the teacher's methods strongly influence how books will be used. You can help teachers explore the possibilities.

You will also face the question of quality versus usefulness. In other words, the demand for information about a person, place, or thing may be so strong that you end up selecting a title that isn't of the highest quality. In such situations, one can only hope that a "better" book will soon appear. The "teachable moment" could disappear before the "better" item is available.

For the collection to be responsive to the curriculum, if literature or fictional works are not incorporated, you can find yourself in a situation where you depend on the local public library to provide the majority of the books to fill children's recreational needs. One hopes in such situations, that the children have easy access to the public library. If they don't, consider creating some working relationship with the public library to ensure that children have access to the wide range of books.

ASSESSING THE WORTH

Other aspects of a book that will influence your decision are the organization of information, the literary merit, special features, the reputation of author and illustrator, and possible uses.

Organization of Information

Organization affects how easily a reader can locate information. A well-organized text helps the reader move through the information. Common ways of organizing informational books include alphabetically, using classification schemes, geographically, chronologically, in tables, or statistically. Questions to consider:

- Does the information flow from one section to another?

- Does the author develop the content logically?
- Can chapters or sections of a book be used independently, or must they be read in sequence?
- Does the author emphasize important ideas?
- Is there a summary or review of the major points? (This may occur at the beginning of the book, at the end of each chapter, or in the final chapter.)
- Are differently sized types or fonts used to emphasize sections or ideas?

Literary Merit

Literary merit in narratives (fiction works) refers to how the author deals with the literary components (theme, plot, setting, character, and style). How literary merit applies to expository writing used for information books (nonfiction) is discussed in Chapter 10, "Information and Reference Books." For fiction works, the effective author uses these literary components to create a unity of presentation. One way to test for this unity is to read the book aloud, regardless of the genre. The significance of each component and the techniques for creating unity of presentation vary from genre to genre. Later chapters will discuss these differences.

Basic questions to ask:

- What is the theme or main idea?
- How does the author present the theme or main idea?
- Is the theme relevant to the child's age, life circumstances, and developmental stage?
- Are the plot, setting, characters, and style consistently organized?
- Does the author catch the reader's interest in the beginning?
- Does the author develop the plot logically?
- Does the story have a beginning, a middle, and an end?
- Is this a book in which the reader creates the ending, as in interactive stories in which the child chooses from several actions, each of which can lead to a different outcome?
- Does the author create plausible, but not predictable, changes and developments?
- Is the description of the time and place clear?
- Are time and place historically, geographically, culturally, and politically accurate?
- Are the characters convincing in their actions?
- Is the presentation style or genre appropriate to the theme?
- Does the choice of words and syntax create a mood or convey ideas?
- Does the author use an appropriate point of view (first person, second person, or third person) to tell the story?
- What is your impression of the total effect of the book?

Special Features

Special features (maps, tables, graphs, photographs, and other illustrative materials; additional text in the margins, glossaries, appendixes, indexes, bibliographies, and recommended reading lists) can be used independently of the main content. Questions to consider:

- Is this information accurately and completely indexed?
- If the information is chronologically arranged, is there a subject index to help the reader locate specific information?
- If the information is alphabetically arranged, are cross-references provided so the reader knows the terms used for the subject?
- Do chapter headings help locate information?
- How does the index help the reader locate information?
- What types of entries are included?
- Given the purpose of the book, will entries (access points) for authors, titles, illustrators, illustrations, first line of a poem, or other subjects be helpful?
- Are there cross-references in the index? (Test the index by using differing terms that mean the same thing.)
- How easy is it to find information in the book?
- Is a different size of type used to emphasize selections or illustrations?
- Are the titles in the bibliographies and recommended reading lists for the child, an adult, or both?
- Is the bibliography limited to books, or are other media recommended?
- Is the bibliography annotated?

The value you see in these features can be a decisive factor when faced with a less-than-clear-cut selection decision.

Considering Author and Illustrator Reputation

There may be well-known authors and illustrators whose classics you want children to know. Questions to consider:

- Is this a title I want to introduce to children?
- With reissues of classics, is the artwork true to the original?
- Is this title up to the standard I expect from this person?
- Do children and adults use other works by this individual?
- Will adults help introduce these works to children?

Stoplight 2.1:   Author's or Illustrator's Reputation
Do not select solely on an author's or illustrator's reputation. Even well-established authors may have works of lesser quality and relevance.

Box 2.1:   Using Award Books as Guides: The Laura Ingalls Wilder Award

There will be other authors and illustrators whose works you think are important. The winners of the Laura Ingalls Wilder Award include such individuals. The award recognizes authors and illustrators for their substantial and lasting contribution to children's literature published in the United States. The award is annually announced at the midwinter meeting of the American Library Association, is available on the ALSC Web site at www.ala.org/alsc, and published in the spring issue of *Children & Libraries* and in the February issue of *School Library Journal*.

Laura Ingalls Wilder

American author, 1867–1957. The first recipient of the award named in her honor is the beloved author of the "Little House" stories, which chronicle her life in the Midwest from 1870 to 1894.

Figure 2.1: Laura Ingalls Wilder Award Recipients, 1992–2007

1992	Marcia Brown
1995	Virginia Hamilton
1998	Russell Freedman
2001	Milton Meltzer
2003	Eric Carle
2005	Laurence Yep
2007	James Marshall

Note: The Association for Library Service to Children administers the Laura Ingalls Wilder Award.
Source: www.ala.org/ala/alsc/awardsscholarships/literaryawds/wildermedal/wilderpast/wildermedalpast.htm (January 27, 2007).

EXAMINING PRACTICAL FEATURES

Possible Uses and Possible Users

As you evaluate books, you will want to think of each one's potential use. Basic questions to ask:

- Who will use the book?
- How will they use it?
- When will they use it?
- Is the subject or genre of interest to children?
- Will this book appeal to children who are not skilled readers?
- Is there more then one audience for this book?

Spotlight 2.2:   Asking Practical Questions

Spotlight on Public Libraries

- Do high circulation figures indicate more titles or copies are needed in a particular subject area?
- Which subject areas are of fleeting interest and could be served by less expensive paperbacks?
- Which titles should be purchased in sturdy library binding because they will get much use?

Spotlight on School Libraries

- Is this a subject of study in the curriculum?
- Is this subject or genre of interest to children?
- Will a student use this book to do a class assignment?
- Could a child use this book for personal information?
- Will a child seek this title for recreational reading?
- Will this book appeal to children who are not skilled readers?
- Can a teacher use this book in an instructional situation?
- Could a teacher or parent use this title for reading aloud?
- Is there more than one audience for this book?

Quality of Translations

Words translated into English from another language pose additional questions:

- Does the translation interfere or deter from the reading of the story?
- Are the translator's credentials listed?
- Additional questions are posed in Chapter 3, "Selecting a Diverse Range of Works."

Stand-Alone Title or Part of a Series

Titles in series often share common characteristics, but you need to judge each book separately. Several authors may write for an information series; not all of the writers may be equally effective.

Questions to consider:

- Does the author of each individual title meet the criteria you use with similar books?
- If one person is the author of all the titles in a nonfiction series, is that individual qualified to write on that range of subjects?

- If one person is the author of a series of fiction titles, is that writer able to sustain the reader's interest throughout the series?
- Can titles be read independently and out of sequence?
- If they are to be read in sequence, is it clear to the reader which title to read first?
- Is this information readily available on the cover, the title page, or the page facing the title page?

Physical Characteristics

The physical characteristics of the book include **binding**, size, weight, paper, cover, illustrations, and typography. You will judge them independently and collectively. A **trade edition** is a hardback book, such as one found in bookstores. A textbook is designed to be used in an instructional situation. A **prebound book** is one with a reinforced binding put on prior to its being sold. A **paperback edition** is a book with a paper binding. Which do you need? If you anticipate a high number of circulations of a picture book, you may want to consider a prebound or library bound edition. These bindings are sturdier than those found on trade editions. If you want duplicate copies or anticipate that the book will have limited use, paperback editions may be the best investment. If your school sponsors nature field trips, you may want a hardback identification book for the reference collection and a paperback copy to carry on the field trip. Professional reviews and selection tools frequently identify the editions available.

Box 2.2: Board Books

Board books are books with sturdy cardboard covers and pages. They are designed to withstand some rough handling by very young children. Alphabet books, concept books, wordless books, and very simple stories in this format serve as a fine introduction to books and reading.

Choose a variety of themes to please different ages. Babies like books with images of people's faces. They respond to illustrations with stark contrast, such as black and white. They hear the rise and fall of the voice reading the text to them. The text should be brief and direct. Toddlers "read" the illustrations in order to understand the concept or story. Attractive illustrations serve as a first introduction to art. In fact, board books can be a bridge to lengthier picture story books by the same authors and illustrators.

Questions to ask yourself as you evaluate board books:

- Is the art appealing?
- Is the subject of interest to toddlers?
- Is the text sparse?
- If a concept is being taught, is the language simple enough?

Some families and doctors' offices use this sturdy board format for practical reasons. They may wish to purchase titles appealing to older children, although this is not the primary audience for board books. Parents state their appreciation for public library collections having a good selection of board books. They can encourage their children to use these books without fear there will be torn pages. Providing short stories and wordless board books for children from birth to 2 years of age sends a powerful literacy message: share books with babies.

Stoplight 2.2: Board Books

Not all stories packaged as board books are suitable for babies and toddlers. Some have too many words or too sophisticated a text.

Spotlight 2.3: Board Books

Spotlight on School Libraries

When the school or an outside agency sponsors programs for toddlers, board books should be considered for the collection.

Oversize paperback books, or **big books**, are designed for use with large groups of children reading together. They require storage spaces similar to the bins one sees in poster and print shops. When evaluating these books, consider the following:

- Does this edition have the original artwork and text?
- Do the illustrations help the children read the text?
- How will you store this book?
- Does the content merit purchase as a big book?
- Do you have an easel to hold the book?

Books vary in size and weight. Think about the children who will use them. Can a young child turn the pages and handle the book with ease? To use one oversize atlas, children quickly learn they need to lay the book on the floor. Naturally this necessitates their lying on the floor as they locate the information they need. It is important to consult with adults serving children with special needs. You will then be able to provide materials in accessible formats.

Don't be surprised when children select books because of their size or weight. Some will pick a book they can carry in their pocket. Others will look for the thickest book in order to impress others. In these cases, recognize that the books are not being chosen for content, and indeed they may not be read.

The quality of paper in a book affects its use. Paper so thin that one can see the print from the next page through it is difficult for a new reader to use. Such thin paper also discourages students who are having reading problems.

Use of white spaces, lines, and size of **type faces** (points less than 1/72 of an inch) affect the ease with which a book can be read. **Leading**, the white space between lines, may be as big as the size of the type face (in this example, the typical 18 points) for beginning readers. Illustrations, border designs, and color can draw a reader's attention to information. Lines help outline figures, set off charts, and draw attention to a feature.

In *John Jeremy Colton* by Bryan Jeffrey Leech (Hyperion, 1994), illustrators Byron Glaser and Sandra Higashi use different point sizes of 22 fonts to emphasize the flow of the text and to underscore this story about differences. The opening endpapers are in black and white with only one house in green. The closing endpapers show multiple colors in the houses. This reflects the changes that take place in the story. The layout of the text moves around the page, making squiggles and other shapes. This adds to the aesthetic appeal; however, the reader ends up moving the book around in order to read the text, which is sometimes upside down. Trying to read this book aloud, while showing the illustrations to a group of children isn't easy, but it is fun.

Today's school-age children have discovered **graphic novels**. The term refers to a format for nonfiction titles as well as for novels. A graphic novel is a story told through a combination of pictures and text, usually in comic format.

Manga is a type of graphic novel, generally associated with Japan. The English versions may read from right to left and from "back" to "front." The comic panels vary in size and position. The **manga** reader can usually follow the story by moving to the panel where the character's eyes are directed.

Although many graphic novels deal with adult themes and contain adult images and language, others meet the needs of children who:

- are visual learners
- enjoy quick reads
- are intrigued by the extraordinary powers described
- like the page-turning action
- admire the graphics
- delight in a series of similar works

As you examine the book's physical characteristics, here are questions to consider:

- Is the spacing of words and lines suitable for the ability of the children?
- Does white space help the reader see the words?
- Are the size and style of type suitable for the reader?
- Are the illustrations close to the appropriate text? Note: Illustrations bound together in one section slow the reading process.

As you observe children using books, notice which formats attract them. Books with movable parts (toy books, engineered books, and books with transparency overlays) present other challenges. Can the intended reader manipulate the parts? You can anticipate that parts will become torn after several uses, since the reader gets involved with the book. The technique is effective for showing relationships between parts of an object, such as in the human body or in an automobile.

Box 2.3:   Criteria for Selecting Graphic Novels
• Do text and illustrations work well together?
• Are illustrations effective and well executed?
• Will children understand the plot?
• Will children have access to other books in the series?

Stoplight 2.3:   Graphic Novels
Graphic novels vary widely in content. Read the reviews if you cannot examine a book before purchase.

JUDGING THE AESTHETIC QUALITY

Aesthetic qualities can add to the appeal and informative value of a book. Questions to consider are:

- Are the illustrations clear and eye catching?
- Is the packaging attractive?
- Is the book jacket or binding appealing?
- Are colors chosen to express the theme?
- Is there a balance of illustrations to text?
- Is the typeface appropriate for the reader?
- Do the endpapers give a hint of the content?
- Can the viewer see the entire illustration in double-page spreads? (The way the book is bound may eliminate parts of a map or portions of an illustration.)

CONTRASTING WITH LIKE BOOKS

Availability of Similar Books

The lack of other books on the subject can influence a selection decision. An example is the election of a new president. Biographies about that individual may be hard to find. By the end of the president's first term of office, more choices will be available. Questions to consider:

- Is there a need for this particular subject or type of story?
- Has someone requested this title or a similar one?

Comparison with Similar Books

Each book has unique characteristics. As you compare books, you will develop the ability to distinguish the elements that make a quality book. To do this, ask yourself these questions:

- How is the book similar to another title by this author or illustrator?
- How is this book different from other titles by this author or illustrator?
- How is this book similar to another title on the same subject or about the same theme?
- How is this different from another title on the same subject or about the same theme?
- What do reviewers say about this title? Do I agree with their comments? If not, why do I disagree?
- What does the author or illustrator say about this title?

- Do I think this title will appeal to children over a number of years, or will interest in it be for a short time, like a fad?

VERIFYING THE BOTTOM LINE

What Is the Actual Cost?

Finally, the cost of the book cannot be ignored.

The average price of children's hardcover books was $21.60 in 2006, up from $19.31 in 2004. Books for preschoolers through grade four rose from $17.51 to $21.60 in 2006. The cost of fiction books for fifth grade and up was up three cents, while nonfiction titles rose from $23.25 to $26.81 (Kenney, 2006). Ask yourself:

- Can I afford this book?
- Is this book a good investment?
- Does my evaluation of the book indicate that it will be used?
- Does the book have enough strengths to justify purchasing it?
- If I cannot afford to buy the book, can I borrow it from other sources?

Here's a tip. Is this book one I would recommend when someone wants to make a gift or donation? (If the answer is yes, start a wish list. Sometimes people want suggestions for memorials and gifts for other occasions, and it is well to be prepared at the moment of interest.)

The Role of Jobbers

In schools and public libraries you may be using a **jobber**, a company that sells books from many publishers. Jobbers may have print or electronic catalogs that list available titles. Remember, the jobber is selling books to a wide range of libraries and individuals, who may not share your needs or goals. They list what's available—not necessarily what's recommended. Even when they list staff or consultants as selectors, the listing is merely that and serves a different function than does the reviewing media. Your use of the reviewing media and the knowledge you gain from your personal examination of new books will guide you as you use these lists. Learn about other people's experiences with a jobber: the company's reputation on order fulfillment, delivery schedule, costs, and replacement policies.

Box 2.4: Books Designed for Beginning Readers

Easy readers or beginning readers (books designed for independent use by new readers) often appear in series. They exist in a variety of genres (fiction, fantasy, historical fiction, folklore, poetry, and information books).

Design is a key factor in these works. The books range in length from 31 to 64 pages and are often nine inches by six inches in size. The size of the typeface is larger than that found in books for more experienced readers. The leading (the space between the lines), the wide margins, and the overall use of white space are all designed to help the new reader determine where sentences begin and end. The short text lines consist of one phrase or a very short sentence. Usually there is an illustration on each page.

Some "beginning-to-read" series titles have controlled vocabularies. A classic example is Dr. Seuss's *Cat in the Hat* (Random House, 1957), which is based on a limited vocabulary list of approximately 200 easy-to-read words. The primary audience for these series is first through third graders. The characteristics of the three levels are displayed in Figure 2.2. A child reading at level three is ready to move into transitional books, with their greater number of words per line, fewer illustrations, justified right margins, and longer chapters.

Questions to ask yourself as you evaluate easy readers:

- Does the story begin with short sentences?
- Does the story begin with a simple concept?
- Are the characters introduced within the first two pages?
- Is the setting introduced within the first two pages?
- Is the number of words per line appropriate for the intended reader?
- Do new sentences start at the beginning of a line?
- Is there action on every page?
- Is the author able to create appealing repetition?
- Does the author provide a context for new words?
- Will the new words be familiar to the child?
- Is the print large and clear?
- Is space used to separate words and lines?
- Do the illustrations give clues to the text?

Figure 2.2: Characteristics of Easy Reader Levels		
Level One	**Level Two**	**Level Three**
first grade	second grade	third grade
17- to 20-point type	18-point type	18-point type
5 words per line	5 words per line	Up to 8 words per line
5 to 7 words per sentence	Slightly more sentences alternating with simple ones	Both compound and complex sentences
Sight (recognized words) vocabulary	Increased sight vocabulary	Increased sight vocabulary
One-syllable words of 5 letters or fewer	Occasional multisyllabic words	Multisyllabic words
2 to 7 lines per page	4 to 15 lines per page	Up to 15 lines per page
2/3 page used for illustrations and white space	Balance of text with white space and illustration	Text may cover 3/4 of page. Illustrations may be on alternating pages.

CHAPTER BOOKS

As children develop their reading skills beyond those that are required for the beginning-to-read books, they turn to **chapter books**. These have more words and fewer pictures than the easy-to-read books and are divided into chapters. Ranging from 45 to 100 pages, they have fewer words, a narrower focus, fewer characters, and are less complex than novels for older children. Their audience is the six- to nine-year-olds.

SUMMARY

Although selection decisions can be subjective, through consistently applying objective criteria you will develop your ability to evaluate books. You will evaluate each book's idea, the presentation of the intellectual content, and the packaging of the book. You will consider criteria relating to treatment of multicultural aspects, characteristics of the genre or subject, possible use, intended user, need, and cost. These are the general criteria one uses in evaluating books.

Selection is a complex process. As you make selection decisions and gain a comparative knowledge of children's books, you will find it easier to apply criteria.

REFERENCES

American Library Association. "Wilder Medal Past Winners." Chicago, IL: ALA. (January 27, 2007) Available: www.ala.org/ala/alsc/awardsscholarships/literaryawds/wildermedal/wilderpast/wildermedalpast.htm

Kenney, Brian. 2006. "The Price You Pay." *School Library Journal* 52, no. 3 (March): 13.

RESOURCES

Canadian Children's Book Centre. CCBC. (August 26, 2006) Available: www.bookcentre.ca
  Provides guides to children's books and information about Canadian children's authors, illustrators, and the book trade.

Canadian Children's Book Centre. 2000. *The Storymakers: Writing Children's Books: 83 Authors Talk about Their Work.* Markham, Ontario: Pembroke.
  Provides biographical information, including awards received and descriptions of how they work. Companion volume to *The Storymakers: Illustrating Children's Books* (1999).

Children's Book Council (CBC). (August 26, 2006) Available: www.cbcbooks.org
  Provides information about children's trade books, publishers, authors, illustrations, and a directory of sites for authors and illustrators.

"Children's Literature Web Guide: Internet Resources Related to Books for Children and Young Adults." (August 26, 2006) Available: www.ucalgary.ca/~dkbrown/
  Provides extensive links to information about awards, lists, authors, illustrators, publishers, booksellers, associations, conferences, events, journals, and resources for parents, teachers, storytellers, writers, and illustrators. David K. Brown of the Doucette Library of Teaching Resources, University of Calgary. Comprehensive in scope.

Christelow, Eileen. 1995. *What Do Authors Do?* New York: Clarion.
  Written for children, this title follows an author and an illustrator from the time they get a creative idea to the publication of the book.

Cullinan, Bernice E., and Diane G. Person, eds. 2003. *The Continuum Encyclopedia of Children's Literature.* New York: Continuum.
  Articles about all aspects of children's literature, including biographical sketches of authors and illustrators with some photographs.

"The Internet Public Library." (August 26, 2006) Available: www.ipl.org/youth/
  Resources for teachers and parents with links to authors' Web sites and organizations involved with reading and children's literature.

"Kay E. Vandergrift's Special Interest Page." (August 26, 2006) Available: www.scils.rutgers.edu/~kvander
  An extensive resource for discussions about children's literature and of links to sites for authors and illustrators.

Leech, Bryan Jeffrey, Byron Glasser, and Sandra Higashi. 1994. *John Jeremy Colton.* New York: Hyperion.

Leedy, Loreen. 2004. *Look at My Book: How Kids Can Write and Illustrate Terrific Books.* New York: Holiday House.

Written for children, it presents directions—from getting an idea to several ways of creating the physical book. Identifies magazines that publish children's works.

Macaulay, David. 1999. *Building the Book Cathedral.* Boston, MA: Houghton Mifflin.

In honor of the 25th anniversary of *Cathedral*, Macaulay describes through words and illustrations the development of an idea into a book with the changes that took place. This book will appeal to children, especially potential illustrators.

Park, Linda Sue. 2005. *Project Mulberry.* New York: Clarion.

Two stories in one. Alternating chapters, with one telling a contemporary growing up story and the other a dialogue between one of the characters and the author, providing insight into the creative writing process. Share with potential authors.

Rochman, Connie C. 2004. *Ninth Book of Junior Authors and Illustrators.* New York: H. W. Wilson.

Includes statement by each author and illustrator, biographical information, bibliography of representative works, list of suggested readings, and Web sites. The index covers this edition and others in the Junior Book of Authors series, since the second edition in 1951.

Scieszka, Jon. 1998. "Design Matters." *Horn Book Magazine* 74, no. 2 (March/April): 196–208.

Describes through text and illustrations the role and the influence of the designer in creating a picture book.

Silvey, Anita, ed. 2002. *The Essential Guide to Children's Books and Their Creators.* Boston, MA: Houghton Mifflin.

Focuses on contemporary American authors and illustrators with updates of information on these individuals from her earlier work, *Children's Books and Their Creators* (1995). Both works include essays by some of the creators.

RECOMMENDED BOARD BOOKS

Bang, Molly. 1983. *Ten, Nine, Eight.* Dorset, VT: Tupelo Books.
Counting backward from ten to one. Vivid illustrations of a child's room at bedtime.

Carle, Eric. 1999. *From Head to Toe.* New York: HarperCollins.
Children try to do what various animals do.

Dyer, Jane. 1998. *Animal Crackers: Nursery Rhymes.* London: Little, Brown.
Traditional and modern rhymes with engaging illustrations.

Falconer, Ian. 2001. *Olivia Counts.* New York: Atheneum.
Olivia is her dramatic self, itemizing her accessories and counting her cousins.

Hill, Eric. 1986. *Spot Looks at Shapes.* New York: Putnam.
  Seven shapes are demonstrated in bright colors against a white backdrop.
Hines, Ann Grossnickle. 1999. *What Can You Do in the Rain?* illustrated by Thea Kliros. New York: Greenwillow.
  Creative approaches to children enjoying a rainy day.
Hoban, Tana. 1993. *Black on White.* New York: Greenwillow.
  Everyday objects against a white background. Babies like the stark contrast.
Hudson, Cheryl Willis. 1992. *Good Morning;* illustrated by Gerald Ford. New York: Scholastic.
  One in a series featuring African American babies and toddlers in their daily activities.
Long, Sylvia. 2001. *Twinkle, Twinkle Little Star: A Traditional Lullaby;* illustrated by Sylvia Long. San Francisco: Chronicle Books.
  Charming illustrations make this a standout.
McDonnell, Flora. 2001. *Flora McDonnell's ABC.* Cambridge, MA: Candlewick.
  Upper- and lower-case letters with whimsical paintings demonstrating two usages of an initial letter.
Martin, Bill, Jr. 1967. *Brown Bear, Brown Bear, What Do You See?* illustrated by Eric Carle. Austin, TX: Holt.
  Each rhyme leads into the next. Children delight in guessing what's coming.
Miller, Margaret. 2001. *Peekaboo Baby.* Part of the "Look Baby Series." New York: Little Simon.
  Colorful photographs of babies' faces. Very young children respond to other children's expressions.
Oxenbury, Helen. 1999. *All Fall Down.* New York: Little Simon.
  An oversize board book full of adorable bouncing babies.
Rosa-Mendoza, Gladys. 2004. *Lupe, Lupita, Where Are You? Lupe Lupita, ¿Donde Estas?* Wheaton, IL: me + mi publishing.
  Colorful paintings of young children demonstrate prepositions in both English and Spanish.
Shannon, David. 2005. *Oops!* New York: Blue Sky Press.
  David wreaks his usual havoc while introducing his first words: *ball, dog, ride, eat, bath,* and *mama.*
Sweet, Melissa. 2002. *Fiddle-I-Fee.* London: Little, Brown.
  Lively illustrations add to the fun of this traditional song.
Yee, Wong Herbert. 2000. *Here Come the Trainmice!* Boston, MA: Houghton Mifflin.
  Simple colored pictures chronicle a train journal, from "All Aboard" to arrival at the station.

RECOMMENDED BOOKS FOR BEGINNING READERS

Adler, David A. 2003. *Young Cam Jansen and the Zoo Note Mystery;* illustrated by Susanna Natti. New York: Viking.
  Cam's excellent memory helps Eric find his permission note. Readers will fol-

low the picture clues and solve the mystery, too. A game page completes the book and encourages memory development. Many Cam Jansen mysteries await those who like this adventure.

Capucilli, Alyssa Satin. 2004. *Biscuit Wins a Prize*; illustrated by Pat Schories. New York: HarperCollins.

Biscuit, a very curious puppy, is more interested in playing than in entering the pet show. Pleasant pictures give clues to the story line. Minimal text. An engaging companion to the other Biscuit books.

Dr. Seuss. 1963. *Hop on Pop*. New York: Beginner Books.

A favorite book for those just beginning to sound out words. Sparse rhymes and fun antics. This is just one of the very popular Seuss readers.

Guest, Elissa Haden. 2004. *Iris and Walter: Lost and Found*; illustrated by Christine Davenier. Orlando, FL: Harcourt.

Pen-and-ink drawings and an animated text tell of Iris's deep concern when she loses the harmonica she promised to keep for just one night. Part of a series.

Haskins, Lori. 2000. *Ducks in Muck*; illustrated by Valeria Petrone. New York: Random House.

Silly rhyming story with very few words and bright clear illustrations.

Lobel, Arnold. 1971. *Frog and Toad Together*. New York: HarperCollins.

These two friends challenge and respect each other. The short chapters show them facing all-too-common human challenges, like trying to resist eating all the cookies in the cookie jar. Other adventures of Frog and Toad are available.

Nichols, Catherine. 2005. *Madam C. J. Walker*. New York: Children's Press.

This carefully documented first biography honors Walker, who knew her hair products would please other African Americans. Primary materials add interest to this inspiring story.

Paterson, Katherine. 2001. *Marvin One Too Many*; illustrated by Jane Clark Brown. New York: HarperCollins.

Marvin is having trouble learning to read, so he hates school. Once they know how left out he feels, the family offer to help. Paterson knows the importance of acceptance. Fans of this book have other Marvin books to explore.

Rylant, Cynthia. 2005. *Henry and Mudge and the Great Grandpas*; illustrated by Sucie Stevenson. New York: Simon & Schuster.

Three warm stories about Henry and his dog, Mudge, and their adventures with Great-Grandpa and his housemates. Winner of the Theodor Seuss Geisel Award.

Thomas, Shelley Moore. 2006. *Happy Birthday, Good Knight*; illustrated by Jennifer Plecas. New York: Dutton.

The three little dragons, who appeared in two earlier books, make a mess while having the very best intentions. Repetition of some of the text lends a pleasing rhythm. Comical pictures suit the text.

VanLeeuwen, Jean. 2005. *Amanda Pig and the Really Hot Day*; illustrated by Ann Schweninger. New York: Dial Books.

From a water hose to a lemonade stand, clever Amanda beats the heat. One of several books about this charming family.

Wardlaw, Lee. 1999. *Hector's Hiccups*; illustrated by Joan Holub. New York: Random House.

Telling a story to Senor Fur, Hector's stuffed bear, is the most successful of his brother Carlos's and sister Maria's attempts to cure Hector's hiccups. For readers ready for several sentences per page.

Weeks, Sarah. 2004. *Baa-Choo!*; illustrated by Jane Manning. New York: HarperCollins.

The cover art shows Sam the lamb holding his handkerchief, ready to sneeze. Half-sneeze, that is, so lamb enlists the help of his barnyard friends. Rhyming and original with a satisfying finale.

Zollman, Pam. 2005. *A Chick Grows Up*. New York: Children's Press.

Clear color photographs, an interactive format, information given in various ways (text, timeline, photos, glossary) add up to a fun learning experience.

Chapter 3

Selecting a Diverse Range of Works

EXAMINING BOOKS FOR DIVERSITY

As global interaction shrinks our world, the responsibility to help children recognize the similarities and appreciate the differences among people becomes more crucial. Growing diversity exists in our families, communities, and schools. We work with children with physical, emotional, or developmental disabilities; from a variety of cultural and ethnic backgrounds; and with native tongues other than English.

Books portraying the similarities and differences include:

- Books with persons with disabilities
- Books with lesbian and gay families
- Books with people of diverse cultural and ethnic backgrounds (**multicultural literature**)
- Books originally published in countries outside the United States (**international literature**)
- Books translated from their original language into English (**translations**)

EVALUATING LITERATURE ABOUT PEOPLE WITH DISABILITIES

A challenge for any adult working with children is to help the children question stereotypical or negative attitudes. As with other forms of diversity discussed in this chapter, the goal is to recognize and appreciate the similarities and differences in human beings. A favorite poster clearly states the message: "Label cans, not people." Books portraying people with disabilities can be found in a number of genres including picture storybooks, fiction, and informational works. In fiction, the story may be told from the perspective of a brother, sister, or friend or by the person with the disability. Photo-essay formatted information books can be effective in showing the daily lives of people with disabilities and the type of help they find effective.

Questions to consider:

- Are the children presented as unique individuals with the interests, concerns, activities, and behaviors typical of all children?
- Is the person's ability rather than disability stressed?
- Is the accurate description of the disability presented as only one aspect of the person's life?
- Is the emphasis on the positive aspects of the person's life?
- Does the character experience the range of achievements and pleasant times that other people do?
- Do the characters solve problems with appropriate help from others?
- Is communication handled in a natural manner?
- Do the characters represent a variety of backgrounds in terms of family, economic level, ethnic groups, and geographical settings?
- Are people with disabilities shown in various roles in society, such as workers, community leaders, and participants in social and sports activities? Linda Lucas Walling Collection. (August 26, 2006) Available: www.libsci.sc.edu/facst/walling/bestfolder.htm

Spotlight 3.1:   Selecting for Diversity

Spotlight on Public Libraries

The public library supports our democracy by being inclusive rather than exclusive in its selection. It does not serve *in loco parentis* as do the public schools. It can provide controversial material that may fall outside the school's selection policy.

Spotlight on School Libraries

School libraries do include books on what may be perceived by some people as controversial subjects. Diversity within the school's population needs to be represented. Another goal is to have the collection represent a variety of viewpoints. In some cases this consists of books that discuss both sides of an issue, rather than separate position papers. This representation is noted in some schools' selection policies that address the goal of helping students explore the various viewpoints.

APPRAISING MATERIALS ABOUT LESBIAN AND GAY FAMILIES

When children with gay or lesbian parents see their family situation in books, they feel acknowledged. When children from other households read about gay and lesbian families, they gain in understanding. To recognize the diversity in our society, we need to make books with gay and lesbian characters available to children.

In addition to applying the same general criteria one would use for any book, Frances Day, in *Lesbian and Gay Voices: An Annotated Bibliography and Guide to Literature for Children and Young Adults*, suggests these guidelines for the evaluation of lesbian/gay-themed books for young readers:

- Will this book bolster or diminish self-esteem?
- Is only heterosexuality presented as normal?
- Are books mentioning homosexuality available to children?
- Are lesbian and gay characters portrayed as multifaceted? Are they from different backgrounds and age groups?
- Does the book use language that is respectful of lesbian and gay people?
- Does the book portray lesbian and gay characters involved in healthy, loving relationships?
- Does the book promote or debunk stereotypes of lesbian and gay people?
- Are biographers honest about the sexual identity of their subjects? (Day, 2000: xxiii-xxv)

ASSESSING MULTICULTURAL LITERATURE

People interpret the term *multicultural literature* in a variety of ways. Terms such as *parallel cultures* and *salad bowl* rather than *melting pot* recognize the value of many perspectives within a society.

As more people choose partners outside their own culture, traditional labels and categories fail. Children's books should reflect this diversity of lifestyles. In this chapter, *multicultural literature* refers to books depicting characters from many backgrounds. One or more cultures may be represented in a single book, as they are in life.

Multicultural books should be judged and selected using the same standards of quality and relevance as with any book. In addition, there are other factors to consider:

Text

- Is the behavior of the characters consistent with the belief systems of those portrayed?
- Is there a clear distinction between fact and conjecture in the text or notes?

- Do the events show the diversity of personalities and behaviors present in any subgroup, or are there stereotypes?

Illustrations

- Is there a variety of individual features portrayed, or do all characters look alike?
- Do the characters have authentic, typical dress for whichever region or time period is portrayed?
- Does the setting reflect the habits or values of the people portrayed?

Author(s)

- If the author is not from the group depicted in the book, what is the author's source of knowledge? Is this source documented?
- Were people from the group depicted involved as consultants and reviewers?

Deborah A. Miranda, in *A Broken Flute: The Native Experience in Books for Children*, urges writers who are not from the culture they are describing to ask themselves, "What can I write about this experience that is authentically from within myself, rather than a projection of what I think happened" (Seale & Slapin, 2005: 367).

Collection of Books Available to a Child

- Can each child find a book that reflects his or her experience?
- Are there stories with different types of homes, families, and jobs?
- Are there stories that show the range of subdivisions within a group, such as individual tribes of Native Americans?
- Are there books set in contemporary times and those with a historical setting?

**Box 3.1:   Using Award Books as Guides:
The Coretta Scott King Award and the Pura Belpre Award**

Since 1970 the Coretta Scott King Award has recognized the efforts of African American authors and illustrators on an annual basis. This American Library Association (ALA) award is administered by the Coretta Scott King Book Awards Committee of the Ethnic and Multicultural Information Exchange Round Table. A third category, "New Talent," was first awarded in 2002.

Latino writers and illustrators, whose works may be in English, Spanish, or bilingual, are honored on a biennial basis by the Pura Belpre Award. A joint committee of the Association for Library Service to Children (an ALA division) and REFORMA (National Association to Promote Library Services to the Spanish Speaking (an ALA affiliate) makes the selection.

These two awards are announced at the ALA Midwinter Meeting and on the ALSC Web site at www.ala.org/alsc and published in the spring issue of *Children & Libraries*, the February issue of *School Library Journal*, and the February issue of *American Libraries*.

SELECTING INTERNATIONAL LITERATURE

The increasing number of students for whom English is a second language and the wide range of countries of origin represented by new students serve as reminders of the international basis of diversity in our schools. To help students understand the similarities and differences among these groups, we can turn to international literature (Tomlinson, 1998).

Examples can be found in a wide range of genres including books about religion, myths, legends, folklore, poetry, picture storybooks, information, fantasy, and fiction. Many classics fall within this category. Representative works include the tales gathered by the Grimm Brothers, *Anno's Journey* (New York: Putnam, 1977), and Anne Frank's *The Diary of a Young Girl* (Mattituck, NY: Amereon, 1967).

To determine if a book may be considered international, locate information about the place of original publication. This is usually found with the book's cataloging in publication (CIP) information on the verso (back) of the title page or on the last page.

In *Adventuring with Books: A Booklist for Pre-K–Grade 6*, Tomlinson reports what he and the committee used as the "Criteria for Excellence" for the titles included in the chapter "International Children's Books or Literature":

- originally published in a country other than the United States
- an original concept or story that reveals how people in other countries live now or have lived in the past

- a theme concerned with the interests, problems, customs, and ways of thinking of people who live in countries other than the United States
- a story that both entertains and educates
- excellent writing
- original, evocative illustrations that help tell the story
- concept and theme appropriate for children in grades K–6 (Tomlinson, 2002).

**Box 3.2:   Promoting International Literature:
International Board on Books for Young People (IBBY)**

A group that actively promotes international understanding and world peace through children's literature is the International Board on Books for Young People (IBBY) founded in 1953.

International Children's Book Day is observed on or around Hans Christian Andersen's birthday, April 2. IBBY also sponsors the prestigious Hans Christian Andersen Medal book award. Member countries may nominate a living children's author and illustrator from which an international jury selects the award winners. Five U.S. authors have won the medal: Meindert DeJong (1962), Scott O'Dell (1972), Paula Fox (1978), Virginia Hamilton (1992), and Katherine Paterson (1998). Maurice Sendak (1970) is the only illustrator from the United States who has won the award.

CONSIDERING TRANSLATIONS AND ENGLISH-LANGUAGE IMPORTS

Although no records are kept concerning translations, it is estimated that less than 1 percent of the total number of children's books published annually in the United States are translations. The number of books from other countries written in English and then published in the United States is greater. The majority of these English-language titles are from Great Britain, Canada, and Australia.

Both types of books call for careful consideration. Books published in English from other countries may include variants on spelling unfamiliar to children in the United States or use an unfamiliar vocabulary. This can be particularly confusing with information or reference works. When examining such titles, check to see if terms are explained either in the text or in a glossary.

Translations present more complex problems. Clues about the translator may be found in a listing on the title page, the verso of the title page, or on the book jacket. An effective translation is not a simple word-by-word process. The successful translator

- Rewrites the original text while maintaining the author's tone, voice, and emotion

- Knows how to make the foreign terms and place names interesting but not confusing to the child reader
- Uses appropriate idioms or substitutes to portray authenticity
- Understands the role of illustration in telling the story

**Box 3.3: Using Award Books as Guides:
The Mildred L. Batchelder Award**

To experience the work of effective translators, try some of the books that have received the Mildred L. Batchelder Award. The Association for Library Service to Children (ALSC) administers this award, which is presented to an American publisher of a translated children's book. The award is announced at the ALA Midwinter Meeting, is available at the ALSC Web site (www.ala.org/alsc), and is published in the spring issue of *Children & Libraries* and in the February issue of *School Library Journal*.

The award recognizes the title as being the outstanding translation of a book originally published in a country other than the United States in a language other than English. The award includes books recommended for children up to age 14.

Spotlight 3.2: Bilingual Titles

Books written in two or more languages provide opportunities for children to read and hear both languages while sharing a story, folktale, or poem. Two examples are provided.

Spicy Hot Colors/Colores Picantes by Sherry Shahan and illustrated by Paula Barragan (Harvest House Little Folk, 2004) presents an energetic English text with color names in English and Spanish. The stunning pictures, musical text, and original examples combine to create a read-aloud or dance-along experience. The work includes a vocabulary and pronunciation guide. Jose Aruego's *Moony Lunca/ Luna Lunita Lunera* (Children's Book Press, 2005), illustrated by Elizabeth Gomez with native reader Laura Chastain, captures the first day of school jitters in Spanish and English. Warm colors soothe as Luna's inner voice goes from fear to excitement at meeting new friends at school.

Spotlight 3.3: Selecting Foreign-Language Titles

Spotlight on School Libraries

Consult with foreign-language teachers regarding the identification and selection of foreign-language books and bilingual ones.

SUMMARY

Helping children develop positive attitudes about themselves and an understanding of others is an important goal. As you select books for children to help them achieve this goal, you need to consider the criteria identified in this chapter about the treatment of people with disabilities, those with different family configurations, our own multicultural society, and our diverse world.

REFERENCES

Day, Frances Ann. 2000. *Lesbian and Gay Voices: An Annotated Bibliography and Guide to Literature for Children and Young Adults*. Westport, CT: Greenwood Press.

International Board on Books for Young People. "Hans Christian Andersen Awards." (August 26, 2006) Available: www.ibby.org/index.php?id=273

Seale, Doris, and Beverly Slapin, eds. 2005. *A Broken Flute: The Native Experience in Books for Children*. Walnut Creek, CA: Altamira; Berkeley, CA: Oyate.

Tomlinson, Carl M., ed. 1998. *Children's Books from Other Countries*. Lanham, MD: Scarecrow. Sponsored by the United States Board on Books for Young People.

Tomlinson, Carl M., and International Children's Books on Literature Committee. 2002. "International Children's Books or Literature" in *Adventuring with Books: A Booklist for Pre-K–Grade 6*. 13th ed. Edited by Amy A. McClure and Janice V. Kristo. Urbana, IL: National Council of Teachers of English.

RESOURCES

Bookbird: The Journal of International Children's Literature (1962–) is a refereed journal published quarterly by IBBY, the International Board on Books for Young People. The journal includes feature articles, news of local chapters, children's literature awards and reading promotion projects. Activities and membership information for USBBY, the United States section, are available as links from the IBBY homepage, www.ibby.org (August 26, 2006).

Bruchac, Joseph. 2003. *Our Stories Remember: American Indian History, Culture, and Values through Storytelling*. Golden, CO: Fulcrum.
Bruchac's commentary and recommended reading aid in understanding the many stories from different native groups. Each chapter begins with a poem, song, or quote. Story sources, other versions of the stories, and an index are included.

Circle of Inclusion Project. "Nine Ways to Evaluate Children's Books That Address Disability as Part of Diversity." Lawrence, KS: University of Kansas. (September 2, 2006) Available: www.circleofinclusion.org/english/books/section1/a.html

Cooperative Children's Book Center. University of Wisconsin at Madison (CCBC). (August 26, 2006) Available: www.education.wisc.edu/ccbc/
"Fifty Multicultural Books Every Child Should Know" plus lists and links to multicultural award Web sites. The Alternative Press Collection listed in the center's MADCAT contains over 1,700 books from 325 small presses.

Day, Frances Ann. 2000. *Lesbian and Gay Voices: An Annotated Bibliography and Guide to Literature for Children and Young Adults*. Westport, CT: Greenwood Press.
Includes detailed descriptions of 275 recommended titles. Suggests guidelines for evaluating books with lesbian and gay content to aid teachers and librarians selecting books for use with children and young adults.

Hansen-Krening, Nancy, Elaine M. Aoki, and Donald T. Mizokawa, eds. 2003. *Kaleidoscope: A Multicultural Booklist for Grades K–8*. 4th ed. NCTE Bibliography Series. Urbana, IL: National Council of Teachers of English.
Includes criteria for the annotated bibliography of books published from 1999 to 2001 and having protagonists who are African American, Asian American, Latino American, or Native American, including bilingual and multilingual literature.

Immroth, Barbara, and Kathleen de la Peña McCook, eds. 2000. *Library Services to Youth of Hispanic Heritage*. Jefferson, NC: McFarland.
A collection of essays describing a variety of services to youth of Hispanic heritage. Part III ("Collections") addresses Spanish language selection issues and includes a selected list of distributors.

International Reading Association. (August 26, 2006)
Sponsors an annual list of 25 "Notable Books for a Global Society" (fiction, nonfiction, and poetry for K–12). Criteria for inclusion are given on the Web site. The list is published in the fall issue of *Dragon Lode*. Available: www.reading.org

Kuharets, Olga R., ed. 2001. *Ventures into Cultures: A Resource Book of Multicultural Materials and Programs*. 2nd ed. Chicago, IL: American Library Association.
Different authors contribute chapters on individual cultures; includes comments about the culture, recommended fiction and nonfiction materials with grade levels, program ideas, Web sites, and a resource list.

Linda Lucas Walling Collection in The Best Center, South Carolina State Library. (August 26, 2006) Available: www.libsci.sc.edu/facst/walling/bestfolder.htm
In addition to describing this collection for and about children with disabilities, the Web site also provides evaluative criteria specific to categories of disability.

Lindsay, Nina. "I Still Isn't for Indian." *School Library Journal* 49, no. 11 (November 2003): 42–43.
Dismayed by the lack of excellent books on native people, Lindsay recommends reading several reviews for a title, seeking the advice of native people, and striving to improve the accuracy and quality of future books by contacting publishers, educating ourselves, and then writing reviews.

Marantz, Sylvia, and Ken Marantz. 2004. *Multicultural Picturebooks: Art for Illuminating Our World: 1997–2004*. 2nd ed. Lanham, MD: Scarecrow Press.
Identifies the criteria used in selecting the books in the descriptive annotated bibliography. Sections are arranged geographically. Provides a chapter on multicultural and cross-cultural experiences. Indexes by author, illustrator, title, and subject.

Multicultural Review: Dedicated to a Better Understanding of Ethnic, Racial, and Religious Diversity. 1992– Westport, CT: Greenwood Press.
Articles and reviews of multicultural materials. December issue includes cumulative index for that year. Subscription information available: www.mcreview.com.

Oyate. "Oyate is a native organization working to see that our lives and histories are portrayed honestly, and so that all people will know our stories belong to us." (August 26, 2006) Available: www.oyate.org
They evaluate and distribute materials, conduct workshops, and manage a small resource center.

Schon, Isabel. 2003. *The Best of Latino Heritage, 1996–2002: A Guide to the Best Juvenile Books about Latino People and Cultures*. Lanham, MD: Scarecrow Press.
Arranged alphabetically by country. Lists noteworthy books defined as quality writing and illustrations plus appeal. Suggests grade level. Indexed by subject, title, author, grade level, and series. Identifies strengths and weaknesses in the annotations.

Schon, Isabel, director. (August 26, 2006) Barahona Center for the Study of Books in Spanish for Children and Adolescents.
See "Recommended Books" section at: www.csusm.edu/csb

Seale, Doris, and Beverly Slapin, eds. 2005. *A Broken Flute: The Native Experience in Books for Children*. Berkeley, CA: Oyate.
A collection of essays, poems, reviews, and criteria for evaluating children's books depicting native life. Both recommended and nonrecommended titles are critiqued for authenticity and accuracy. Over 400 children's and teen titles are examined.

Smith, Henrietta M. 2004. *The Coretta Scott King Awards: 1970–2004*. Chicago, IL: American Library Association.
Traces the history of the awards. Provides biographical information about the African American authors and illustrators receiving the awards. Includes some samples of their work.

Stan, Susan, ed. 2002. *The World through Children's Books*. Lanham, MD: Scarecrow Press.
Companion work to *Children's Books from Other Countries*, edited by Carl M. Tomlinson (1998). The earlier book covered works published from 1950 to 1996; the newer one covers 1996 to 2000 publications. Both provide an overview of international children's literature and suggestions for sharing these books with children.

The second part offers descriptive annotations of both "quality international and domestic books organized by region of the world and country" (p. ix). Information and electronic and print sources are interspersed throughout these chapters. The third part identifies other resources: children's book awards, organizations, publishers, and distributors of foreign-language and bilingual books. Indexes included are for author, illustrator, title, translator, and subject.

Steiner, Stanley F. 2001. *Promoting a Global Community through Multicultural Children's Literature.* Westport, CT: Libraries Unlimited.

An extensive annotated bibliography arranged by subject; includes picture books, fiction, and nonfiction. Suggests activities. Includes publishers of multicultural materials and resources for infusing literature into content areas.

Trevino, Rose Zertuche. 2006. *The Pura Belpre Awards: Celebrating Latino Authors and Illustrators.* Chicago, IL: American Library Association.

Provides a history of the award and the work of Pura Belpre, describes the award winners, includes biographical sketches, and suggests booktalks and activities. With Internet resources, photographs of the winners, sample illustrations, and a DVD disc.

Ward, Marilyn. 2002. *Voices From the Margins: An Annotated Bibliography of Fiction on Disabilities and Differences for Young People.* Westport, CT: Greenwood Press.

The 200 books for children K–12 are accessible by title, author, age level, and subject. All titles were published between 1990 and 2001. Ward includes favorable and critical comments, although inclusion constitutes her recommendation.

York, Sherry. 2002. *Children's and Young Adult Literature by Latino Writers: A Guide for Librarians, Teachers, Parents and Students.* Columbus, OH: Linworth Publishing.

Inclusion does not constitute recommendation. Provides bibliographic and ordering information, number of chapters, summary, subjects, genre/form, setting, interest level, reading level, test coverage, where received, awards, and inclusion on lists. Chapter 8, "Resource Materials for Cultural Education," includes: short stories, novels, folklore, drama, poetry, nonfiction, resource materials, and lists of writers.

Chapter 4

Using Selection Tools Effectively

EXPLORING SELECTION TOOLS

Where can you find recommended titles to consider for purchase? Ideally, selectors would examine each book, but often this is not feasible. There are approximately 5,000 juvenile titles published each year. Few people have access to all of them.

Fortunately, there are many resources to guide you. Each has its advantages and disadvantages. Four commonly used evaluative sources to help you are databases with reviews, journals with reviews, selected bibliographies, and bibliographic essays.

Databases with Reviews

Commercial electronic databases such as BWI, Mackin, and Follett provide an extensive variety of titles with links to reviews. They also offer other services, such as cataloging and processing of materials. Several online bookstores offer titles with reviews. These reviews evaluate books and can also be read offline in journals and other publications.

Electronic access to reviews and bibliographic information provides convenience and efficiency. Networks allow input from different work sites. Selectors with a password can purchase materials. One can check a personal list of titles selected in a particular account. Managers can easily review expenditures. The benefits are enormous. If you recognize an ongoing need for a title or type of book, ask your supplier to carry it. Your argument will be more persuasive if you document your need by describing the anticipated audience.

Carefully scrutinize each entry. Note the illustrator and edition. Otherwise, inadvertently, you may receive a paper, abridged version of the classic title you wanted. The number of pages and cover art help identify the specific edition. If budget permits, err on the side of two rather than one copy of a replacement title of proven recent popularity. Books go out of print with frightening regularity!

Online booksellers like Amazon and Barnes & Noble offer both editorial and customer reviews. Carefully study the book description to be sure you are receiving a durable, attractive edition.

Stoplight 4.1:   Utilizing Multiple Sources
In order to build a collection tailored to your specific needs, use more than one source. Purchasing books from small presses, books published by associations, books presenting a unique perspective or language other than English may require shopping in several places.

Journals with Reviews

Whether online or in print, journals with their reviews of current titles provide the major source of information that aids selection decisions. They may cover a broad range of subjects or focus on one subject. An example of a subject-oriented journal is *Science Books & Films* (American Association for the Advancement of Science, 1975–).

Each reviewing journal has unique features. These differences create advantages and limitations for the user. The journals may:

- be produced by different types of publishers (commercial firms, professional associations, or education agencies)
- be aimed at specific audiences, such as media personnel, children's librarians, or classroom teachers
- focus on one format, such as books, or cover a wide range of formats
- focus on materials for potential users—children in kindergarten through sixth grade, preschoolers through adult
- focus on a particular perspective, such as the consciousness-raising efforts of *Multicultural Review* (1992–)

Four commonly used reviewing journals—*Bulletin of the Center for Children's Books* (Graduate School of Library and Information Science, University of Illinois, August 1945–), *School Library Journal* (Reed Business Information, 1954–), *Booklist: Includes Reference Book Bulletin* (American Library Association, 1905–), and *Horn Book Magazine* (Horn Book, 1924–)—illustrate the different approaches. *Bulletin of the Center for Children's Books* clearly explains the symbols used for its recommendations, including titles not recommended. School library media specialists, children's librarians, and library educators write the reviews in *School Library Journal. Booklist* includes reviews of books for preschoolers through adults. *Horn Book* chooses about 70 items to review in each issue and is therefore very selective. You will learn the importance of reading more than one review, since no single journal provides all the information you need to make selection decisions. Databases that provide several reviews with each title make this easy to do.

Examine the journals to become familiar with their purpose, coverage, and selection process. You may be able to access them at nearby public libraries and school district offices. You will also learn to pick up clues about the background of reviewers, who may be journal staff members with a wide range of experience with children's books or professionals working with children. Look for signed reviews or a list of reviewers with information about each person's position and background.

Some things to look for as you read reviews:

- descriptive reviews with objective statements about plot, characters, theme, and illustrations
- evaluative statements including comparison of the title with similar books
- identification of potential appeal, curriculum use, and possible controversial aspects
- description of binding and format

When you cannot actually handle a book and must rely on a review, be aware of the following:

- Time lag between publication and review. Check the journal's policy about how close to a book's publication date it will include a review. Conversely, after what period of time will it not include a review? If the journal uses reviewers working with children, there may be a delay due to the shipping and handling of the book. The advantage to this is that children's reactions may be noted in the review.
- Lack of access to reviewing journals for specific subjects. For example, reviews about mathematics and science books receive greater coverage in subject-oriented reviewing journals than in the commonly used broad-based journals.
- Lack of reviews in more than one journal for specific titles. The number of issues per year varies from journal to journal, as does the number of titles reviewed each year. Study the journal's policy to identify limitations on what or when it reviews.
- Uneven quality or relevance of reviews. Even if you are able to locate the reviews, the assessments can vary in quality or applicability to your collection. Note the job title and location of the reviewer to decide if his or her situation could be similar to your own.

Features	Booklist	Bulletin of the Center for Children's Books	Horn Book Magazine	School Library Journal
Frequency	Biweekly	Monthly	Bimonthly	Monthly
Publisher	American Library Association	Illinois: Graduate School of Library and Information	The Horn Book, Inc.	Reed Business Information, Inc.
Age targeted in reviewed materials	Preschool through adult	Three-year-olds to ninth graders	Infancy through young adult	Preschool through young adult
Formats reviewed	Books, video, DVD, audio	Books	Books	Books, video, audio, computer software, professional books
Index for each issue	No	Yes	Yes	Yes
Index for year	Cumulative index on Web site	Annual, July/August issue	Annual, November/December issue	Searchable review database
Selectors	Staff	Staff	Staff and guest reviewers	Volunteer practicing librarians
Other coverage	Articles/Columns	N/A	Articles	Articles
Cost	$89.95	$75, institution; $70, individual	$59, institution; $49, individual	$124

Figure 4.1: Comparison of Commonly Used Reviewing Journals

Selected Bibliographies

Sometimes called "**selection tools**" or "**selection aids**," these bibliographies recommend specific titles. They may be extensive works, such as *Children's Catalog* (19th ed.; H. W. Wilson, 2006), or shorter lists, such as "Capitol Choices: Noteworthy Books for Children," http://capitolchoices.communitypoint.org (accessed August 27, 2006). Typically, for each title they provide bibliographic information, cost, a description, and an evaluation.

Extensive selected bibliographies may:

- recommend more than one book on a topic, so you can obtain comparative information
- identify resources for an instructional unit
- recommend titles for reading aloud
- identify books for readers at various levels

Because it takes time for reviewers to evaluate new titles, there is a gap between the publication date of the most recent item and the publication date of the selection bibliography itself. Therefore, use reviewing journals for current publications.

DETERMINING THE BEST BIBLIOGRAPHIES

You will want to read the introduction to the bibliography to learn how the selections were made and who was involved in the process. Three common practices for deciding which titles to include are: 1) recommendations by an individual; 2) recommendations by a committee; or 3) books that received positive reviews in other sources. Also look for the selection criteria used. This important information is frequently not provided, leaving the user in a "buyer beware" position. The introduction to the selection tool should provide clues as to whether a title not included would even have been received in time to be considered.

Criteria for Judging Bibliographies

To judge a bibliography, read the introduction, the information about how to use the tool, and sample entries. As you do this, think about the following questions:

- What is the purpose of the bibliography? Does that purpose meet your needs?
- Does the introduction provide adequate directions for using the bibliography?
- Does it describe the basis for recommending titles in the bibliography? Are the criteria stated?
- Does it explain any symbols or abbreviations used in the entries?
- Is the bibliography in print, on a CD-ROM, online, or in another format? Do you have access to the equipment needed to use the bibliography?
- Who selects the books? Who is responsible for writing the annotations? What are the reviewers' qualifications? Are the reviews signed? Is there a list of the reviewers?
- What information is provided for each entry?

    - Check for bibliographic data: full title, authorship (author, editor, reteller), illustrator, translator, series titles, place of publication, publisher; date of publication, distributor (if not the publisher), and ISBN (International Standard Book Number).

- Check the annotation: Is it descriptive, evaluative, or both? Does it recommend the book for specific situations, uses, or audiences? Does it compare this title with other titles? Does the work recommend all titles equally, or are there different levels of recommendation?
- Do symbols indicate level of recommendation, interest level, readability level, or audience?
- What other information about the book is included? This information could be about various editions available, books available in more than one language, or bilingual text.

- What is the coverage of the bibliography? Does it include only books or all formats used by children? Does it includes books for a wide audience, or is it limited to books for children? Does it cover all subjects, or is it specialized? What periods of publication does it cover?
- How are the entries organized? Common patterns include classification scheme, such as the Dewey Decimal System of classification by broad subjects; audience for the book; author; or title.
- Does it have indexes to help locate items? Does it provide cross-references? Are there indexes for author, title, series title, audience, reading level, and subject as well as analytics to sections of the books recommended? Are these individual or combined indexes?

A Sample of Selection Bibliographies

Children's Catalog provides "how to use" directions, identifies selection criteria, explains symbols used, and identifies the format of each title. Each entry has full bibliographic information: full title, author, illustrator, series title, publisher, date, and ISBN. Annotations are critically descriptive and include interest levels. There is a "Recommended Web Resources" list and a directory of publishers and distributors. The online *Children's Catalog* provides access to 10,000 titles. One can link to the library's catalog to check holdings. The print version includes approximately 8,500 entries in the 2006 volume plus paperback supplements for 2007, 2008, and 2009. There are over 5,000 new titles since the 2001 edition was published, including graphic novels and recommendations of periodicals for children and professionals.

Spotlight 4.1:   Using Selected Bibliographies

Spotlight on Public Libraries

A selected bibliography can provide a reference point when buying books to stock a new or enlarged library. This is one check to ensure that you are including different categories and not just buying titles from the current publishing year.

Spotlight on School Libraries

Using selected bibliographies, especially in the subject areas, can help you identify titles that may not be covered in the regular reviewing sources.

There are annual publications that include far fewer recommendations than *Children's Catalog* but are less expensive to obtain. As you study Figure 4.2, note the differences. The coverage in these annual lists is limited to titles published during the preceding year.

Capitol Choices: Noteworthy Books for Children is an annual list of noteworthy books published in the preceding year in the United States. Originally issued by the Children's Literature Center of the Library of Congress, the list is now a joint project of several dozen Washington, D.C. area librarians, teachers, booksellers, magazine editors, and children's literature specialists and can be viewed at the Capitol Choices Web site.

The Best Children's Books of the Year (Children's Book Committee at Bank Street College) is an annual publication by the Child Study Children's Book Committee at Bank Street College, in New York. The Bank Street Book Committee was established over 75 years ago.

Although both lists cover a wide range of subjects, the limited number of recommended titles hampers their usefulness in identifying books to meet a specific subject need. Such lists and those that follow are useful for checking to see if you have overlooked any outstanding titles.

Figure 4.2: Comparison of *Capitol Choices* and *The Best Children's Books of the Year*		
Characteristics	***Capitol Choices***	***The Best Children's Books of the Year***
Purpose	Recommend "Best of the Year"	Recommend "Best of the Year"
Directions?	No	Explains symbols
Lists selection criteria	Yes	Yes
Material types	Books, audiobooks	Books
Identifies selectors	Yes	Yes
Provides bibliographic data	Yes	Yes
Displays cover art	Yes	No
Type of annotation	Descriptive	Descriptive
Arrangement	Subjects, age of audience	Age and interest
Includes indexes	Searchable online	By author and title
Other information	None	Publishers list, children's book awards list, tips for parents
Number of titles	Over 100	Approximately 600
Cost	Free	$8.00

Other sources of inexpensive annual listings include those of recommended titles selected by members of professional associations. To obtain the lists described here and similar ones, you can contact the issuing professional association, or look for the list in the association's electronic or print publications. If you do not subscribe to these publications, you may be able to access them through a school or public library subscription.

As with other bibliographies, you need to read the criteria for selecting titles for inclusion on the list. The label "notable" or "outstanding" title usually indicates a book of quality; however, the title may not meet your particular needs.

The Association for Library Service to Children's annual "Notable Children's Book" list uses the terms notable as including

> books of especially commendable quality, books that exhibit venturesome creativity, and books of fiction, information, poetry and pictures for all age levels (through age 14) that reflect and encourage children's interest in exemplary ways (Association for Library Service to Children, 2006).

Usually the list includes sixty-some titles including all genres. The list is available online and is published in *Booklist*, usually in the April issue, and in the March issue of *School Library Journal*.

The National Science Teachers Association's annual "Outstanding Science Trade Books for Children K–12" appears in the March issue of *Science & Children* and is available online. The panel looks at both content and presentation. Selection is based generally on the following criteria:

- The book has substantial science content.
- Information is clear, accurate, and up to date.
- Theories and facts are clearly distinguished.
- Facts are not oversimplified to the point where the information is misleading.
- Generalizations are supported by facts and significant facts are not omitted.
- Books are free of gender, ethnic, and socioeconomic bias.
  (National Science Teachers Association, 2006)

A parallel list, "Notable Trade Books for Young People" by the National Council for the Social Studies, appears annually in the April/May issue of *Social Education*. The books must:

- be written primarily for children in grades K–8
- emphasize human relations
- represent a diversity of groups and be sensitive to a broad range of cultural experiences
- present an original theme or a fresh slant on a traditional topic
- be easily readable and of high literary quality
- have a pleasing format and, when appropriate, illustrations that enrich the text

Recommended titles include works of fiction, poetry, folklore, and information. These are arranged by the thematic strands of the social studies curriculum: culture, time, continuity, and change; people, places, and environments; individual development and identity; individuals, groups, and institutions, power, authority, and governance; production, distribution, and consumption; science, technology and society; global connections; and civic ideals and practices (National Council for the Social Studies, 2006).

"Children's Choices" is printed in the October issue of the International Reading Association's (IRA) journal, *The Reading Teacher*, and is available in a single copy.

The list is an annual project of the IRA and the Children's Book Council, begun in 1974. Each year an average of 100 favorite books are chosen by approximately 10,000 children ages 5 to 13 from different regions of the United States. U.S. publishers supply approximately 460 titles for voting (International Reading Association, 2006).

Additional selected bibliographies are identified throughout this book.

EXAMINING BIBLIOGRAPHIC ESSAYS

These articles may evaluate the treatment of a specific topic in old and new titles, compare books within a specific genre, or assess books for specific readers or users. They describe books on a particular subject, theme, or use or for a specific audience. These frequently appear in *School Library Journal* and in *Book Links*. The essays can be very helpful, but they demand careful reading. An omitted item may not be recommended; the reader does not know whether the writer simply overlooked the item or does not recommend it. Bibliographic essays usually focus on a specific component of an item and often do not provide an overall assessment of each title mentioned in the essay.

CHOOSING THE RIGHT SELECTION TOOLS

If you want to compare selection guides, identify a recently published children's book with which you are familiar. Then compare your evaluation of it with the comments of the reviewers. Do you agree with the reviewer's evaluation? Does the reviewer raise questions about the book or offer new insight you hadn't considered? Reread the book to consider if your assessment will change in light of the reviewer's comments. When you look at the reviewer's qualifications, can you better understand why the perspective is different from yours? Is this a perspective you need to consider?

SUMMARY

Few book selectors have an opportunity to personally evaluate the thousands of children's books that are published annually. They consult selection sources including databases with reviews, selected bibliographies, professionally recommended annual best book lists, and bibliographic essays. They get to know children well enough to understand their book interests and needs.

Knowing that selected lists and reviews are expressions of the reviewer's opinion, selectors can compare their own assessments of a specific book with those of the reviewers. This process helps to evaluate the selection tool and at the same time may provide the opportunity to learn to examine books in new ways.

REFERENCES

Association for Library Service to Children. "Children's Notable Books: Terms and Criteria." Chicago, IL: American Library Association. (August 26, 2006) Available: www.ala.org/ALSCTemplate.cfm?Section=childrensnotable& Template=/Content Management/ContentDisplay.cfm&ContentID=156423

International Reading Association. "Children's Choices." (August 26, 2006) Available: www.reading.org/resources/tools/choices_childrens.html

National Council for the Social Studies. "Notable Trade Books for Young People." (August 26, 2006) Available: www.socialstudies.org/resources/notable

National Science Teachers Association. "Outstanding Science Trade Books for Students K–12." (August 26, 2006) Available: www.nsta.org/ostbc

PART II

SPECIAL SELECTION CRITERIA FOR SPECIFIC GENRES

Chapter 5

Picture Books

EXPLORING PICTURE BOOKS

When one hears the term **picture book**, one often thinks first of the genre in which pictures and text play equally important roles in the narrative. These types of picture storybooks will be discussed in another chapter. Picture book also refers to books with a specific format. Usually 32 pages in length, these books may be 48 or 64 pages long. The pictures alone may tell the story, as in the case of wordless books, such as David Wiesner's *Tuesday* (Clarion, 1999).

There are a wide variety of books in which pictures convey the story or information. Examples include alphabet books, counting books, and concept books. Fiction examples include picture storybooks, historical fiction, modern realistic fiction, fantasy, and other genres. Nonfiction examples are folk literature, myths and legends, information books, and poetry. Audience range for the picture book format is wide. Picture books can be **cross-over books**, a marketing term for books of interest to both young readers and adults.

The content of the book may be a simple story or a complex one. The content of a story may be less obvious in a work like *Times Flies* by Eric Rohmann (Crown, 1994). This wordless book can be viewed at several levels. The reader who has prior knowledge of the debate about the relationship between dinosaurs and birds brings a greater appreciation to the experience than one who does not; yet, both readers can enjoy the book. Another complex example is David Macaulay's *Black and White* (Houghton Mifflin, 1990), which tells four related stories simultaneously on each double-page spread.

A picture book differs from an **illustrated book**, in which occasional illustrations serve a decorative purpose rather than extending the text. In some works of fiction each chapter is introduced by an illustration. Another example is found in anthologies, in which an illustration may indicate the subject of the section.

Barbara Elleman, former editor of *Book Links*, argues that

> we need to give time and attention to children's aesthetic growth and to looking quietly and thoughtfully at well executed art. . . . The artwork available in children's books is wide-ranging in style, technique, and media, and offers a natural opportunity for introducing children to art (Elleman, 1994: 5).

As you examine the pictorial elements, composition, media, book design, and styles found in children's books, you will appreciate Elleman's observation about the wide range of artwork available to children.

Because illustrations play a major role in communicating the message in picture books, the quality of these illustrations is of the utmost importance. To evaluate picture books, you have to use your knowledge and appreciation of the techniques of illustration and book design. One way to improve your skill is to consult books about art. Two useful titles are *Looking at Pictures: An Introduction to Art for Young People* by Joy Richardson (Harry N. Abrams, 1997) and *The Painter's Eye: Learning to Look at Contemporary American Art* by Jan Greenberg and Sandra Jordan (Delacorte Press, 1994). Books to help you with artistic terms and provide various visual approaches are listed at the end of this chapter under the heading "Resources."

Box 5.1:   Randolph Caldecott

Randolph Caldecott was a 19th-century English illustrator known for the action in his illustrations, the vitality of the drawings, and the display of humor. The Caldecott Medal bears reproductions of his illustrations of John Gilpin's ride in William Cowper's poem "The Diverting History of John Gilpin" and "four-and-twenty blackbirds baked in a pie" from the Mother Goose nursery rhyme "Sing a Song of Sixpence."

AWARD BOOKS AS GUIDES: CALDECOTT AWARD

You can examine the Caldecott Award and Honor books for examples of excellence in picture books. This award honors the illustrator of the most distinguished picture book for children published in the United States during the preceding year. The Association for Library Service to Children, a division of the American Library Association (ALSC), administers the award. The Award and Honor books are announced at a press conference during the Midwinter Meeting of the American Library Association, are listed on the ALSC Web site at www.ala.org/alsc, and are published in the spring issue of *Children & Libraries* and the February issue of *School Library Journal.*

The purpose of the award is to encourage original and creative works in the field of books for children up to age 14. The artist must be a citizen or resident of the United States. The committee may select additional distinguished books as Honor books.

Distinguished is defined as:

- marked by eminence and distinction; noted for significant achievement
- marked by excellence in quality
- marked by conspicuous excellence or eminence
- individually distinct
  (Association for Library Service to Children, 2004)

Dorothy P. Lathrop received the first Caldecott Medal in 1938 for *Animals of the Bible,* with text selected by Helen Dean Fish from the King James Bible (Lippincott, 1937).

		Figure 5.1: Caldecott Award Books, 1995–2007	
Award Year	**Illustrator and author**	**Title**	**Publisher Date**
1995	David Diaz; text by Eve Bunting	*Smoky Night*	Harcourt, 1994
1996	Peggy Rathmann	*Officer Buckley and Gloria*	Putnam, 1995
1997	David Wisniewski	*Golem*	Clarion, 1996
1998	Paul O. Zelinsky	*Rapunzel*	Dutton, 1997
1999	Mary Azarian; text by Jacqueline Briggs Martin	*Snowflake Bentley*	Houghton Mifflin, 1998
2000	Simms Taback	*Joseph Had a Little Overcoat*	Viking, 1999
2001	David Small; text by Judith St. George	*So You Want to Be President?*	Philomel Books, 2000
2002	David Wiesner	*The Three Pigs*	Clarion/Houghton Mifflin, 2001
2003	Eric Rohmann	*My Friend Rabbit*	Roaring Brook/ Milbrook, 2002
2004	Mordicai Gerstein	*The Man Who Walked between Towers*	Roaring Brook Press/ Milbrook Press, 2003
2005	Kevin Henkes	*Kitten's First Full Moon*	Greenwillow, 2004
2006	Chris Raschka; text by Norton Juster	*The Hello, Goodbye Window*	Michael di Capua Books, 2005
2007	David Wiesner	*Flotsam*	Clarion Books, 2006

Source: Association for Library Service to Children. "Caldecott Medal Winners, 1938–Present." Chicago: Association for Library Service to Children. (January 27, 2007) Available: www.ala.org/ala/alsc/awardsscholarships/literaryawds/caldecottmedal/caldecotthonors/caldecottmedal.htm

EXAMINING THE ELEMENTS OF PICTURE BOOKS

How do you examine picture books? One technique is to look at the book several times. Each time concentrate on a different aspect. What clues do the cover and book jacket give you about the content and purpose of the book? Next, look for clues on the endpapers inside each cover. Does the color of the paper or the illustrations suggest the book's content? Can you find clues on the title page and its facing page? Even the illustrations on the dedication page can add to your anticipation of the book's content. Read the book attentively. Concentrate on both the illustrations and the text. Ask yourself, "How does the overall presentation of the literary and pictorial elements of the book tell the story?"

Then reread the book and concentrate on the illustrations. Questions to consider:

- How do the pictures tell the story or present the information?
- Do they convey meaning and emotion?
- Do they show the relationship of shapes?
- What do they tell you about the setting of the story?
- If there were no text, could you tell the story?
- How are colors used in the books?
- Are the illustrations limited to the primary colors (red, blue, and yellow)?
- Are the colors bright or pale, soft or harsh, cool or warm?
- Can you determine the medium the artist used?
- What overall impression do you have of the uniqueness of this book?

Next concentrate on details in the illustrations. Do any of the details reappear in the various illustrations? In books designed to motivate the young child, look for details that would involve the child or flaps covering an object to be identified.

As you use picture books, you and children can answer the following questions: What information do the details provide? Do they reflect a historical period or culture?

Evaluate the pictures as art. What techniques did the artist use? How do these techniques create a mood, provide information, focus the reader's attention on the action of the story, reveal the setting, or show changes in the characters? And finally, do you think the qualities of the book will bring enjoyment to a child?

Spotlight 5.1:   Selecting Picture Books

Spotlight on Public Libraries

Children and adults learn about art by being exposed to many different styles using various media. Offer a wide selection meant to stimulate and engage their minds. From folk art to computer graphics, from pleasant paintings to offbeat fun, be inclusive.

Spotlight on School Libraries

Bring the range of art represented in the collection's picture books to the attention of art teachers. Seek out their knowledge to increase your own. Educate teachers and students to the ageless appeal of picture books, which often can be read on several levels of meaning.

ASSESSING PICTORIAL ELEMENTS

Artists, regardless of their style or choice of medium, decide how they are going to effectively use the **pictorial elements** of shape, line, space, edge, color, proportion, and detail to tell the story. One can equate the pictorial elements with an artist's vocabulary; these elements serve the same purposes as words and syntax for authors.

The artist can use lines, colors, and value to create shapes or to outline some mass. **Shapes** can be recognizable objects, animals, or people; they may be geometric or abstract. The shapes may be flat and two-dimensional or fully rounded, giving a three-dimensional impression. Shapes can suggest rather than portray objects.

Look for shapes that suggest feeling and ideas. The shape of an object may give the viewer a sense of its perspective. The viewer may sense the dimensions and volume of the object. You will find many effective examples of the use of line and shapes.

Eric Carle, well known for his collages, uses shape, space, and color to create contrast, motion, and unity in *From Head to Toe* (Plate 9, HarperCollins, 1997). The call for physical exercise is delivered with an upbeat approach. The large black letter text and large areas of white space contrast with the clear colors of the figures. The double-page illustrations' use of facing shapes communicates how to do the exercise. The paint strokes suggest motion and textures. The blue-and-black of the cat directs the viewer's eye to the hat of the child. The position of the eyes and body stances unite the two sides of the illustration.

An artist creates a **line** with dots that can go in any direction. It may be a straight line, a shaped one, an angular one, or one that curves. The line may be broken. It may be thick or thin, dark or pale. Lines may be soft, fluid, following contours, or quickly drawn; both can create movement. Lines can define an object and give substance, shape, and mass. All this can be done in black and white or in color.

Lines vary in their angle, width, length, motion, and color. Each use helps the artist communicate in a different way. Lines can visualize the character's actions, interactions with others, inner thoughts, and feelings. Often lines are used to outline a shape or form or to imply depth and texture.

In *Smoky Night* (Plate 10; Harcourt, 1994) by Eve Bunting, David Diaz uses shape, line, color, and proportion and creates balance, emphasis, and focus. Yellow is used throughout this story of the Watts riot. In this illustration the protagonist's cat has been found after the fire. Yellow—the color of the sun and suggestive of new beginnings—is used as a dominant and hopeful color. Heavy black lines set off the illustration from the border and outline the figures. The large curving shape of the woman is balanced by the vertical stance of the boy and cat. The extended arms of the woman and the elongated shape of the cat direct our focus to the dish of milk. This event plays a role in moving the story forward, foreshadowing the book's climax. A unique feature of this book is the collage used as background for the text and illustrations. Photographs of harsh, heavy, and sharp objects capture the chaos of a riot.

Artists use **space** in illustrations to create negative areas (empty) or positive (enclosed). The artist's use of these two types of spaces can create balance in the illustration. Whether dealing with an abstract or realistic painting, artists use the same techniques to create perspective or the illusion of depth. They may use overlapping planes, converging lines, color, scale, size, and placement to create a two-dimensional or three-dimensional effect. For example, paler and less intense colors may be used to create a faraway effect. Colors in the background may be softer and blur. In the two-dimensional illustration the objects or figures might overlap. The artist thus focuses our attention by creating a point of view in the space.

In *Hosni the Dreamer* (Plate 3; Farrar, Straus & Giroux, 1997), Uri Shulevitz uses shape, space, line, color, and detail to create exaggeration, perspective, and rhythm. A shepherd travels across the desert to the city to spend his fortune. Using the authentic desert colors of the region, Shulevitz enlivens the text with his charming drawings. This is a good example of the importance of the integration of text and illustrations in a picture storybook. Here the illustrations play a key role in establishing the setting and mood of the story. Shulevitz fills the space with the rhythm of people moving to capture the busyness of the marketplace. While exaggerating the shape of buildings, he pays attention to details such as the Arabic writings on the buildings and the architectural ornaments. His strong use of line to define shapes creates patterns, and with his use of watercolor shadows, he brings a three-dimensional quality to the illustration.

Other artists use **edge**, rather than a line, to create shape. To create the edge, the artist may use a contrasting color to distinguish the shape from the background or another object. When an artist makes a collage, different materials create the edge.

Picture books can be color or in black and white. Variations in black-and-white illustrations can be created by adding black to mix shades or by adding white to mix tints.

When using **color** the artist is involved with its three attributes: hue, intensity, and value. **Hue** refers to the six pure colors: red, orange, yellow, green, blue, and violet. You can find color wheels online and in encyclopedias or dictionaries. For an example of how artists use the primary colors of red, yellow, and blue with other colors see Joy Richardson's *Looking at Pictures: An Introduction to Art for Young People* (Abrams, 1997). Colors with red in them are considered warm, while colors with blue in them are cool. The artist's choice of color thus affects the mood of the picture.

Intensity refers to the brightness or dullness (the strength) of a color, which can be made duller by adding the color opposite it on the color wheel. For example, adding blue makes orange duller.

Value refers to the lightness or darkness of a color and can be changed by adding white or black. Artists also use shape, line, and texture to create value contrasts. Changing the value with color or shadings of black and white helps create space, identify characters, suggest a change of time, create mood, reflect action, and give a sense of setting.

In *Grandfather's Journey* (Plate 1; Houghton Mifflin, 1993), Allen Say uses shape, space, line, color, value, and detail with balance and repetition. The muted soft watercolors capture the mood of this story of remembrance. In these realistic, almost portraitlike drawings, viewers feel they are looking at a family photo album. The positioning of the bodies and the details of facial expressions reveal a dignified and reflective spirit. The weight of the three characters as one shape is balanced by the white (lack of color) crisp lines of the ship's railing. Horizontal lines of the decking repeated in the background shapes show that this is a docked boat. Usage of grays close in value provides a background setting without distracting from the emphasis on the family. The contrast of the hazy details and faded background further add reality to the setting.

Proportion, the relationship of the size of one object with another, may be realistic or highly exaggerated. Dr. Seuss's use of exaggerated proportions adds to the humor of his stories. In contrast, realistic proportions are more desirable in a concept book dealing with the relationships of objects. (**Concept book** is a term used to describe the category of books in which basic information is presented, usually for the young child.)

The amount of detail used by the artist also influences the message being delivered. Many objects can be complex or create a very busy illustration. This approach can effectively present an activity involving many people or reflect a character's state of mind. Fewer details provide a simpler style, one desirable in helping very young children focus on a particular object.

Michael McCurdy, in *The Gettysburg Address* by Abraham Lincoln (Plate 6; Houghton Mifflin, 1995), uses line and detail with contrasts and perspective to create a realistic scene. The black-and-white illustrations depict the somber tone of the Civil War through detailed and accurate drawings of the battle scenes and war maneuvers. The struggle of the people is rendered so realistically that it brings new energy to this historical era. Using fine lines and high contrast, McCurdy emphasizes ethnic and gender diversity as well as action in his realistic portraits. In this particular scene, the detailed features of the audience watching Lincoln point the viewer's attention to McCurdy's focal point, Lincoln on the stage. The inclusion of their reactions to his famous words provides a vehicle for involving the viewer in the event. The mood of the illustration mirrors the impact of the text.

Contrast this illustration with that of Malcah Zeldis. A folk artist, Malcah Zeldis in *Honest Abe* (Plate 5; Greenwillow Books, 1993) by Edith Kunhardt, uses intense colors and exaggerated sizes of Douglas and Lincoln to suggest their power as speakers. The naïve style and typical intense use of colors highlight the presence of Lincoln in each of the paintings. In using two-dimensional figures with details reflecting the historical period and setting, Zeldis focuses on Lincoln's grandeur and importance, making him larger than life. Notice how effectively the exaggerated size of Douglas and Lincoln suggests their power in contrast to the sizes of the audience figures, which reflect their lesser role in history. Here these smaller figures function as a decorative element in the illustration.

Stoplight 5.1:   Picture Books—Buyer Beware!
Beware of picture books whose sole purpose is to showcase an artist's work. Insist on books that have meaning to children.

Composition

Artists also make decisions about how they are going to organize the elements. This involves unity, balance, rhythm, perspective, and proximity. Writers arrange words to provide a message; artists arrange pictorial elements to create a message. The artist aims to achieve a sense of unity within the illustration. **Unity** is the result of the artist's technique in relating various parts of an illustration to one another to create an integrated whole. To determine whether this was achieved, Jan Greenberg and Sandra Jordan assert that when you look at a unified work of art, you feel it. If you were to remove one line or shape or color, the painting might fall apart. If you were to add another part, it would be too much (Greenberg and Jordan, 1994: 68).

The artist rearranges the elements in the composition to achieve unity.

In *Tuesday*, David Wiesner (Plate 8; Clarion Books, 1991) uses color and detail to create perspective, rhythm, and unity. Flying frogs travel over a city in a nighttime adventure. In this fantasy voyage Wiesner uses his humorous paintings to give the reader a bird's-eye view of the frogs' adventure in flight. Looking down on the houses from the frogs' perspective, we see the realistic detail of setting, emphasized by perspective, muted colors, and moonlight shadows, making the impossible believable. The reoccurring image of frogs on each page reinforces the central theme of the book and unifies the story. The placement of some of the frogs moving off the page leads the viewer on to the next scene.

Balance is one of the important aspects of composition. Balance may be symmetrical or asymmetrical. If the parts of the illustration are arranged so the shapes, patterns, and colors are identical on either side of a central boundary, then the work is **symmetrical**. When the halves are not identical, the work is **asymmetrical**. Colors, lines, shapes, and sizes are used to create the balance. A smaller shape of a bright color may attract more attention than a larger space of a dull color on the page.

In *John Henry* (Plate 4; Dial Books, 1994), Jerry Pinkney uses line, color, proportion, detail, asymmetrical placement, and perspective. In this retelling by Julius Lester of a legendary African American hero, John Henry's forward-leaning position presents a statement of his eagerness to face this new challenge. This stance portrays not only his eagerness but also his strength. John Henry dominates this scene in terms of size, body position, and placement on the page. His body is in an asymmetrical position. Line, light, and color and the use of shadow give volume and movement, creating a three-dimensional appearance that adds depth to the illustration while focusing the viewer's attention. The choice of lighter and brighter colors for John Henry enables the viewer to notice more detail in his features and clothing than for the other people in the illustration. The darker colors and lack of contrasts limit the impact of the boss's clothing and steam drill and provide a balance for John Henry.

The **rhythm** in the illustration expresses movement by repeating colors, shapes, lines, or texture. The sense of motion in the picture causes the eye to move from one part to another. The artist may use techniques such as repetition of patterns or lines to create this effect.

In *Freight Train*, Donald Crews (Plate 2; Greenwillow Books, 1978) uses shapes, space, edge, and color to create motion and balance, and the influence of graphic art is evident in this book about colors. The color of each car flows into the color of the following car. Motion is also seen in the blurred lines from the wheels. An airbrush technique creates a sense of motion; the soft edge of the airbrush contrasts with the linear drawing of the trestles. The asymmetrical placement of the train suggests its motion onto the next page and is contrasted with the flatness of the rest of the illustration. The large-size text on white space balances the black of the engine and the smoke, while the bottom half of the illustration is balanced by the soft yellowish green background.

Variety in textures, lines, colors, and shapes provides contrasts and visual interest. All of these in turn can direct the viewer's eye to the movement and help us see from the artist's viewpoint.

The artist uses lines and patterns to direct the viewer's eye to what the viewer is supposed to see (**perspective**), whether it be motion, activity, stability, or calm. One way the artist might do this is to use a character's arm or an arrow to direct the viewer's attention to a specific place in the painting.

There are other ways the artist engages the eye or evokes feelings. **Proximity** refers to the location of various objects in relationship to one another. The artist may choose one dominant object or a visual element to catch the eye. For example, one character or object may be placed closer to the viewer and thus appear larger than the other characters or objects. The artist may accent or highlight certain features by exaggerating them and may choose to use objects similar to or very different from each other.

David Wisniewski, noted for his cut-paper illustrations, uses shapes, color, detail, contrast, and exaggeration to help the reader focus in his *Wave of the Sea-Wolf* (Plate 7; Houghton Mifflin, 1994). An Indian princess is rescued from drowning and saves her people. An original story based on Northwest Indian lore inspires the dramatic cut-paper illustrations. Wisniewski layers intricate shapes on each other to build to a diorama filled with excitement and action. In this scene the figures of Tlingit people, wearing customary clothing, point the viewer to the distant mountain. The exaggerated waves of the water forewarn of coming events. The high contrast of the brightness and jaggedness of the white paper against the blue sky draws the viewer's attention from the more evenly colored foreground to the background wave. All the figures cast a shadow on the background, making this a three-dimensional drama. A border of traditional Northwest Indian motifs continues the theme by framing the text.

Medium

Artists employ various media—each with unique qualities—to create distinct effects. You will find a wide range in picture books. Information about the medium used may be provided in the book, usually on the **verso** of the title page, in the blurb on the inside of the book jacket, or in a biographical sketch about the illustrator on the back flap of the book jacket.

The original artwork may be drawn using pencils, pen and ink, pastels, watercolor, or paints. Other illustrations are the result of printmaking in which woodblock prints, engravings, or silkscreen are used. And still other illustrations may be photographs. Artists may use a combination of materials or may create collages.

The artist might do a preliminary sketch using pencils and then use them again for the final illustrations. A graphite pencil is used to create lines; a hard pencil is used to create a thin line, and a soft one to create a heavy line. An array of neutral tones can be achieved using only black and white. Colored pencils can create various hues. Other tools used in drawings that can create lines, shading, and shadows include pen and ink, markers, crayons, and chalk.

Pastels, soft chalky drawing material similar to charcoal, are available in a wide range of colors. The artist can create a slightly textured, flaky surface by pressing heavily with the pastel or create a softer effect by blending the colors. When the artist uses a light touch, the results are sketchy marks and less intense colors.

Watercolor, a powder color mixed with water, can be used on watercolor paper, which is usually white. With the transparency of the watercolors, the paper creates the light areas. Artists may use ink lines on the watercolors to define forms.

Gouache (opaque watercolors), made by mixing water directly into a powdered pigment, is opaque and hides what is under it. This can create intense color because the amount of pigment prevents the reflection of light. **Tempera** is formed by mixing colored pigment with a binder and water; it dries quickly and permanently, so it is harder to achieve subtle colors with it. **Poster paint** is a form of tempera.

Acrylic paint is water soluble until it dries and then becomes water resistant. It can be applied with a brush or palette knife to achieve different effects.

Mixing color pigments into an oil base makes **oil paints**. As the oil dries slowly, the artist can mix colors or remove mistakes. Different degrees of thickness result in different textures.

In **printmaking** the drawn item is reversed when printed. The artist chooses from a variety of materials to transfer one image to another. In an early method, one seen less frequently today, the artist cut into a wood block, removing pieces, and creating a raised surface (in relief). When inked, this surface pressed against the paper creates a reversed impression of the design or image as a **woodblock print**. The artist may do a similar process using a **linoleum block** creating a linocut. **Etching** is the process in which the drawings are reproduced from a metal plate on which acid has been used to create the lines. Another common form of printmaking is **silk screening**. In this process the artist creates a stencil by blocking out parts of the silk. The ink is squeezed through the open mesh of the silk on the paper. The image is not reversed as in the other forms of printmaking.

Scratchboard gives the appearance of a woodcut. Artists scratch a picture into the surface of a two-layer board. The result is a high contrast between the remaining and scratched-away areas.

Some illustrations are composed of multiple materials, including fragments of colored papers, photographs, fabrics, or pieces of wood. These materials are then glued to a flat surface, creating a single picture. To create a three-dimensional effect, the artist may use objects, such as safety pins, or embossing.

Photographers using black-and-white or color film create other illustrations. As an artist, the photographer uses techniques of framing, composing, and printing pictures. As the painter presents a viewpoint, so does the photographer. Tana Hoban effectively uses the camera to make small objects large or the distant close in her concept books.

Graphic artists can also use technology. David Pelletier's *The Graphic Alphabet* (Orchard, 1996) is an example of the use of computer-generated images reproduced in full color. Other artists may use images from X rays and photographs that were scanned and computer coded to create clear, colorful illustrations.

Sculptured media can be created using plastine, which is then photographed. This form of modeling clay never gets hard, so the artist can reshape the piece.

Design

The appearance and appeal of a picture book reflect the work of the book designer. These individuals make decisions about the shape, size, binding, endpapers, paper, typefaces, and page layout.

The shape of a picture book is usually a rectangle. In some cases the height of the rectangle exceeds the width. Other books may be wide, allowing the illustrators to create larger pictures using facing pages. *Time Flies* by Eric Rohmann provides an example of this artist using the two-page spread to give a sense of movement and size of the objects. While the shape of a book can give a hint of its content, the variety of shapes also makes these books the most difficult to shelve. They often require deeper shelves than many classrooms, homes, or libraries have. Dividers in the shelves for these books can help keep them straight, whether they are picture storybooks or information books.

The **front matter**, or the pages between the front endpapers and the first page of text, also may be illustrated. Illustrations may appear on the half-title page, the frontispiece, the title page, and the dedication page. Here one may find clues to the mood, characters, setting, theme, or subject of the book. Patricia Polacco's dedication page in *Pink and Say* (Philomel Books, 1994) is a good example of how authors and illustrators use illustrations on this page. Polacco uses a double-page spread portraying a black family seeing the eldest son off to the Civil War. The text, "To the memory of Pinkus Aylee," introduces the reader to this black Union soldier who saved the life of a white Union soldier.

Page shape can vary from book shape. You will find half pages, where the top might contain one story and the bottom another, or the top page can be used with various bottom pages, or a variation of the above. The technique of trimming pages so each one is bigger than the page before can help direct the reader's attention to the movement of the story or a change in size and detail. Other techniques include die-cutting a part of the page so that the reader sees something from the following page, or using a clear transparent page with information about the illustration under it.

Sizes range from very small, such as Beatrix Potter's books, to very large ones like *Time Flies.* The larger size permits sharing with a group of children.

Binding refers to how the book is encased. The designer is interested in creating an appealing book with a durable exterior. This is an important factor for libraries or other settings where the book will be used by many children over a period of time. Sometimes an illustration appears on the cover, other times a design motif.

Book jackets, protective covers for the book, also provide information about a book. They prepare the users for what will come. The illustration used may be the one that is on the cover, one from the book, or one from a separate work. When the illustration extends over both sides, you have a double-page spread. Sometimes the book jacket has two illustrations: the front one giving a hint of the content, the back reflecting the end of the story. Information provided on the inside of the book jackets includes biographical information about the author and illustrator and a description of the contents.

Endpapers are the first and last spreads inside the front and back cover. The endpapers may be plain or introduce a motif used throughout the book. Pictures used on the endpapers may forecast the content, provide information, or create the mood for a story. Characters may be introduced. The colors of the endpapers may feature colors used throughout the book, suggesting the mood of a story.

The choice of paper can add to the sensory experience of handling a book. The paper may have a matte finish (a dull surface) or be coated with a shiny surface. The paper should not dominate or weaken the artwork. For young readers or those having difficulty reading, avoid thin pages in which the text from one page can be seen on the reverse page.

Typefaces used in the text (text faces) also affect the look of the book. For beginning readers the selection of text faces can facilitate access to the information or make it easy to read. These may differ from the **display faces** used on the title page or for chapter headings. The size of the text face (measured in points) also affects the appearance and accessibility of the book. As you examine books, look to see if the typeface is aesthetically pleasing with the illustrations.

Typefaces used on title pages and for chapter headings are called *display faces.* They are usually larger and more decorative than the text faces.

Introduce children to typography with books using different fonts, typefaces, and levels of boldness. Children may want to use a word processor to create different fonts and different sizes to see the effect.

Page layout refers to how the type and illustrations are placed on the page. In some books a frame or border sets off the text or pictures. In other books the text may be above, below, to the right, to the left, or in a combination of locations in relation to the pictures. The text can also be on the illustration. As you look at the book, ask yourself if the child will be able to follow the flow of words or if the busyness of the page is confusing.

The term **double-page spread** refers to two facing pages. An illustrator may do one painting using the two pages, which gives the artist the advantage of having more space and room in which to illustrate. The place where the two pages come together is called the **gutter**. In a carefully prepared book the picture (created by the artwork on each of two pages) matches. Illustrations in the gutter create a problem when one is thinking about having a book rebound and there is not enough room for the necessary trimming.

So far we have looked at the characteristics of the traditional book format of flat two-dimensional pages. Today there are many books that involve construction details used by book designers and paper engineers. Within this category are pop-up books and lift the flap, pull the tab, revolving wheels, sliding panels, and toy books. The interactive characteristics of these books attract users. Some of the information books help children see the relationships of parts of an object or person. The big drawback for libraries and classroom collections is the limited number of times these books can be used or circulated without needing replacement. A part pulled completely out of the book is not easy to replace.

Other books contain movable parts, such as game pieces, or materials for science experiments or handicraft activities, and audiocassettes or CDs in the book or attached to the cover. The first user enjoys the combination; the second may not be able to use the book if a part is missing. If you work with preschoolers, pay attention to warning labels on some board books with parts potentially harmful to children.

PLATE 1

Illustration from *Grandfather's Journey* by Allen Say. Copyright © 1993 by Allen Say. Reprinted by permission of Houghton Mifflin Company. All rights reserved.

Medium: Gouache paints

The use of grays close in value provides a background setting for the weight of the three characters, which form one shape balanced by the white (lack of color) crisp lines of the ship's railing. The horizontal lines of the decking repeated in the shapes in the background show this is a docked boat.

PLATE 2

Illustration by Donald Crews from his *Freight Train.* Copyright © 1978 by Donald Crews. By permission of HarperCollins Publishers.

Medium: Paint applied with an air brush

Shape, space, edge, and color are used to create motion and balance. The color of one car flowing to the color of the following car and the blurred lines of the wheels create motion. The asymmetrical placement of the train suggests its motion onto the next page. The soft edge of the airbrush is in contrast with the linear drawing of the trestles.

PLATE 3

Illustration from *Hosni the Dreamer: An Arabian Tale* by Ehud Ben-Ezer, pictures by Uri Shulevitz. Text copyright © 1997 by Ehud Ben-Ezer. Illustration copyright © 1997 by Uri Shulevitz. Illustrattions reprinted by permission of Uri Shulevitz.

Medium: Watercolors

Shape, space, line, color, and detail create exaggeration, perspective, and rhythm. Authentic desert colors establish the setting. The rhythm of people moving fills the space and captures the busyness of the market place. Although the buildings are exaggerated, care is given to details such as the Arabic writings on the buildings and architectural ornaments. Strong use of line defines shapes and creates patterns combined with watercolor shadows to bring a three-dimensional quality to the illustration.

PLATE 4

From *John Henry* by Julius Lester, illustrated by Jerry Pinkney. Copyright © 1994 by Jerry Pinkney, illustrations. Used by permission of Dial Books for Young Readers, A Division of Penguin Young Readers Group, A Member of Penguin Group (USA) Inc., 345 Hudson St., New York, NY 10014. All rights reserved.

Medium: Pencil, colored pencil, and watercolor

John Henry dominates this scene in terms of his size, position of his body, and his placement on the page. Line, light, color, and shadow give volume and movement creating a three-dimensional appearance adding depth to the illustration, while focusing the viewer's attention on John Henry. John Henry's body's asymmetrical position is balanced by the darker colors of the boss's clothing and the steam drill.

PLATE 5

Illustration from *Honest Abe* by Edith Kunhardt. Illustrations by Malcah Zeldis. Copyright © 1993 by Malcah Zeldis. Used by permission of HarperCollins Publishers.

Medium: Gouache paints

This folk artist uses intense colors and exaggerated sizes for Douglas and Lincoln to suggest their power as speakers. In using flat, two-dimensional figures with details reflecting the historical period and setting, Zeldis focuses on Lincoln's grandeur and importance, making Lincoln appear larger than life. Smaller figures function as a decorative element in the illustration.

Finally, when his daughter was nearly grown, he could wait no more.
He took his family and returned to his homeland.

Plate 1

Crossing trestles.

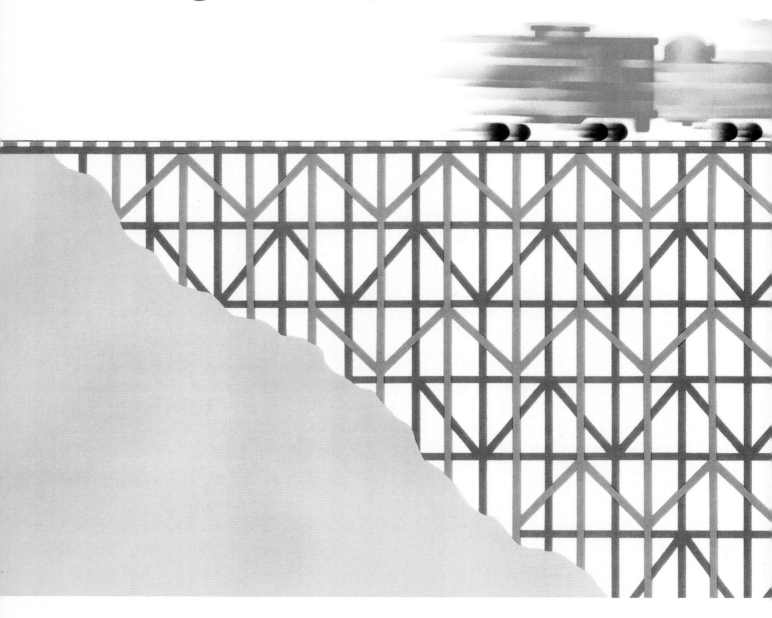

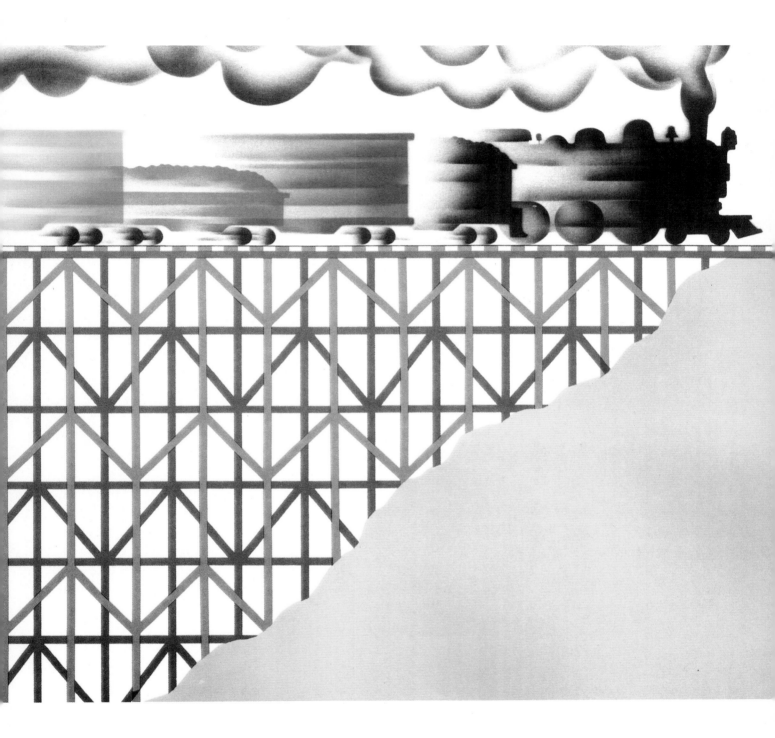

Plate 2

Plate 3

Plate 4

A few years later Abe decided to run for the United States Senate. He ran against Stephen A. Douglas. Douglas believed that slavery should continue. Lincoln believed that slavery should end. Lincoln and Douglas traveled all over Illinois, debating each other. When the people voted, Douglas won, but the debates made Lincoln famous.

Plate 5

The world will little note, nor long remember what we say here, but it can never forget what they did here.

Plate 6

Thereafter, Kchokeen could foretell the giant waves that marked Gonakadet's travels at the mouth of the bay. The trembling of the earth and the sound of the sea told her much, but it was the howl of the bear that meant a wave was coming. The fishermen were grateful for her predictions, because now they could travel the waters in safety. The village prospered, and the people accorded Kchokeen great honor and wealth.

Plate 7

Plate 8

I am a cat
and I arch my back.
Can you do it?

I can do it!

Plate 9

plate 16

Plate 10

PLATE 6

Illustration by Michael McCurdy from *The Gettysburg Address*. Illustration copyright © 1995 by Michael McCurdy. Reprinted by permission of Houghton Mifflin Company. All rights reserved.

Medium: Scratchboard

Line and detail with contrasts and perspective create a realistic scene. The black-and-white illustrations depict the somber tone of the Civil War. In this particular scene, the carefully detailed features of the audience help the viewer focus on Lincoln. The inclusion of their reactions to his famous words provides a vehicle for involving the viewer in the event. The mood of the illustration mirrors the impact of the text.

PLATE 7

Illustration from *The Wave of The Sea-Wolf* by David Wisniewski. Copyright © 1994 by David Wisniewski. Reprinted by permission of Clarion Books, an imprint of Houghton Mifflin Company. All rights reserved.

Medium: Cut paper

Layers of intricate shapes, exaggerated waves, and high contrast of the brightness and jaggedness of the white paper against the blue sky draw the viewer's attention to the background wave that forewarns of coming events. Wisniewski layers intricate shapes upon each other to build a diorama filled with excitement and action.

PLATE 8

Illustration from *Tuesday* by David Wiesner. Copyright © 1991 by David Wiesner. Reprinted by permission of Clarion Books, an imprint of Houghton Mifflin Company. All rights reserved.

Medium: Watercolors

The realistic detail of setting, emphasized by perspective, muted colors, and moonlight shadows makes the impossible believable. The placement of some of the frogs moving off the page leads the viewer on to the next scene.

PLATE 9

From Head to Toe by Eric Carle. Copyright © 1997 by Eric Carle. Used by permission of HarperCollins Publishers.

Medium: Collage

Large white spaces contrast with the bold, clear colors. The blue and black of the cat directs the viewer's eye to the child's hat. The position of the eyes and body stances unite the two sides of this double-page spread.

PLATE 10

Illustration from *Smoky Night* by Eve Bunting, copyright © 1994 by David Diaz, reproduced by permission of Harcourt, Inc.

Medium: Collage, acrylics, linocut

Heavy black lines set off the illustration from the border and outline the figures. The large curving shape of the woman is balanced by the vertical stance of the boy and cat. The extended arms of the woman and the elongated shape of the cat direct our focus to the dish of milk. Yellow is a dominant and hopeful color at this turning point in the story.

JUDGING PICTURE BOOKS

The following questions are designed to help you examine picture books. No one book will or should have all the qualities mentioned. They are options to look for in the illustrations, and there is not one right answer. You will need to judge the appropriateness of the question for the book you are evaluating.

Overall questions:

- Does the artwork extend or clarify the text?
- Does the artist make the viewer see something in a new way?
- Is the content of the illustrations appropriate for the book's purpose?
- Is the number of illustrations appropriate for the book's purpose?
- Are pictorial conventions from specific groups used to add realism to the content?
- Do the illustrations lend themselves to sharing with a group?

Color

- How is color used? Do the colors convey mood and emotions? Do the colors provide movement? Are they passively in the background?
- Are colors appropriate for the text?
- What role does color play in the layout of the page?
- Are contrasting colors, tones, shades, and tints used to create variety, texture, and perspective?

Line

- Are lines used effectively?
- Are the lines strong and solid or diminutive and quick?
- Do they express movement?
- Does the width of the lines or cross-hatching add perspective to the person or subject?

Shape

- Is shape handled effectively?
- Does shape help tell the story?
- How do shapes on the same page relate to one another?
- Is the page crowded and cluttered with shapes?

Composition

- Do the layout and size of the pictures carry the eye from page to page and create a rhythm in keeping with the meaning of the book?
- Is there a balance between the pictures and the text?
- Do the pictures and text create a pleasing effect?
- Is there variety and unity?
- Is there a focus to the illustration?

Design

- Is the choice of medium in keeping with the mood of the story or the concept being presented?
- Is the typeface appropriate to the book and the intended user?
- Is the paper in keeping with the original medium (acrylic on shiny paper, watercolor or pencil on a matte finish)?
- Does the book represent excellence in bookmaking?

EVALUATING WORDLESS BOOKS

In **wordless books**, the story line is told entirely with pictures or with a minimum of words. Their appeal is wide. *A Day, A Dog* by Gabrielle Vincent (Front Street, 2000) is one enjoyed by children and adults. Wordless books vary in style and sophistication. Those for younger children have basic line drawings, crisp format, clear plots, and straightforward story lines. They require focus and unity, created through the illustrations and story lines. For older children the artwork is more detailed and the themes are more highly developed and complex. For younger children, telling the story in a wordless book can facilitate interactive experiences for several readers, two children, or a child and an adult. Such books provide basic cognitive exercises in sequencing and language development. Reading these books involves the literary elements of character, plot, setting, style, and theme. For older children wordless books can serve as a take-off point for creative writing. Books in this format accommodate viewers using languages other than English.

Another variation on the wordless book format is the wordless form of graphic novels.

Criteria

Questions to consider:

- Is action shown in each illustration?
- Does the story move from the familiar to the unfamiliar?

- Is the sequence of the action clear?
- Is the story line distinct?
- Is the information clearly developed?
- Do the illustrations clearly present the literary elements of character, plot, setting, style, and theme?

SUMMARY

Illustrations play a significant role in communicating the story or presenting information in picture books. Artists choose pictorial elements, decide on the composition of the illustrations, and select appropriate media to create unified works. Compatible book design can enhance the illustrations. In wordless books the illustrations must communicate both the visual and literary elements. Careful use of criteria can guide the evaluation of picture book illustrations.

REFERENCES

Association for Library Service to Children. 2004. *The Newbery and Caldecott Awards: A Guide to the Medal and Honor Books.* Annual. Chicago, IL: American Library Association.

Association for Library Service to Children. 2007. "Caldecott Medal Winners, 1938–present." Chicago, IL: Association of Library Service to Children. (January 27, 2007) Available: www.ala.org/alsc/awardsscholarships/literaryawds/caldecottmedal/caldecotthonors/caldecottmedal.htm

Banta, Gratia J. 2004. "Reading Pictures: Searching for Excellence in Picture Books." *Children & Libraries* 2, no. 3 (Winter): 30–34.

Codell, Esme Raji. 2003. *How to Get Your Child to Love Reading.* Chapel Hill, NC: Algonquin Books of Chapel Hill.

Elleman, Barbara. 1994. "The Visual Connection." *Book Links,* 3, no. 5 (May): 5.

Greenberg, Jan, and Sandra Jordan. 1994. *The Painter's Eye: Learning to Look at Contemporary American Art.* New York: Delacorte Press.

Richardson, Joy. 1997. *Looking at Pictures: An Introduction to Art for Young People.* New York: Harry N. Abrams.

RESOURCES

Association for Library Service to Children. "Caldecott Medal Home Page." Chicago, IL: Association for Library Service to Children. (August 26, 2006) Available: www.ala.org/ala/alsc/awardssholarships/literaryawds/caldecottmedal/caldecottmedal.htm
Provides information about the award and honor books.

Banta, Gratia J. "Reading Pictures: Searching for Excellence in Picture Books." *Children & Libraries* 2, no. 3 (Winter 2004): 30–34. Also available in *The Newbery and Caldecott Awards: A Guide to the Medal and Honor Books* (ALA Editions, 2004), pp. 9–18.
Identifies elements of design, describes how adults can increase their understanding of cultural context, and suggests ways to develop visual literacy.

Carle, Eric. 1996. *The Art of Eric Carle.* New York: Philomel Books.
Includes his autobiography, essays about his work, a step-by-step photo essay on his collage techniques, and examples of his illustrations.

Eric Carle Museum of Picture Book Art. (August 26, 2006) Available: www.picturebookart.org
Provides information about the museum and features illustrators.

Janson, H. W., and Anthony F. Janson. 2003. *History of Art for Young People.* New York: Abrams. Or their *History of Art*, 5th ed. (Abrams, 1996).
The latter has 1,266 illustrations. Comprehensive in coverage providing additional information through maps and a glossary.

Leonard, Marcia. "The Start of Something Big: How an Unusual Exhibit Revolutionized the Way We View Picture-book Art." *School Library Journal* 51, no. 9 (September 2005): 50–55.
Describes the beginnings of The Original Art annual exhibition sponsored by Society of Illustrators in New York City. An article to share with aspiring illustrators. Identifies locations of original artwork and offers advice to young artists.

Reading Is Fundamental. 2005. *The Art of Reading: Forty Illustrators Celebrate RIF's 40th Anniversary.* With a foreword by Leonard S. Marcus. New York: Dutton.
Each illustrator describes a children's book that influenced him or her and provides an illustration for that work. Enhanced by photographs of the illustrators and of books they knew as a child.

Shulevitz, Uri. 1997. *Writing with Pictures: How to Write and Illustrate Children's Books.* New York: Watson-Guptill.
An excellent resource based on his works and teaching.

Society of Illustrators. Museum of American Illustration. (August 26, 2006) Available: www.societyillustrators.org/index.cms
Presents annual retrospective of illustrations from children's books.

RECOMMENDED WORDLESS PICTURE BOOKS

Anno, Mitsumasa. 2003. *Anno's Spain.* New York: Philomel Books.
Why are some people upside down? This is just one of the puzzles in Anno's delicate detailed drawings of Spain's villages, towns, and countryside. From kindergarteners to curious adults will have much to study as they journey with Anno.

Aruego, Jose, and Ariane Dewey. 2006. *Last Laugh.* New York: Dial Books.

From the lighthearted "hiss" repeated over and over on the endpapers to the mocking "quacks" hounding the bullying snake to the "hee" repeated at the end of the book, this story cautions bullies everywhere. Bright, humorous paintings dance across the pages.

Briggs, Raymond. 1978. *The Snowman*. New York: Random House.
A boy's snowman comes to life and discovers new wonders indoors. Then, they hold hands and fly through the snowstorm for more adventures until the sun melts the snowman. Muted snowscapes combine with cozy indoor scenes.

Burke, Tina. 2006. *Fly, Little Bird*. La Jolla, CA: Kane/Miller.
When a little girl and her dog discover a baby bird in the woods, they encourage it to fly, but it does not know how. After some tender care, the bird leaves its human home to join the other birds. Soft watercolors depict endearing characters.

Geisert, Arthur. 2005. *Lights Out*. Boston, MA: Houghton Mifflin.
One page of text explains little pig's challenge—to obey his parents' lights-out rule yet still keep his bedside lamp lit until he falls asleep. Detailed drawings show his ingenious step-by-step solution.

Lehman, Barbara. 2006 *Museum Trip*. Boston, MA: Houghton Mifflin.
Watercolor, gouache, and ink illustrations record a boy's literal entry into a museum exhibit. He follows a maze, receives a gold medal, and then rejoins his class in time to board the school bus. The fact that the museum guide wears a similar medal adds a note of intrigue.

McCully, Emily Arnold. 2001. *Four Hungry Kittens*. New York: Dial Books.
Four adorable little kittens investigate their rural surroundings unaware of the hazards on a farm. A loyal dog takes care of them until their mother returns. Watercolors seem just right for this warm story.

Rogers, Gregory. 2004. *The Boy, the Bear, the Baron, the Bard*. New York: Roaring Brook Press.
An impish child follows his soccer ball into a theater and is transported to Elizabethan England, where Shakespeare himself chases him through a village. In the middle of this graphic novel–format book, a riveting bird's-eye perspective uses the double spread to full advantage. The effect is gorgeous. When the boy and bear unlock the baron's cell, the baron joins their adventure. A knowledge of Shakespeare informs these shenanigans.

Rohmann, Eric. 1994. *Time Flies*. New York: Crown.
Dramatic vantage points of a bird's flight through modern times back to the age of the dinosaurs. Potentially frightening for the young child, but fascinating for five- to seven-year-olds.

Schories, Pat. 2006. *Jack and the Night Visitors*. Birmingham, UK: Front Street.
The third in a series of wordless books about a clever dog named Jack. Fascinated with the parade of robots entering his bedroom, a young boy puts one of them in a glass jar. Fortunately, Jack is nearby and frees the distressed captive. Simple plot with engaging illustrations.

Varon, Sara. 2006. *Chicken and Cat*. New York: Scholastic.

Visual clues invite the "reader" to join Cat as he visits his city friend, Chicken. Clean, outlined illustrations resemble animation. A book that invites speculation.

Weitzman, Jacqueline Preiss, and Robin Preiss Glasser. 2002. *You Can't Take a Balloon into The Museum of Fine Arts.* New York: Dial Books.

A street map of Boston prepares the viewer for the journey of a green balloon as it floats away from the intrepid grandmother who had offered to hold it while the rest of the family enjoyed the art museum. Characters in this wordless story mimic famous works of art appearing on the same page. Many amusing detailed Boston scenes to study. The book ends with listings of the paintings and of famous people appearing throughout.

RECOMMENDED PICTURE BOOK ILLUSTRATORS

Browne, Anthony. English author and illustrator praised for his creativity and concern for sensitive children. He is the 2000 recipient of the Hans Christian Andersen Award for Illustrations. *My Dad* (Farrar, Straus & Giroux, 2000) and *My Mom* (Farrar, Straus & Giroux, 2005) are told from the child's perspective. The warm browns of Dad's plaid bathrobe and the bright color flowers of Mom's bathrobe are carried throughout the other illustrations. Both texts end with the simple statement of Mom and Dad loving the child. Look for one of his familiar characteristics, the use of surreal events, in *The Shape Game* (Farrar, Straus & Giroux, 2003). A family visits the Tate Britain museum in London and is drawn into the paintings for real and surreal adventures. On the way home the family plays the shape game, an excellent way for readers to explore the world of art and how we each perceive things in different ways.

Carle, Eric. Illustrator and author noted for his bright, colorful tissue paper illustrations that are photographed after the layered papers are pasted to cardboard. Two recent examples include Bill Martin, Jr.'s *Panda Bear, Panda Bear, What Do You See?* (Holt, 2003), with its focus on endangered species, who respond to "What do I see?" and *"Slowly, Slowly, Slowly," Said the Sloth* (Philomel, 2002), with an introduction by Jane Goodall, which captures the setting and creatures of the Amazon rain forest. The back endpapers identify each animal in this story. See Carle's Web site at www.eric-carle.com

Dillon, Leo and Diane. This highly respected and honored team continue to add new artistic techniques as they enrich children's visual experiences. Their *Rap a Tap Tap: Here's Bojangles—Think of That!* (Blue Sky Press, 2002; also available with disc narrated by Charles Turner) has two-page spreads; on one side are the people with boldly painted, overlapping flat images, almost transparentlike; while the second side features the movement of Bojangles in browns, grays, and blacks. Bring this to the attention of those interested in music and movement. For *Earth Mother* by Ellen Jackson (Walker, 2005), the Dillons use soft shades of earth tones (browns, greens, blues). An eye appealing book for all.

Folk motifs with thick outlines and muted colors enhance Howard Norman's *Between Heaven and Earth: Bird Tales from Around the World* (Harcourt, 2004). Both text and illustrations capture the oral tradition, providing a perfect selection for reading aloud or storytelling. In Virginia Hamilton's retelling of a folktale, *The People Could Fly: The Picture Book* (Knopf, 2004), the Dillons provide deep-hues paintings and a framing scheme to encase the art and text in thick lines on three sides. Another for the read-aloud list. For John Herman's *One Winter's Night* (Philomel Books, 2003), the Dillons show the cow's story in full-page naturalistic paintings, while the human couple resemble woodcuts. An engaging modern version of the Nativity story.

Ehlert, Lois. Author and illustrator of picture books. Ehlert's background as a designer and graphic artist is evident in her books, with their vivid colors, interesting shapes, varying layouts and page sizes, and use of collage. *Leaf Man* (Harcourt, 2005) has die-cut tops of pages creating a sense of distance and perspective. Leaves are identified on the endpages. *Waiting for Wings* (Harcourt, 2001) includes identification and discussion of butterflies' parts and how to create a butterfly garden. A counting book that includes 0 is *Chicka Chicka 1, 2, 3* (Simon & Schuster, 2004) written by Bill Martin, Jr., and Michael Sampson, which involves numbers climbing a tree and falling to the ground, so the numbers are first heard in ascending order and then descending. Die-cut "steam holes" on the cover of *Pie in the Sky* (Harcourt, 2004) add appeal to the story of a father and child watching the cherry tree bloom, leading to the making of a pie (recipe included).

Gerstein, Mordicai. Illustrator also known for his paintings, sculptures, and prizewinning films. *Charlie Heard* (Farrar, Straus & Giroux, 2002) tells the life of Charles Ives through the sounds he heard (expressed through differently colored and sized typefaces, ducks quacking, two marching bands—one in blue and one in yellow—moving toward each other and playing different tunes). The text is boxed on white in contrast to the colorful overlapping of sounds. This is a unique visual approach to explaining this composer and his music.

For Eric A. Kimmel's retelling of *Three Samurai Cats: A Story from Japan* (Holiday House, 2003), Gerstein uses cartoon-style illustrations to depict the loathsome rat whose own greed is used by a tattered, disreputable old feline to work against him. Other recent titles include *Sparrow Jack* (Farrar, Straus & Giroux, 2003) and his Caldecott Award winner, *The Man Who Walked between the Towers* (Roaring Brook Press, 2003). The latter two titles, based on real events, show his skillful composition and dramatic use of perspective, and they have various framing patterns and multiple-page spreads to draw the reader into the scene.

Pinkney, Brian. Illustrator who uses oil paints over scratchboard to create sweeping lines, repeated contours, and vibrant colors to express energy. He often works with his wife, Andrea Davis Pinkney, as in the lively *Ella Fitzgerald: The*

Tales of a Vocal Virtuosa told through the voice of Scat Cat Monroe (Hyperion, 2002, with disc). In *The Stone Lamp: A Hanukkah Collection: Eight Days of Dark, Eight Nights of Light* by Karen Hesse (Hyperion, 2002), both author and illustrator bring warmth, light, and respect as a child's viewpoint records events from 1665 (the Clifford Tower episode during the Crusades) to Rabin's assassination in 1995. Each day opens with a biblical quote in a frame around a brief text describing the event, which is then told in the child's voice. Each event opens with a boxed symbolic small illustration and a full-page illustration.

Rohmann, Eric. Author and illustrator. His *My Friend Rabbit* (Millbrook, 2002; Caldecott, 2003) uses bold black lines to outline figures, plus black border around each of the hand-colored relief two-page spread prints, including the one that is read vertically. There's lots of humor in the antics and in the expressive portrayals of the animals. This is a delightful adventure of friendship. Black frames on wide white borders set off the brightly colored illustrations in *Pumpkinhead* (Knopf, 2003). Rohmann returns to the use of oils in *Clara and Asha* (Roaring Brook, 2005) and uses softer tones in the illustrations bordered by white background with minimum text in this nighttime tale of adventures with one's imaginary friends.

Sabuda, Robert. Considered a master paper engineer and certainly one who has brought this format to the attention of the American public. *America the Beautiful* (Simon & Schuster, 2004) illustrates the words of the song with the pop-ups, predominately in white against a colorful background with a label of the location of the subject of the pop-up. Another example of his appeal to all ages.

Don't overlook the nonfiction titles he does with Matthew Reinhart. Their *Encyclopedia Prehistorica: Dinosaurs* (Candlewick Press, 2005) is a fascinating book. At the physical and visual level, there are 35 flaps, each revealing more information. Unlike some pop-ups, the pages here are colored on both sides so viewers from the back of the page can gain information, such as comparative sizes. On the information side is the latest information and recognition of what is to be explored by future scientists. For some of the multiple flaps small hands with manipulative skills are needed. Visit Sabuda at www.RobertSabuda.com

Shulevitz, Uri. Author and Illustrator. For his *The Travels of Benjamin of Tudela: Through Three Continents in the Twelfth Century* (Farrar, Straus & Giroux, 2005), a rich palette of colors enhance the text of a Jewish man's 14-year journey to Italy, Greece, Palestine, Persia, Egypt, and Sicily. The author's note describes the original documents on which this fictional work is based. The personalized account weaves Jewish history and conditions of the times into a fascinating travelogue. Extensive bibliography and acknowledgments provide evidence of the research behind this retracing of Benjamin's journey. A Guggenheim Fellowship supported Shulevitz's research and travel for this work. He received the Caldecott Medal for his illustrations for Arthur Ransome's *The Fool of the World and the Flying Ship*.

Sis, Peter. Illustrator known for his ability to visually lead his reader to new sights and information, whether in storybooks or nonfiction titles. His illustrations for *Madlenka's Dog* (Frances Foster Books, 2002) add the fun of looking under tabs as Madlenka, while walking her imaginary dog, meets dogs associated with the neighbors on her block. Sis's use of cross-hatching to give texture to the buildings is in contrast to the use of white background for Madlenka in the early part of the book. Effective white silhouettes clearly show how the parents feel about a dog.

For Diane Ackerman's *Animal Senses* (Knopf, 2003), a book of poetry featuring images of how animals use their senses, Sis uses appropriately subtle pictures and white space to match the text.

Smith, Lane. Illustrator and author who offers a fresh perspective and humor with appealing pen-and-ink drawings enriched with a variety of textures created by use of oil paint, collage, and other techniques. A variety of page layouts (split pages, a double-page spread, where the arrow leads the viewer) help move the plot of *Pinocchio, The Boy: Incognito in Collodi* (Viking, 2002), in which the Blue Fairy turns the puppet into a boy who does not know that. For a fresh look at history, see *John, Paul, George, Ben* and *Independent Tom* (Hyperion, 2006), which closes by separating fact from fiction. Both should be added to your read-aloud list.

Smith's works with Jon Scieszka (author) entertain children and adults with their parodies of familiar songs, folk literature, and poems. Cartoon drawings set against solid backgrounds and readable font feature the expressive face of a boy caught up in the "poetry of science" in *Science Verse* (Viking, 2004; includes a sound disc). The appeal goes beyond those interested in spoofs, parody as a poetic form, or science. The endpages present the table of elements. Their *The Stinky Cheese Man and Other Fairly Stupid Tales* (Viking, 1992) is considered a "classic" of parody. The team continue their fresh approach to their subjects with *Seen Art?* (Viking, 2005) and its introduction to MoMA, the Museum of Modern Art, in New York City, and its collection.

Van Allsburg, Chris. Author and illustrator of the contemporary classic *The Polar Express* (Houghton, 1985), drawn using pastels. A board book, *All Aboard the Polar Express,* based on the movie, was issued by Houghton Mifflin in 2004. Van Allsburg's use of black and gray pencil sketches, textured paper, and scale is found in *Zathura: A Space Adventure* (Houghton Mifflin, 2002), in which Walter and Danny Budwig from *Jumanji* (Houghton Mifflin, 1981; Caldecott) face further adventures involving time, space, and perspective shifts.

Wiesner, David. Picture storybook author and illustrator known for his attention to detail and use of line and proportions, which lead the viewer on an imaginative exploration of the subject. Recall the pigs in *Tuesday* (Clarion, 2001; Caldecott, 1992) and follow their adventures in *The Three Pigs* (Clarion/ Houghton Mifflin, 2001; Caldecott, 2002), where they step out of the traditional tale. Wiesner uses frames for the old tale with characters moving outside as they fly to meet other traditional characters. Note the use of white spaces and moving parts of the familiar tale with the pigs adding circled comments. Also note the blending of art styles as the new adventures unfold.

In *The Loathsome Dragon* (Clarion, 2005) by Wiesner and his wife, Kim Kahng, one finds rich colors and traditional double-page spreads in a story about a jealous stepmother who turns the king's daughter into a finely scaled, seagreen dragon. Add this to your read-aloud list. For an artistic contrast, see Wiesner's pencil drawings for his adaptation of Fritz Leiber's Hugo and Nebula Award-winning *Gonna Roll the Bones* (Simon & Schuster, 2004).

Willems, Mo. Author-illustrator of books for young children, Emmy Award-winning script writer for such television programs as *Sesame Street*, and animated filmmaker. Recent titles demonstrate his ability to create a humorous story with appeal and identification for young children. *Your Pal Mo Willems Presents Leonardo the Terrible Monster* (Hyperion, 2005), with its cartoon drawings, well-paced story, and letters that change color, is typical. Can a terrible monster and a boy become friends? Yes. *Knuffly Bunny* (Hyperion, 2004) traces Trixie and her father's trip to the laundromat and their return to retrieve her stuffed bunny from the laundry, whereupon Trixie utters her first words, "Knuffle Bunny." In *Time to Say "Please"!* (Hyperion, 2005), via a cast of mice and multicultural children, the basics of polite conversation are introduced. Check Willems out at www.mowillems.com

Wisniewski, David. Author and illustrator noted for his detailed three-dimensional cut-paper illustrations and a selection of colors that capture the spirit and setting of the story. Compare his Caldecott Award-winning *Golem* (Clarion, 1996) with the following works, with their slanted panels and inserts in a nonlinear layout, with lots of action by the characters, and with different fonts and sizes for action words such as *SWOOOSH!*

In *Sumi Mouse* (Chronicle Books, 2002), a story of good versus evil set in Japan, brightly colored purples and golden oranges serve as background roles, as well as accent costumed key characters supported by active small grey mice. In *Master Man: A Tall Tale of Nigeria* (Lothrop, Lee & Shepard, 2001), the use of oranges and browns is contrasted with white space setting off sections of the page, as well as background for much of the dialogue. The power, strength, size, and action of the characters in both titles are graphically portrayed. For *Halloweenies* (HarperCollins, 2002), a short-story collection, Wisniewski captures the black-and-white photography of old monster movies with his pen-and-ink drawings. Check him out at www.davidwisniewski.com

Wormell, Christopher. Internationally recognized (Graphics Prize at the Bologna International Children's Book Fair in 1991) English illustrator known for his stunning, colorful linoleum-block prints. Characteristics of his work include bold, black lines around the images and effective use of light and shadow, creating simple but clear and dramatic illustrations. Wormell also works as a wood engraver in the fields of advertising, design, and editorial illustration. *Mice, Morals and Monkey Business: Lively Lessons from Aesop's Fables* (Running Press Kids, 2005) provides an opportunity for a visual literacy experience as the viewer sees the moral and interprets the message. A fuller version of the fable and a smaller version of the illustration appear at the end of the book.

Similar techniques and qualities are found in *Teeth, Tails and Tentacles: An Animal Counting Book* (Running Press Kids, 2004), which features the numbers 1–20 by depicting each numeral, spelling it in capital letters, and featuring a body part or characteristic of an animal. Information about each animal is provided at the end of the book.

Chapter 6

Fiction

EXAMINING NARRATIVE FICTION

A **fiction** book is a narrative product of the writer's imagination. Its purpose is to amuse, entertain, or stimulate our understanding of the human condition. **Realistic fiction** refers to stories about people, animals, or objects set in current times (**contemporary realism**) or in the past (historical fiction). In both, believable characters exist in realistic settings and face problems appropriate for that time and setting. **Fantasy** refers to authors' imaginative stories about people, animals, and objectives in settings outside of our daily lives.

As in adult fiction, there are several subcategories of fiction for children: stories about adventure, animals, sports, mysteries, humor, school, and other common experiences. Since realistic fiction deals with everyday life, the topics cover a wide range of life experiences. Topics that were once taboo in children's literature are treated openly, honestly, and with sensitivity by the more skillful authors. These topics include alcoholism, child abuse, divorce, death, drugs, diverse society, homelessness, single-parent families, same-sex parents, and interracial families.

The differences between an effective writer and a less effective one are displayed in Figure 6.1.

Figure 6.1: Effective vs. Less Effective Writing	
Effective Writer	**Less Effective Writer**
Well crafted	Poorly written
Characters carefully developed	Characters flat or stereotypical
Conflict development	Conflict resolved or problem solved in too pat a manner
Character and conflict interrelated	Character neither causes action nor grows from it
Universal theme	Sentimentality or didacticism
Entertains rather than instructs	Tone is didactic, sensational, or sentimental

The chief characteristics of fiction are:

- discernible characters
- developing characters
- interrelationship of character and conflict
- credible setting
- realistic plot
- particular point of view
- unique style or tone in the telling of the story
- insights into personal problems
- explorations of the reader's feelings and those of other people
- often written in the first person
- use of dialogue
- use of prose paragraph style
- relating concrete concepts to experience
- events and characters that give meaning to the story
- reader suspends disbelief
- plot holds reader's attention
- reader may read material quickly
- illustrations may extend the text, set the mood at the beginning of a chapter, or be purely decorative

Foreseeing some of the trends we see today, Eliza T. Dresang and Kate McClelland predicted in 1996 the following changes in fiction works:

- Plots: multilayered, nonlinear, and nonsequential; various points of entry; ambiguous resolutions; provocation of further thought; and lack of the traditional "happy ending."

- Characters: multiple or uncommon points of view, deeply personal expression, reflection of children's own voices, and focus on growth in inner resilience and on connections with adults or peers, usually nonparents.
- Settings: more likely to be specifically described, rather than generic, including heretofore uncommon or underrepresented places, and defining home and family in nontraditional ways.
- Themes: universal ramifications, unlimited in their range of "acceptable" topics.
- Style/tone: innovative graphics leading to interactive involvement of the reader. In some books, words and pictures may transform one another, becoming one another.
(Dresang and McClelland, 1996)

Spotlight 6.1:   Expanding Your Collection

Spotlight on Public Libraries

When a customer presents a list of titles and the library has few of them, ask if you can make a photocopy to consult for future selection consideration. Adding titles that meet your selection criteria will send the message that the library is interested in being inclusive. Often, one patron's requested title is of interest to others. Be humble enough to know that we miss some relevant titles and need suggestions from the public.

Spotlight on School Libraries

Solicit suggestions from teachers and students. Notify them when their suggestions arrive and offer to "hold" the title for them for a specified time. If you are not able to purchase the title, suggest alternatives.

ASSESSING COMPONENTS OF NARRATIVE FICTION

The interdependent elements of theme, plot, setting, characters, style, and point of view comprise a fictional work. The theme is the main idea or the central meaning of the story. The plot presents the action, whereas the setting is where and when the action takes place. The characters are the people, animals, or inanimate objects that carry out the actions. Style is the manner in which the author says something. The story is told from a point of view.

Theme

Theme is the central idea of the story, what the story means. It reveals the significance of the action. It is a comment, observation, or insight about the subject of the story. In order to accept the theme, the reader must believe both in the character and that the character could have the experience described in the story. The theme can be judged for its relevance (an external force) and for its coherence (an internal factor ordering the parts of the book to form a sequential, cohesive whole). The theme may be remembered long after the details of the plot are forgotten.

A theme may be explicit or implicit. An **explicit theme** is stated by a character or flatly stated in the narrative. Such a flat statement may sound preachy. **Implied themes** are revealed through the characters' actions and reactions.

Books for younger children usually are limited to one primary theme. Older readers can handle the complexity of secondary themes, which are generally linked to the primary theme.

Didacticism, or instruction, is not appropriate in fictional narratives written for children. These novels and short stories are designed to give pleasure and increase understanding rather than to instruct. The one area in which didacticism in children's books is justifiable is in science fiction titles, when the author is trying to explain new views and values.

Theme may be hard to identify in nonsense and fantasy stories, with their treatment of illogical and inconsistent aspects of life. These books cause the reader to look at and begin to understand the order and disorder in life and how anomalies fit together.

Questions to consider:

- What is the theme?
- How does the author present the theme?
- Is the theme relevant to the child's experiences and developmental stage?
- Is the theme universal?
- Is the story coherent?
- Is the story internally consistent, creating a convincing and unified whole?
- Is it entertaining without being moralistic?
- Does the story provide a new perspective for the reader?
- Is the theme intrinsic to the story?
- Is the protagonist believable?
- Is the character's adventure one that leads the reader to accept the theme?

Stoplight 6.1:   Book Authors—Buyer Beware!
Avoid the didactic, preachy, and moralistic writer. Avoid the writer who has joined the bandwagon in response to a current concern in society, without the expertise to address the issues.

Plot

Plot involves the actions (what happens in the story), the story line (the sequence of events), and how the writer chooses these to present and resolve the conflict. As characters act and react to conflicts, the plot grows. Plot answers the question What if? or What will happen next? For young readers, plot is the key literary element. Tension moves the story and holds children's interest.

The author can create several types of **conflict** and may use more than one in a story. The main character (**protagonist**) may face a conflict against

- self (internal conflict of feelings within the protagonist)
- nature (as seen in survival stories)
- a person (the antagonist)
- society (the rules at one's school can represent society)

In some series the characters are minimally developed and the conflict carries the story. These books often have predictable plots, which appeal to the inexperienced reader. At the same time, the predictability can eventually become boring to more able readers. Even able readers may choose to read series for the comfort of predictability and connectivity to peers reading the same series. In the more carefully crafted series, the character is more fully developed and the incidents occur because of the protagonist's personal traits.

The author usually chooses one of three basic **narrative structures**. In **chronological** order, time of day or days in the week are the same for all characters. A second way is to arrange the events in one or more **progressive plots**, in which the rendition of the event is dictated by dramatic structure; the conflict is introduced, a climax is reached, and the story ends with resolution of the conflict. This is the pattern of many folk tales. A third option is to use the **episodic structure**, in which there is a conflict and resolution in each character linked to the other chapters through characters or theme.

The reader of **interactive fiction** books selects from several choices to determine the progress of the story. The reader chooses the end of an episode.

To keep the story moving, the author chooses different action patterns: suspense, the cliffhanger, foreshadowing, sensationalism, and climax. **Suspense** raises anticipations and expectations about what will happen, when it will happen, why it happened, the solution of the problem, the outcome of events, and the well being of the character. Using suspense at the end of the chapter to set the stage for the next chapter is a device known as a **cliffhanger**. This is effective in stories for reading aloud to a group of children in several sittings. In **foreshadowing** the author provides clues to what will happen later on, providing a pattern of predictability. If the author does not relieve the suspense, the story becomes **sensational**. Adults may enjoy this in mystery stories and murder thrillers, but children may find it an uncomfortable form of tension.

The **climax** is the moment of high interest and may be the crisis or the turning point for the protagonist. Children may realize that at this point they know how a book was going to end. This resolution of the conflict is also called a **denouement**. When the twists and turns of the story have been unraveled and the reader finds a satisfactory ending, the plot has a **closed ending**. This type of conclusion is reassuring to young children. An **open ending** leaves the conclusion up to the reader.

Questions to consider:

- Does the author catch the reader's interest in the beginning?
- Does the story have a beginning, a middle, and an ending?
- Does the beginning introduce the reader to the conflict?
- Does the author develop the story logically?
- Is the conflict developed in the middle of the story?
- Is the conflict resolved at the end of the story or left for the reader to decide?
- Does the author use events to develop the action and unity of the story?
- Are the incidents determined by the local nature of events and consistent with the narrative?
- Do the incidents involve change and development, with tensions and complications that are plausible but not predictable?
- Is the plot based on some element of novelty, surprise, or the unexpected?
- Is the movement of the story maintained?
- Will the pace of the story maintain the reader's interest?
- Is the plot structure appropriate for the intended audience?
- How does the author weave events, actions, conflicts, characters, and setting to develop the plot?
- Are the plot, setting, characters, and style consistently presented?

Setting

The term **setting** refers to when and where the story takes place and the descriptive details about the place of action. Setting can function to establish the mood of a story, to influence the lives of characters, or to provide local color. To test the importance of the setting to a specific story, one can ask, "Would this be the same story without this setting?"

There are two types of settings: backdrop and integral. The **backdrop setting** is like the scenery in a drama; it sets a place for the action but doesn't take a role in the story. Different stories could be set against the same background. The **integral setting** plays a more active role. Examples can be found in historical fiction, in which the setting clarifies a conflict, or in survival stories, in which the setting becomes the antagonist threatening the protagonist. The setting can also explain the character's beliefs and actions. If the author uses the setting as an integral part of the story, then the setting must be so clearly described that the reader is aware of the relationship. A one-dimensional setting, like a flat character, will not be as believable as a more fully developed setting will be in influencing the plot.

Functions of setting:

- clarifies conflict

  - in historical fiction, gives reality to the story
  - in regional literature, shows how time and place affect the story
  - in fantasy, author manipulates the description of the setting, to lengthening or shortening, simplifying or elaborating, as appropriate to the story

- serves as antagonist in survival stories
- illuminates character
- acts as a symbol, such as good or evil found in folk tales

In picture storybooks the illustrations rather than the text may present the setting. Whether in text or illustrations, the setting must be consistent throughout the story.

Questions to consider:

- Does the setting serve as a backdrop to the story, or does it play an integral role?
- Does the setting contribute to the credibility of the action?
- Is the setting one that children will recognize or accept?
- Does the description of the setting give a sense of the authenticity of the time period?
- If the setting is an actual place, is the description accurate?
- Does the description of an imaginary place provide sufficient details to be a credible setting for the story?

Character

Character means a person, personified animal, or inanimate object whose actions and personal qualities are limited by that character's role in the story. The writer is responsible for making the main character believable. The character in the center of the conflict (the protagonist) will be developed more fully than one in the background.

A **flat character** is not fully developed. In picture storybooks and in fables the character may have only one facet or personality trait. A **rounded character** is three-dimensional, with contradictions and realistic complexities. The character's traits are demonstrated in the action of the story. Character and action need to be unified. Flat characters do not grow out of the action; rounded characters do. By the same token, action can stem from the rounded character but not from the flat one. Rounded characters are thus integrated with the action.

When a character has only a few traits and these are generally attributed to the social or racial group of which the character is a member, the character is called a **stereotype**. This type of stereotyping is misleading to the child reader, who may think this is a realistic description of each member of the group portrayed. Another type of stereotype for a minor character is the **stock character**, who has a specific personality trait that is often used in other stories or who has a specific role in society. Examples include a spoiled younger sister in a story or a trickster found in a folktale.

For young children, the protagonist may be a rounded character, with secondary figures being flat characters. Books for older children include both major and minor characters with fuller development.

A story may have a **dynamic character**, who changes as a result of the impact of the events. These changes can help the reader understand the action. A character who does not change is called a **static character**. Minor characters tend to be static. A minor character who is too fully developed can change the plot and cause the loss of unity that the author seeks between characters and plot.

Characterization is the method a writer uses to describe and reveal the characters. Authors use techniques such as action and dialogue to introduce characters. There are three common methods: 1) directly describing the character, 2) presenting the character in action, and 3) revealing the character's thoughts and emotions.

The deft author is able to use action and speech to reveal how the character and event generate change. This creates a unity of character and action.

Questions to consider:

- Is the author's delineation of the character appropriate for the intended audience?
- Are the characters believable?
- Do the characters cause action?
- Do the characters grow and develop?
- Is at least one character fully developed?
- Is each character unique?
- Is the character's action appropriate for his or her personality?
- Do the characters represent universal qualities without becoming stereotypes?
- Can the reader identify with the actions, motives, and feelings of the protagonist?
- How does the author reveal the characters?
- Are the characters convincing in their actions?

Style

Style refers to how the book is written, how the author uses words to communicate ideas, establish moods, and anticipate understanding. As the illustrator uses pictorial elements, the writer uses literary devices. Styles vary from author to author and in the books of a particular author. Style can be simple or complex depending on the mood and setting of the story.

Styles can be examined in terms of

- arrangement of ideas
- choice of words
- use of figurative language
- structure and variety of sentences
- rhythm
- repetition of words and phrases
- coherence of sentences, paragraphs, and chapters
- emphasis on words or passages
- unity of the parts. The source of unity may be plot, characterization, form, theme, mood, imagery, or symbolism.

The author chooses the devices of style.

- **Connotation**: the associations, images, or impressions that a word brings to a reader, not the literal meaning of the word.
- **Imagery**: an appeal to the senses (taste, smell, hearing, touch, sight) and to the reader's emotions.
- **Figurative language**: use of figures of speech to create comparison or associations, use of words in the nonliteral sense.

    - **Personalification**: attributing human traits to animals, plants, inanimate objects, natural forces, or abstract ideas.
    - **Simile**: use of *as*, *like*, or *as if* to directly compare two different objects, actions, or attributes that share some point of similarity.
    - **Metaphor**: implied comparison or identification of one thing with another without using the terms *as* or *like*.
    - **Hyperbole**: exaggeration or overstatement meant to create humor or emphasis, not be taken literally.

- Rhythm: the patterned flow of sound. Writers use sound devices to contribute to the rhythm of the story, which is evident when the story is read aloud.

Diction, or word choice, is how the writer gives the flavor of the time, place, and events. This is found in history and regional works using language that appears to be of that period and locality. In high fantasy, dignified language seems appropriate for the struggle between good and evil.

Questions to consider:

- Does the author treat the young reader with respect?

- Does the author avoid using sentimental language, talking down to the reader, preaching, and oversimplifying?
- Is there a rhythm to the story?
- How does the author use words in relation to objects?
- What is the relationship among the words?
- Does the author use an objective or subjective style?
- What literary devices does the author use?
- Is the author's style accessible to children?
- Is the style appropriate for the subject?
- Is the dialogue natural?
- Is the use of language fresh and imaginative?
- Does the narrative flow easily?
- Is the style appropriate to the theme?
- Does the choice of words and syntax create a mood or help convey ideas?
- Does the author tell the story with sensitivity rather than in a sensational manner?

Point of View

Point of view refers to the teller of the story who may be the author or one of the characters. In the first person approach, the character speaks as "I"; in third person, characters are referred to as "he," "she," or "they." Examples of point of view are:

- First person: tells the story from inside the head of the character. This approach establishes credibility and brings a sense of intimacy between character and reader.
- First-person observer: A character not directly involved in the action tells what he or she observes using the first person "I."
- Author-observer: A third person tells about deeds, words, gestures in an objective manner without going into the minds of characters or offering the author's comments.
- Omniscient: The author, using the third person, relates every detail of action as well as the characters' conscious or unconscious thoughts and feelings. The omniscient narrator knows the present, past, and future and sometimes comments on the actions of the characters.
- Combination: Author may combine several of the above points of view through the use of dialogue, diary entries, and other techniques.

The author will vary the point of view depending on subject matter, type of conflict, and maturity level of the intended readers. The third-person form is the one most commonly used in children's literature.

Questions to consider:

- Who is telling the story?

- Does the narrator have credibility in knowing that point of view?
- Is the point of view appropriate for the story?
- Is more than one point of view used, and is there a reason for that change?
- Is the change in point of view one the reader can understand?
- If the author shifts the point of view between chapters what clues will help the reader to be aware of the change?
- Does the point of view give a perspective that is believable and that enriches the story?

Tone

Tone in literature tells us how the author feels about his or her subject, characters, and readers. Sentence structure, choice of words, word patterns or word usage, and arrangements all influence tone. Tone can be described as humorous, kindly, affectionate, pleasant, brusque, friendly, serious, lighthearted, mysterious, insinuating, or teasing. Different readers will respond to different tones in various ways. The response will be based on their preferences and their experiences.

Certain tones used in adult literature are not as acceptable in children's literature. The ironic humor and wit in satire may be an intellectual exercise beyond children's experiences. They may lack the ability and maturity to see and interpret the irony, the understatements, the sarcasm, and the innuendos.

When a writer creates a tear-jerking situation that plays excessively upon the reader's sentiments, the results (**sentimentality**) evoke an exaggerated response. A writer who talks down to children with a condescending attitude is insulting and disrespectful of the child reader. Examples can be found in the retelling of folk literature and of the "classics." The overuse of sentiment is a form of condescension.

A sensational tone may occur in mysteries when a writer includes unnecessary and overly descriptive violence. Rebecca J. Lukens observes, "Like overused sentimentality, sensationalism may dull the reader's reaction to emotional pain or physical discomfort in real life" (Lukens, 2003: 223).

Another negative element is found in works in which the author is deliberately preaching (didacticism). While this is not appropriate in any genre but science fiction for children, clearly stated moral lessons are appropriate elements in fables.

JUDGING CLASSICS

Another area of literature that raises questions is that of the classics. A **classic** is a book with permanence, one that remains a favorite for more than one generation of children. Children's classics are not adult classics, even watered-down versions. There are many children's books that are classics, and they appear in all genres, including historical fiction, high fantasy, and picture storybooks. Common characteristics are:

- strong, unique, credible characters
- engaging style
- appeal to children of more than one generation
- universal theme
- memorable story

In 1997, children in Seattle, Washington, were asked to write an essay about their favorite book. Some of the classics on their lists were *Ramona the Pest* by Beverly Cleary (Morrow, 1968), *The Hobbit* by J. R. R. Tolkien (Houghton Mifflin, n.d.), *Charlotte's Web* by E. B. White (HarperCollins, 1952), *The Lion, the Witch, and the Wardrobe* by C. S. Lewis (Macmillan, 1988), and *Pippi Longstocking* by Astrid Lindgren (Viking, 1950) (De Leon, 1997).

Selecting Series Books

There are two types of series books available in children's fiction: **formula series** and literary series. A common characteristic of both is one character who appears in several volumes. In the formula book, such as the Nancy Drew mystery, the character is flat and does not grow or develop. In the **literary series**, such as Beverly Cleary's Ramona books, the character is a rounded, three-dimensional person who grows and develops in the story. The formula books focus on a fast-moving plot, while the literary series may have a thought-provoking theme. Some critics consider the formula books to be more commercially driven, while the literary types reflect artistic vision. Both have appeal, provide quick reads, and have a minimum of description to slow them down.

One of the debates faced by people responsible for selecting books is whether the monies should be spent on formula series. The commercial nature of these works, where quantity is more important than quality, puts these titles in a different category than the series of "popular fiction" works. Familiar formula series include Magic Treehouse, American Girl, Series of Unfortunate Events by Lemony Snicket, and manga series like *Tokyo Mew Mew* by Mia Ikumi and Reiko Yoshida (Tokuopo, 2002).

Although recognizing the limited literary merit of such works, some librarians argue that attracting developing readers is sufficient reason to have a limited number of these titles in the collection. Their predictability is satisfying for the inexperienced reader. One drawback is that many are available only in paperback editions, which will not last for many circulations. However, these titles are popular with children, who recommend them to one another. Adults can focus on leading children to more literary titles.

Criteria for Series Books

Questions to consider:
- Is the action fast paced?
- Is the plot logically developed?
- Does the book meet criteria for general fiction?
- Will this book fill a gap for developing readers?
- Will it hold the reader's attention?
- Can this book be used as a stepping-stone to books with more character development and more complex plots?
- Will it physically withstand being read by a number of readers?

Spotlight 6.2:   Selecting Series Books
Spotlight on Public Libraries Select whole series whenever possible rather than purchasing one from each series. Reading the same series as a child's friends is a social as well as literacy activity. **Spotlight on School Libraries** Some school libraries set aside a shelf or other area where students and teachers can swap books.

SUMMARY

The purpose of fiction is primarily to entertain and amuse, to a lesser extent to instruct. Theme, plot, setting, and characters form interdependent elements. The author's style, point of view, and tone affect how the story is communicated.

Series books may be formula driven, or they may be more literary, with characters who develop throughout the sequence of titles.

Additional criteria apply when one is evaluating the various subcategories of fiction. Discussion about picture storybooks, historical fiction, fantasy, animal stories, mysteries, and sports stories will be the subject of Chapter 7.

REFERENCES

De Leon, Ferdinand M. 1997. "Winning Words." *The Seattle Times* (December 8): E1-E3.

Dresang, Eliza T. 1999. *Radical Change: Books for Youth in a Digital Age.* New York: H. W. Wilson.

Dresang, Eliza T., and Kate McClelland. 1996. "Radical Change." *Book Links* 5, no. 6 (July): 40–46.

Lukens, Rebecca J. 2003. *A Critical Handbook of Children's Literature.* 7th ed. Boston, MA: Longman.

Chapter 7

Fiction Genres

EXAMINING FICTION GENRES

This chapter examines the characteristics and criteria for selecting narrative stories in the subcategories of picture storybooks, historical fiction, fantasy, mysteries, animal stories, and sports stories. These stories need to be evaluated with the general narrative criteria in Chapter 6 as well as criteria specific to the genre.

JUDGING PICTURE STORYBOOKS

In **picture storybooks** the pictorial and literary elements are of equal importance. The integration of illustrations with text creates a sense of unity. Barbara Bader describes their relationship: "As an art form it [a picturebook] hinges on the interdependence of picture and words, on the simultaneous display of two facing pages, and on the drama of the turning of the page" (Bader, 1976: vii).

Strong illustrations may overpower a weak text; the reverse of these elements makes the opposite effect, that is, a lack of complementing pictorial works weakens a strong text. Together the pictorial and literary elements should form an artistic unit unachievable separately.

The term **interactive book** refers to titles often designed for children from two to six years old. The child is encouraged to participate. The text may ask a question or suggest that the child clap to the rhythm of the words, repeat a word or phrase, touch something, or look for specific objects. One example is *Bear*

Gets Dressed: A Guessing-Game Story (Sterling, 2004), in which the child guesses what Bear will wear, then opens the flap to see the answer.

Picture books often are housed in the "Easy" section of the library, which is misleading to the person who assumes they are easy to read. Rather, these books are meant for adults or older children to read to younger ones. The vocabulary may be at the sixth- or seventh-grade reading level, while the interest level may be for anyone from very young children to adults. Picture storybooks are commonly 32 pages in length.

Characteristics of picture storybooks:

- presence of action or tension
- wide range of themes
- settings created by text and illustration
- a specific point of view
- use of figurative language
- range of tone

The protagonist is a rounded character who develops through interaction with conflict. The character may be an anthropomorphic animal (an animal with human characteristics) that acts (perhaps also dresses) as a believable human being. Each character should have a relevant role to play in the story. Irrelevant characters can be confusing to young audiences.

As in stories for an older audience, one expects action or tension in picture storybooks. Mood pieces or character studies are less likely to hold the interest of young children than are stories with an engaging plot.

There is a wide range of themes dealing with children's experiences. Today's books reflect the diversity of our society. Families are not limited to a mother, a father, two-and-a-half children, and their pets. Parenting may be carried out by a grandmother, a single parent (male or female), a lesbian or gay couple, two sets of parents after a divorce and remarriage, or a foster family, or with some other caregiver.

Examine each book from a child's perspective. For humor to appeal to children, it should be broad and obvious. Adult-oriented humor should be avoided; however, it is also true that the adult may be called on to read and reread the book, so choose books that will appeal to both of you.

In books dealing with intergenerational relations, look for ones that challenge ageist stereotypes, explore the complexities of aging, and deal with death. Other common themes are a child's everyday experiences, growing up situations, attending school, and exploring nature.

Though always an integral part of a picture storybook, illustrations take many forms. In some books text and illustrations are interwoven to create a setting. In others the illustrations handle all the descriptions of the setting.

In writing picture storybooks, authors use the same range of options they do with other stories. Examples can be found of the objective voice, the observer, the first person, and the omniscient point of view.

And, as with any other genre, styles vary. Authors may use figurative language to add imagery to the story. Some stories have a rhythmic quality that becomes most evident when the story is read aloud. Tone can range from thoughtful and serious to joyous and humorous. The illustrations can enhance the tone.

Criteria

In evaluating picture storybooks one should apply the criteria used for literary merit (theme, plot setting, characters, and style) plus those for pictures identified in Chapter 5.

Questions to consider about literary elements:

- Is the main character well rounded?
- Will the action maintain the young child's interest?
- Do the text and illustrations develop the theme?
- Does the text or the illustrations, or both, describe the setting?
- Does the humor appeal to children?
- Does the author use clear, natural language?

Questions to consider about illustrations:

- Are the illustrations and text integrated, rather than either one dominating the book?
- Are the details in the illustrations consistent with the text? Children will quickly spot differences.
- Are the illustrations authentic in terms of the cultural or geographical setting?

Spotlight 7.1:   Minding School Requirements
Spotlight on Public Libraries
Although it is not the primary mission of a public library to support the school curriculum, keep this curriculum in mind when you are selecting genre fiction. Be aware of repeated school assignments, so that students can find books to meet their homework and leisure needs. Stop to examine the school's curriculum and assignments before you make purchasing decisions each year. Teachers and curriculum may change. A favorite read-aloud of one teacher may have few requests once that teacher is no longer in the local school.

ASSESSING HISTORICAL FICTION

Historical fiction is realistic fiction by a contemporary author about events set in an earlier time period with characters true to that time. Imaginary characters and plot blend with the historical facts. Realistic language and appropriate dialogue are other important elements in historical fiction.

Characteristics of historical fiction:

- The setting represents a specific time period.
- The characters act and speak in a manner consistent with the time period, and they reflect the values of that period.
- Details about everyday life fit the time and place, if known.
- There is a credible problem, goal, or conflict.
- The plot or sequence of events is conceivable.
- The setting influences the plot.
- There is a universal theme or commonly shared truth.
- The story is told from an appropriate point of view or by a fitting narrator.
- The story is told with a unique style or tone.

It is particularly important that the actions of the characters reflect the standards and norms of the historical period. When actual historical figures appear in these novels, the author should include dialogue only when documentary evidence or other records can verify such activity. If a historical story is narrated in the first person, the grammar, vocabulary, and sentence structure should authentically reflect the usage of the time period in which the story is set. Such language may be difficult for children to comprehend, so, at times the authors give the characters names of the period but use contemporary language.

The details of the setting should help the reader clearly visualize the time and place in which the events occur. The setting should be authentic and accurately reflect historical and geographical data.

The concept of historic fiction can be confusing to a child. Stories from earlier times may appear to be history to today's child. A book like Louisa May Alcott's *Little Women* (Little Brown, 1968) was realistic fiction when it was written. It is important to explain to today's reader that the author was not writing historical fiction. The values, opinions, and styles were real for the time in which the book was written. Alcott was, in fact, writing about her own family.

Criteria

Questions to consider:

- Theme

    - Do the episodes in the story center on themes that adhere to facts?
    - Does the author portray the "why" of the event?

- Do the issues of the past appear real to today's readers?
- Do the issues present an opportunity for explanations by adults?

- Plot

  - Does the action reflect the pace of life in that historical period?
  - Are the action and conflict resolution in keeping with the times in which the story is set?

- Setting

  - Are time and place historically, geographically, and politically accurate?
  - Is the setting authentic in terms of what we know about the history and geography at the time of the story?

- Character

  - Do the characters' mannerisms, speech, dress, and attitudes reflect the historical period portrayed?
  - Are the characters drawn convincingly as ordinary or extraordinary people who participated in these events?

- Style

  - Does the story convey a sense of life in that time period?
  - Do the speech patterns sound right for the time period?

- Point of view

  - Are fact and fiction blended in such a way that the background is subordinate to the story?
  - Does the story reflect the values and spirit of the historical time?
  - Does the author present the various points of view on issues of the times?
  - Does the dialogue convey a feeling of the period without seeming artificial?

- Tone

  - Are notes, time lines, bibliographies, and glossaries provided?
  - Are the details of the time, place, and social order authentic?

EVALUATING FANTASY

Fantasy stories are realistic in most details, but they do require readers who are willing to suspend their disbelief about a character, theme, or setting. The characters may be personified animals or inanimate objects. In fantasy the key question of theme is frequently What if? This leads to Then . . . , that is, the consequences of the action. Finally, there is the answer to So what?—the meaning of the story.

Within fantasies by one author the reader will find the cycle format, in which one book is linked to another through characters or settings, or both. Some titles can be read independently of the others, but they make a fuller impact when the cycle is read in sequence. **Cycle format** readers enjoy knowing a specific character and following that character through other conflicts.

Science fiction is the subcategory of fantasy in which scientific laws and technological inventions play a key influence in the conflict and resolution. Science fiction often addresses the question What if? by using scientific thought to explore the question or speculate about a world that could be.

In **high fantasy**, a subcategory of fantasy, the focus is on the conflict between good and evil. The reader judges the story in terms of its internal consistency within the imaginary world or by the protagonist's belief in his or her experience. Thus, point of view influences how the character is accepted. Settings may be the creation of the author, may represent a more worldlike location, or may move back and forth between the two. The author may manipulate time, moving it back and forth. Themes often deal with universal questions about humanity. The tone is somber and in awe of the story. To be believable, there must be logic to the story, even if that logic is one perceived through a sense of humor rather than everyday rational behavior.

Characteristics of fantasy:

- characters that include humanlike animals, stereotypes of good and evil, heroes and heroines with magical powers, or extraterrestrial beings
- a problem, goal, or conflict, sometimes between forces of good and evil
- a plot that may include adventures of the characters, or in science fiction, a heroic battle for the common good
- a climax, resolution of conflict, or accomplishment of the goal
- a theme of universal truth
- a clear point of view
- a tone or style that is special in some way

Criteria

Questions to consider about fantasies:

- Plot

  - Does the story move from reality to the imaginative without breaking the credibility of the story?
  - Are events interrelated?

- Theme

    - Does the story deal with a universal truth?
    - Will the reader understand the symbolic significance of the theme?

- Setting

    - Do the settings reflect originality on the part of the author?
    - Is the setting appropriate for the story?

- Style

    - Does the author skillfully use words, phrases, symbols, and allegories to create images?
    - Are the images credible?
    - Do the supernatural aspects have credibility?
    - Does the reader sense that the author has a creative imagination?
    - Is the science fiction story based on a scientific fact or hypothesis?
    - Does a science fiction novel encourage consideration of the emotional, psychological, and mental effects of futuristic ideas, conflict, and change?
    - Does the science fiction novel involve the reader in considering unlimited possibilities and in raising questions about other forms of life?

STUDYING MYSTERIES

Mystery stories can be set in the present, the past, or the future. Suspense comes from unexplained events and actions, with an explanation or resolution by the end of the story. Plot is the key literary element in moving the story forward, and this high level of movement promotes fast reading. Characters may be flat, as in the formula series, or rounded and fully developed. The setting can be any locale. A popular feature for the regular mystery reader is the author's use of foreshadowing.

Criteria

Questions to consider:

- Is the tension created by unexplained events?
- Do the characters change because of the conflict?
- Does the action keep the plot moving?
- Does the plot hold the reader's interest?
- Does the author involve the reader in solving the mystery?

LOOKING AT ANIMAL STORIES

This subcategory includes stories in which animals behave like human beings, animals behave as animals but with the ability to talk, and animals behave as animals. Animals behaving as human beings are frequently found in picture storybooks for young children. In these cases the author uses **anthropomorphism** (assigns human behavior to the animal) so the animal becomes a believable character.

Authors can also present the animal behaving like an animal. They show the reality of animal life by describing its natural habitat (weather conditions, geographical features), its life cycle, and the activities of its predators. Through these descriptions, the author can explain the influence of these natural phenomena on the animal, and with these realistic elements he or she creates tension in the story. It is with effective descriptions that an author can gain the reader's acceptance of the story.

In realistic fiction the author may choose to have animal characters behave like animals. The author uses the observer point of view to create characters that seem real to the reader. For example, E. B. White, in *Charlotte's Web* (HarperCollins, 1952), tells the story by having animals speak and think as humans but act like real animals.

Criteria

Questions to consider:

- Does the author use the observer point of view to create a realistic story?
- Does the author avoid being unrealistic and sentimental?
- Does the author's description of the setting add to the tension?
- Does the setting add credibility to the story?

CHOOSING SPORTS STORIES

Well-developed characters and the author's style can add depth to a sports story. There are more stories about team sports such as soccer, football, baseball, and basketball than about individual sports.

Criteria

Questions to consider:

- Does the story have a theme beyond the winning of a game?
- Does the main character develop and grow because of events or conflicts in the story?

SUMMARY

Subcategories of fiction, including picture storybooks, historical fiction, fantasy, mysteries, animal stories, and sports stories, have unique characteristics. Books in these categories need to be evaluated using both the general criteria for all fiction works and the criteria unique to them.

REFERENCES

Bader, Barbara. 1976. *American Picturebooks: From Noah's Ark to the Beast Within.* New York: Macmillan.

RESOURCES

Campbell, Laura Ann. 1999. *Storybooks for Tough Times.* Golden, CO: Fulcrum. Under chapter headings such as "Adoption" and "Fears," the author lists picture books that may help children understand the issues they are facing. Summaries of each book, suggestions for discussing them, bibliographic information, and an index of authors and titles make this a welcome resource.

Lima, Carolyn W., and John A. Lima. 2005. *A to Zoo: Subject Access to Children's Picture Books.* 7th ed. Westport, CT: Libraries Unlimited.
Index to over 27,000 titles (fiction and nonfiction) for preschoolers through 2nd graders, including 4,000 published since 2001. Access is by subject, title, author, and illustrator.

Lynn, Ruth Nadelman. 2005. *Fantasy Literature for Children and Young Adults: a Comprehensive Guide.* 5th ed. Westport, CT: Libraries Unlimited.
Author, illustrator, title, series, and subject access to annotations arranged in categories (for example, animal fantasy, high fantasy). The over 7,600 novels and story collections listed were published in English in the United States. Grade levels, review citations, and top recommendations offer guidance.

VandeKieft, Lynette. "Historical Fiction in the Elementary School Classroom." Masters of Art in Literacy Instruction project. East Lansing, MI: Michigan State University. (September 5, 2006) Available: www.msu.edu/~vandeki3 Includes several links to aid selection.

RECOMMENDED CHAPTER BOOK AUTHORS AND TITLES

(Note: Books in this section combine quality with popularity, making these authors good investments.)

Avi. A writer in several genres and for several different ages. *Poppy* (Orchard Books, 1995) exemplifies courage, compassion, and adventure, while *Crispin* (Hyperion, 2002), a Newbery Award winner, describes a boy's maturation as he flees for his life in medieval England.

Cleary, Beverly. Her everyday, funny and insightful neighborhood stories about *Ramona Quinley, Age 8* (Morrow, 1981) and *Henry Huggins* (HarperCollins, 2004) continue to captivate beginning chapter book readers.

Creech, Sharon. For the insightful reader, deep questions of self-esteem and relationships with page-turning plots. Every word in *Heartbeat* (HarperCollins, 2004) helps us learn what is important to 12-year-old Annie. This book-size poem appeals to reluctant readers. *Chasing Redbird* (HarperCollins, 1997) demonstrates the satisfaction of a job well done.

Curtis, Christopher Paul. *Mr. Chickee's Funny Money* (Wendy Lamb Books, 2005) stars a brilliant boy detective who receives a quadrillion-dollar bill. This humorous book contrasts with the hard realities skillfully told in *Bud, Not Buddy* (Delacorte Press, 1999) and The *Watsons Go to Birmingham* (Delacorte Press, 1995).

Dahl, Roald. Imaginative silliness with some tension and absurdity. *BFG* (Farrar, Straus & Giroux, 1982) is gentle; *Charlie and the Chocolate Factory* (Knopf, 1973) reminds us that life can be cruel. Sophisticated, zany humor.

Di Camillo, Kate. *The Tales of Desperaux: Being the Story of a Mouse, a Princess, Some Soup, and a Spool of Thread* (Candlewick Press, 2003), a fantasy, enchants readers and introduces many to a writer who knows children's interests. *Because of Winn-Dixie* (Candlewick, 2000) brings a host of neighbors together through their friendship with Opal, a spunky girl who longs for her alcoholic mother to return home.

Gantos, Jack. *What Would Joey Do?* (Farrar, Straus & Giroux, 2002) completes a trilogy about Joey Pigza, who processes everything around him even while wearing a patch to control his hyperactivity. He labels himself "Mr. Helpful" in a chaotic household, where his parents still argue though they are separated. Gantos inserts humor and hope. One has a sense Joey will thrive thanks to his creativity and sincerity.

Hahn, Mary. Realistic fiction attesting to this author's perfect recall of a child's perspective. Mysteries, ghost stories, and stories of friendship. *The Old Willis Place: A Ghost Story* (Clarion, 2004) combines all three with a surprising plot twist.

Ibbotson, Eva. Plot-driven stories about ghosts with personality. *The Haunting of Granite Falls* (Dutton, 2003) features young heroes and fascinating characters like The Hand.

Jacques, Brian. The Redwall Series, including *Rakkety Tam* (Philomel Books, 2004), proves children will flock to thick, detailed animal fantasy if the characters are real and the dilemmas captivating.

L'Engle, Madeleine. *Wrinkle in Time* (Farrar, Straus & Giroux, 1962) starts a science fiction series with real characters and a chance to contemplate good versus evil.

Lowry, Lois. From the Anastasia Krupnik realistic fiction books to the haunting science fiction series beginning with *The Giver* (Houghton Mifflin, 1993) and continued in *Messenger* (Houghton Mifflin, 2004) to the historical fiction Newbery Award-winning *Number the Stars* (Houghton Mifflin, 1989), Lowry provides imperfect heroes who inspire.

Oppel, Kenneth. *Firewing* (Simon & Schuster, 2003) will engage fans of fantasy and science fiction. Fast-breaking adventure, vividly described creatures, and issues of trust and loyalty. Children will develop "bat-empathy" as they follow the adventures that began with *Silverwing* (Simon & Schuster, 1997) and were continued in *Sunwing* (Simon & Schuster, 2000).

Park, Barbara. *Junie B. Jones and the Stupid Smelly Bus* (Random House, 1992) starts a comical series about a spunky girl full of self-confidence and daring.

Paterson, Katherine. A wide range of genre and age interest, compelling literary stories of life, death, and in between. *The Same Stuff as Stars* (Clarion, 2002) tells us about a great grandma, an 11-year-old girl, and her 7-year-old brother forming a family that works.

Patneaude, David. Popular novels including historical, mystery and sports interest. *Thin Wood Walls* (Houghton Mifflin, 2004) tells a compelling story of a Japanese American family's strength as they're moved from home to detention camps. *Haunting at Home Plate* (Albert Whitman & Company, 2000) offers believable characters that develop throughout the book. Fast action, suspense, and some play-by-play baseball description.

Paulsen, Gary. Once a reader has read the page-turning *Hatchet* (Bradbury, 1997) survival story, Paulsen's many other titles await. Two gamers use their laptops to manipulate history in *The Time Hackers* (Wendy Lamb, 2005).

Pilkey, Dav. Silly and clever, the Captain Underpants books entice reluctant readers.

Rowling, J. K. The humor distinguishes Rowling's Harry Potter series. This is blended with a young, powerful, mistreated hero on a noble mission who is aided by interesting friends and challenged by exotic foes. More mature matter as Harry grows older.

Spinelli, Jerry. The main character in *Maniac Magee* (Little Brown, 1990), as in Spinelli's other books, is recognizable to every reader. Here is someone who dares to be himself! In *Milkweed* (Knopf, 2003), Misha, an orphan who has every reason to ignore the world around him, does the opposite. He squeezes through a hole in the wall separating the Jews of Warsaw so he can bring them food. Mature fifth and sixth graders and older will learn much from this child's eye–view of Nazi occupation.

RECOMMENDED PICTURE BOOK AUTHORS AND TITLES (SELECTED FOR THEIR CHILD-APPEALING TEXTS)

Burningham, John. 1970. *Mr. Gumpy's Outing*. Austin, TX: Holt.
   Children can predict what will happen next in this cumulative tale.

Cronin, Doreen. 2000. *Click, Clack, Moo Cows That Type*, illustrated by Betsy Lewin. New York: Simon & Schuster.
   Combines absurd fun, an expansive vocabulary, and an irresistible refrain for children to repeat.

Dorros, Arthur. 1991. *Abuela*, illustrated by Elisa Kleven. New York: Dutton.

This warm story follows a young girl's imagination as she flies through the air with her grandmother. A glossary translates the occasional Spanish phrases.

Feiffer, Jules. 1999. *Bark, George!* New York: HarperCollins.

A hilarious, cumulative story for all ages.

Freeman, Don. 1968. *Corduroy.* New York: Viking.

Set in a department store, a story of belonging and adventure.

Henkes, Kevin. 1996. *Lilly's Purple Plastic Purse.* New York: Greenwillow.

Started the books featuring a whimsical, resilient mouse with vulnerabilities we humans recognize. *Lilly's Big Day* (Greenwillow, 2006) continues the fine tradition.

Hest, Amy. 2001. *Kiss Good Night,* illustrated by Anita Jeram. Cambridge, MA: Candlewick.

Little Bear can't go to sleep until he has the reassurance of some goodnight kisses from his mother. The author of *Guess Who, Baby Duck!,* illustrated by Jill Barton (Candlewick Press, 2004), knows exactly what children find interesting and important.

Hutchins, Pat. 1971. *Titch.* New York: Macmillan.

Titch is little, but children cheer as he proves he is also an achiever.

Keats, Ezra Jack. 1962. *The Snowy Day.* New York: Viking.

Peter enjoys the security of his mother's warm welcome after a day playing in the snow. *Peter's Chair* (Harper & Row, 1967) is a classic tale of a sibling's concern when a new child joins the family.

Krauss, Ruth. 1945. *The Carrot Seed,* illustrated by Crockett Johnson. New York: HarperCollins.

A boy ignores the skeptical voices of his family and continues to care for his carrot seed.

Martin, Bill, Jr. 1967. *Brown Bear, Brown Bear What Do You See?,* illustrated by Eric Carle. Austin, TX: Holt.

A brightly illustrated guessing game for young children learning their colors.

McMullan, Kate and Jim. 2002. *I Stink!* New York: Joanna Cotler Books.

Responds to a child's natural interest in the noisy, powerful garbage truck showing a typical night's work routine.

Numeroff, Laura. 1985. *If You Give a Mouse a Cookie,* illustrated by Felicia Bond. New York: HarperCollins.

A chance for children to giggle while they predict mouse's behavior. The fun continues with *If You Take a Mouse to the Movies* (HarperCollins, 2000).

Potter, Beatrix. 1902. *The Tale of Peter Rabbit.* New York: Warne.

Children can safely experience the adventure resulting when Peter fails to heed his mother's warning to stay away from Mr. McGregor's garden.

Rey, H. A. 1941. *Curious George.* Boston, MA: Houghton Mifflin.

George follows his curiosity and causes havoc. One of the most popular titles *Curious George Goes to the Hospital* (Houghton Mifflin, 1966) is a collaboration with the Children's Hospital Medical Center in Boston.

Sendak, Maurice. 1963. *Where the Wild Things Are.* New York: HarperCollins.

Max controls his nightmares to the satisfaction of the child reader.

Seuss, Dr. 1954. *Horton Hears a Who!* New York: Random House.
"A person's a person, no matter how small," says Horton, the elephant, when he hears a voice coming from a speck of dust. Adults may tire of the repetition and sound play in Seuss's books, but I've not met a child with this response.

Shannon, David. 1998. *No, David!* New York: Blue Sky Press.
Even though David gets in trouble for disobeying, his mother assures him that he is loved.

Slobodkina, Esphyr. 1940. *Caps for Sale: A Tale of a Peddler, Some Monkeys and Their Monkey Business.* New York: HarperCollins.
The absurdity of monkeys imitating the cap peddler invites listener participation.

Smith, Cynthia L. 2000. *Jingle Dancer*, illustrated by Cornelius Van Wright and Ying-Hwa Hu. New York: Morrow.
A contemporary story of Jenna who goes from home to home, asking to borrow jingles, which will sound when she dances at the powwow.

Van Allsburg, Chris. 1981. *Jumanji.* Boston, MA: Houghton Mifflin.
A haunting adventure for the more sophisticated child begins when a child finds a mysterious game.

Wells, Rosemary. 1973. *Noisy Nora.* New York: Viking.
Nora suffers from being a middle child needing more attention from her parents. *Max Cleans Up* (Viking, 2000) exposes the workings of the toddler mind.

Williams, Vera B. 1990. *"More, More, More," Said the Baby: 3 Love Stories.* New York: Greenwillow.
Parents and a grandparent play and delight in their babies.

Wong, Janet S. 2000. *BUZZ*, illustrated by Margaret Chodos-Irvine. Orlando, FL: Harcourt.
Chronicles a modern family's busy morning routine from the eyes of a child.

Wood, Audrey. 1984. *A Napping House*, illustrated by Don Wood. Orlando, FL: Harcourt.
One by one, the bed is piled with people and creatures until a flea upsets them all in this cumulative tale.

Yashima, Taro. 1958. *Umbrella.* New York: Viking.
Records a milestone in a three-year-old's life when she walks along the street with her new umbrella without holding her parents' hands.

Chapter 8

Folk Literature

EXAMINING FOLK LITERATURE

The term **folklore** refers to the beliefs, manners, customs, observations, superstitions, tales, ballads, proverbs, music, and art of an earlier time. **Folk literature** refers to stories with uncertain origins that were handed down orally from one storyteller to another. This body of traditional narratives includes animal tales (pourquoi, or "why," stories and trickster tales), fables, folktales, humorous tales (drolls, noodleheads, sillies, and numbskull tales), legends, myths, parables, tall tales, and traditional fairy tales.

Folk literature provides a look into other cultures. For instance, in social studies the literature provides a glimpse into history, geography, sociology, language, values, and ethnic heritage. Comparing the same tale from several countries offers an opportunity to learn about the similarities and differences.

Folktales can also present another aspect of a culture—its printed language. For example, a book may have a bilingual text, English and the native language of the culture. In other cases we are finding examples of stories recorded using the language pattern of the spoken rather than written language. Much of the folk literature used in the United States originated in other languages. Our English language contributions are the American regional and tall tales using the language of those regions. The American Indian myths and legends were first told and written down in tribal languages.

Traditional folk literature differs from the tales found in the fiction section of libraries. The latter are **literary fairy tales** written by known authors. Many of Hans Christian Andersen's tales fall in this category. Such writers create a story following the forms and elements of the traditional literature.

The writers of folk literature (traditional stories) are known as **adapters** or **retellers**. They do not create the story; they make an old story available to us through their adaptation or retelling.

A careful writer provides **source notes** to describe the origin of the story and the changes made. Common changes include altering the motif or mood of the story and simplifying or elaborating the original version. Compilers who gather stories together also provide source notes about the background of the stories. Other information about the origin of the story may be found on the inside flap of the book jacket and on the copyright page.

A collection of folklore may include **variants** of the same story. In this case, each of the stories shares common elements, such as the plot or character, but may have different settings or motifs. For example, there are many variants of the Cinderella story from around the world. Cinderella may have a different name in the stories, but the plot or a variation on it is the same.

Spotlight 8.1:   Folktales

Spotlight on Public Libraries

Folktales speak to all ages and are among the most versatile materials you select. They introduce the reader to different cultures and provide recognition of our own traditions. Both illustrated single tales and collections are used by children and adults as well.

EVALUATING FOLKTALES

Folktales have a common tripartite structure: construction (introduction), struggle (development of the story), and major climax (conclusion).

1. Construction
   A few sentences introduce the main characters, the setting of the story, and the conflict to be solved. Most common openings include "Once upon a time," "Long ago and far away," "In olden times when wishing still helped one," "A thousand years ago tomorrow," and "Once in a time, and a very good time too." A brief sketch of the scene lets the reader know where the action will take place. The objectively stated conflict alerts the reader to the magnitude and intensity of the challenge.
2. Struggle
   In the middle section the quest begins, tasks are initiated and performed, and obstacles appear. The action mounts steadily until it reaches a climax. The plot is full of suspense and action. Fast action is a major char-

acteristic of a folktale. The use of motifs can add to the suspense, since the reader or listener looks for the familiar pattern.

3. Major Climax
The last part is as brief as the introduction and completes all that was stated in the introduction. Conventional endings include "And they lived happily ever after"; "If they haven't left off their merry-making yet, why, they're still at it"; "A mouse did run, the story's done"; and "No one need ask if they were happy."

Characteristics

Motif, the smallest part of a tale, exists independently. It is repeated either three or seven times in a story, although four times is characteristic of Native American tales. Common motifs are magical powers, transformations, magic objects, wishes, and trickery. The reteller creates repetitive story patterns by repeating a refrain or episode. As the reteller embellishes with new ideas or episodes and repeats what has gone before, the story becomes cumulative. These characteristics help children learn to anticipate what might happen. The comparison of motifs in folk literature is one method of introducing children to cross-cultural studies.

Many folktales have themes. The same theme can be found in the literature of more than one culture because themes tend to state a universal truth. The reader readily sees the implicit theme through the characters and the conflict.

Characters in folktales are not developed individuals. Flat characters representing good and evil ones are easily recognized, and stock characters, like a trickster or a wicked stepmother, are frequently used. The teller may use a brief phrase to describe the character and repeat it frequently. These character descriptions cannot be long because the action in a folktale moves so quickly. Folktales are normally told in the third person. The tone of these stories may vary from humorous to sentimental, or they may be matter-of-fact.

Characteristics of folktales:

- Words capture sound and rhythm of oral language.
- Characters are easily recognized as good or bad.
- Brief phrases describe characters.
- Stock characters appear frequently.
- Series of episodes maintain a quick flow of action.
- Narrator uses dialogue.
- Figurative language of metaphors and similes creates vivid images.
- Narrative patterns are predictable.
- Language is simple but full of rhythm and melody.
- Conflict is often between personified animals as well as people in "person-to-person" conflicts.
- Action has the inevitable conflict and resolution.

- Story ends briefly.
- Story has universal appeal and deals with common needs of people regardless of culture.
- Language uses idioms that reflect dialect or speech patterns of a particular region or people. (Children may need help in understanding idioms and learning not to read them literally.)

Animal tales consist of animals that act and talk like human beings with exaggerated human characterization. While the tales teach a lesson, they are not didactic as fables.

The **humorous tales** (drolls, noodleheads, sillies, and numbskulls tales) revolve around a character who makes funny mistakes.

Pourquoi, or **etiological**, animal tales explain the why of natural phenomena, basing the explanation of animal traits on characteristics and customs of people. Unlike legends, these tales were meant to entertain, not to instruct their listeners.

Beast tales or **trickster stories** feature one character that is a trickster in animal shapes. The coyote, the raven, Anansi the spider, and Reynard the fox often play this role.

JUDGING FABLES

A **fable** is a brief, didactic tale in which an animal or inanimate object speaks in human language and represents different aspects of human nature. A significant act is used to teach a moral or lesson. The setting is the backdrop for the stated moral.

Western culture has Aesop's fables, which were reportedly told by the Greek slave in about 600 BC. Familiar proverbial phrases, such as "sour grapes" or "a wolf in sheep's clothing," summarize the moral of well-known fables. From Eastern culture come the Jataka tales, or moralistic lessons involving the reincarnation of Buddha as an animal or bird, which have been recorded since 500 BC. English versions often do not include the moral and teaching verses.

Other characteristics of fables:

- three or fewer characters
- single-trait characters
- single-incident plot
- no interpretation of action by narrator
- didactic purpose
- crisp, straightforward style
- abstract idea expressed in relatively few words
- implicit and explicit moral
- moral statement at end of story
- backdrop setting for the action

A **parable** has similar characteristics, but the main character is a human being. These brief stories deal with a moral or spiritual truth.

ASSESSING MYTHS

Myths, like legends, are stories told as if they were facts. They represent beliefs about supernatural forces and are told with dignity and simplicity. Myths

- explain the origin of man and of the world
- interpret natural phenomena
- explain religion
- explore the meaning of life and death

The characters in myths are gods, goddesses, and supernatural powers. The plots usually involve a single incident or a few incidents that are linked by the characters. They deal with issues of ethics and are full of strong emotions. Because myths respond to questions about the universe, they have been enjoyed for generations.
Common types of myths:

- **Creation myths**, or the various ways in which people explained creation.
- **Nature myths**, explaining natural phenomena such as changes in seasons, characteristics of animals, earth formations, astronomy.
- **Hero myths**, in which the hero who accepts a dangerous assignment may be assisted or hindered by the gods, but the person remains the focus of the story.

STUDYING LEGENDS

Legends are tales about a specific historical event, person, or place presented as fact. The characters may be humans, animals as humans, or supernatural creatures. Some characters, such as Johnny Appleseed, are based on real people. Others, like Paul Bunyan, were invented. The setting is in a historic time, and the place is a recognizable world. These stories involve change in creation and heroic deeds.

LOOKING INTO TALL TALES

Tall tales are highly exaggerated accounts of exploits. These hilarious tales involve careful detail and are based on reasonable activities. The language uses vivid vernacular idioms, dialect, and fanciful metaphors.
Common characteristics of tall tales:

- people (real or imagined)

- events (real or imagined)
- subjects that include hunting, agriculture, marvelous feats of strength or speed, or virtues of a place

SELECTING FAIRY TALES

Fairy tales are imaginary tales that involve enchantment, supernatural elements, or magical powers. The term *fairy* is misleading because there are not necessarily any fairies mentioned in the story. Common characteristics of fairy tales:

- elements of magic or enchantment in characters, plots, or settings
- use of magic objects or words to weave their enchantments
- opening and closing conventions such as "Once upon a time" and "They lived happily ever after"
- predictable patterns in which love, kindness, and truth prevail and hate, wickedness, and evil are punished
- characters like fairies, elves, pixies, brownies, witches, magicians, genies, and fairy godmothers
- characters that are all good or all bad
- quickly delineated flat characters
- vague settings

Modern humorous tales include **fractured fairy tales**, in which the reteller uses the features of the original tale while making a spoof of it. Both text and visual references poke fun at the original. A classic example is *The True Story of the Three Pigs* by Jon Scieszka and illustrated by Lane Smith (Viking, 1989). In this version, the wolf tells his view of the events.

Selection criteria for fractured fairy tales:

- Is it written for children?
- Does it use humor that children enjoy?
- Does it follow criteria for other good writing?
- Does it show respect for the original tale?
- Do children need to know the original tale in order to see the humor?

ESTABLISHING CRITERIA FOR ANTHOLOGIES

To select collections of folk literature, consider the following questions:

Purpose

- What is the purpose of the collection?

- Is the purpose stated in the introduction or in an opening section of the book?
- Does the purpose fill a need?
- Is there a description of how and why the tales were selected?
- Do the tales meet the purpose of the anthology?
- Is there a theme or setting that is common to all the tales?
- How does the compiler or reteller relate the stories to one another?

Authority

- Is there evidence of the reteller and the illustrator's scholarship and attention to authenticity?
- Do source notes provide background information about the original versions of the stories?
- Is there an explanation of what changes were made and why?
- Is there information about variants of the tales?
- Do background notes describe the cultural context of the tales?
- Is it clear whether the reteller found the story in a book or actually heard it from a storyteller?

Spotlight 8.2: Flexibility Is Key
Spotlight on Public Libraries In order to include authentic tales in your collection, you may at times need to relax your standards for sturdily bound books or purchase a title and reinforce the binding.

Style

- Is the narrative style preserved?
- Do the tales sound as if they were being told?

Stoplight 8.1   Folktales—What to Avoid
Avoid tales with flat language. Folktales are meant to be read or told aloud. Picturesque language and repeated refrains enliven the experience and build language skills.

Audience

- Were the stories selected for the child reader or the adult storyteller?
- Are the selections appropriate for the intended user?
- Will the size of the book and the illustrations make this a useful book for reading aloud with a group?

Scope

- How many tales are included?
- What types of folktales are included?
- Is the collection limited to folk literature from one nation or ethnic group or representative of many sources?

Organization

- How are the stories arranged and organized?
- Does the organization help relate one story to another?
- Can the stories be read either independently or continuously?

Illustrations

- Do the illustrations enhance the tales?
- Does the artwork reflect the country or the culture of the tale's origin?
- Are the illustrations integral to the story, or are they merely decorative?
- Are the illustrations placed appropriately?

Special Features

- Does the introduction provide guidance for using the anthology?
- Can a reader locate tales by title, source, motif, subject, or country of origin?
- Is there a table of contents?
- Are there one or more indexes? Possibilities include title, author, illustrator, subject, origin of tales.
- Does the book contain additional information that will be of use in the curriculum, such as a genealogy of the gods or a glossary of names?
- Are there commentaries about the tales?
- Is the source of each tale identified?
- Do the acknowledgments and copyright data sections provide more information about the tales?
- Does the subtitle or author's note identify the particular type of story, such as a myth, legend, or fable?

SETTING CRITERIA FOR A SINGLE STORY

General criteria apply to any type of folk literature. For tales published in a single format, the following questions can be used:

- Is the story unique?
- Is the story for the child reader or the adult storyteller?
- Do the characters use figurative language and imagery? If dialect is used, is it accessible to children?
- Does it sound as though a storyteller told it?
- Does the reteller give the origin of the story?
- Does the story remain true to the values, lifestyles, and beliefs of the original culture?
- Does the language maintain the flavor of the country or culture where the tale originated?
- Are the illustrations culturally accurate?
- Is the book intended to showcase an artist's work or, rather, to help tell the story?
- Are the illustrations and tale integrated?
- Is this a new interpretation of the story?
- How does this version compare with others?

SUMMARY

Traditional folk narratives, including folktales, fables, myths, legends, tall tales, and fairy tales, have unique characteristics. When selecting these stories, one should consider the criteria for the book with a single story or for anthologies.

RESOURCES

Frank, Diana Crone, and Jeffrey Frank, sel. and trans. 2003. *The Stories of Hans Christian Andersen.* Boston, MA: Houghton Mifflin.
Notes follow each story. Translators intend to restore the essentially Danish colloquial voices of the tales. Includes the original illustrations by Vilhelm Pedersen and Lorenz Frolich.

Jacobs, Joseph. 1993. *English Fairy Tales,* illustrated by John Batten. New York: Knopf.
One of several volumes of world tales written in language ready for oral storytelling. Source notes.

Library of Congress. "The American Folklife Center." (August 27, 2006) Available: www.loc.gov/folklife
Provides title, subject, geographical, and distributor access to information on the world's cultures, including such entries as "Asian American." Provides Teacher's Guide to Folklife Resources, lesson plans, and titles for further study.

MacDonald, Margaret Read, and Brian W. Sturm. 2001. *The Storyteller's Sourcebook: A Subject, Title, and Motif Index to Folklore Collections for Children 1983–1999.* Farmington Hills, MI: Thompson Gale.

Access points also include geographic or ethnic origin. Provides plots and identifies which collections contain the tale.

Zipes, Jack, ed. 2000. *Oxford Companion to Fairy Tales: The Western Fairy Tale Tradition from Medieval to Modern.* Oxford: Oxford University Press.

Entries arranged in dictionary style provide access to illustrators, authors, subjects, and countries.

RECOMMENDED AUTHORS, RETELLERS, AND ILLUSTRATORS

Ada, Alma Flor. 1999. *The Three Golden Oranges*, illustrated by Reg Cartwright. New York: Atheneum.

The popular character Blancaflor, appears in this story of three brothers searching for their brides. Vivid oil paintings support the text. Ada has also retold *Mediopollito Half-Chicken,* translated by Rosa Zubizarreta, illustrated by Kim Howard (Doubleday, 1995); *The Lizard and the Sun/La lagartija y el sol*, translated by Rosa Zubizarreta, illustrated by Felipe Davalos (Doubleday, 1997); and *The Rooster Who Went to His Uncle's Wedding/El gallo que fue a la boda de su tío*, illustrated by Kathleen Kuchera (Putnam, 1993).

Andersen, Hans Christian. 2001. *Hans Christian Andersen's Fairy Tales*, selected and illustrated by Lisbeth Zweger, translated by Anthea Bell. San Francisco: North-South.

Eleven tales illustrated with engaging, enlightening paintings by a recipient of the Hans Christian Andersen Medal for lifetime contribution.

Bryan, Ashley. 2003. *Beautiful Blackbird.* New York: Atheneum.

Bryan uses drumbeat prose and bold paper collage to retell a Zambian tale. Like a fable, the story urges us to "Just remember, whatever I do, I'll be me and you'll be you." Winner of the Coretta Scott King Medal for *Beat the Story-Drum, Pum-Pum* (Atheneum, 1980) and *Lion and the Ostrich Chicks* (Atheneum, 1986).

Grimm, Jacob. 1993. *The Complete Brothers Grimm Fairy Tales.* New York: Avenel. More than 200 tales by the Brothers Grimm.

Heo, Yumi. Illustrator. *Yoshi's Feast*, written by Kimiko Kajikawa (Dorling-Kindersley, 2000).

In this Japanese fairy tale, two vendors compete, then cooperate. Heo's oil, pencil, and collage artworks add interest and momentum. Heo's artwork has appeared in several folk and fairy tales including *So Say the Little Monkeys* (Atheneum, 1998), *The Green Frogs: A Korean Folktale* (Houghton Mifflin, 1996), and *The Rabbit's Escape* (Holt, 1995).

Hyman, Trina Schart. Illustrator whose treatment of fairy tales typically includes a series of borders that enclose a page of text and a page of illustration. Examples of her detailed and realistic characters and settings can be seen in *Bearskin* by Howard Pyle (Morrow, 1997) and *Sense Pass King: A Story from Cameroon* (Holiday House, 2002).

Kimmel, Eric. 2004. *Cactus Soup*, illustrated by Phil Huling. London: Marshall Cavendish.

Kimmel writes with a keen ear for the oral tradition. The watercolor and ink drawings add humor to this version of Stone Soup. *Hershel and the Hanukkah Goblins*, illustrated by Trina Schart Hyman (Holiday House, 1989), was a Caldecott Honor Book. In January 2005, Kimmel received the Sydney Taylor Lifetime Achievement Award.

Paye, Won-Ldy, and Margaret H. Lippert. 2003. *Mrs. Chicken and the Hungry Crocodile*, illustrated by Julie Paschkis. Austin, TX: Holt.

Bold gouache illustrations with white text and black paper add drama to this tale of vanity and survival. Won-Ldy heard this Northeastern Liberian story from his grandmother. Other titles include: *Head, Body, Legs: A Story from Liberia*, illustrated by Margaret H. Lippert (Holt, 2002), and *Why Leopard Has Spots*: *Dan Stories from Liberia*, illustrated by Ashley Bryan (Fulcrum Kids, 1998).

Pinkney, Jerry. Illustrator and reteller whose realistic African and African American characters are found in picture storybooks and folklore. *John Henry* by Julius Lester (Dial, 1994) provides one example of his ability to create a visual image that stays with the viewer. Other examples are *The Ugly Duckling* by Hans Christian Andersen (Morrow Junior Books, 1999) and *Aesop's Fables* by Aesop (SeaStar Books 2000). Pinkney's *Noah's Ark* (North-South, 2002) brings a rich visual experience of watercolor, pencil, and colored pencil illustrations of a life filled with energy and details, along with an underlying sense of wonder and fragility of our world.

San Souci, Daniel. 2002. *The Rabbit and the Dragon King: Based on a Korean Folk Tale*, illustrated by Eujin Kim Neilan. Honesdale, PA: Boyds Mills.

Textured drawings and cinematic perspectives accompany this tale of mind over matter. San Souci's *The Legend of Scarface* (Doubleday, 1978) was a Horn Book Honor Book.

Scieszka, Jon. Author of parodies of folktales including *The Stinky Cheese Man and Other Fairly Stupid Tales*, illustrated by Lane Smith (Viking, 1992.) This team, known for their playful language and off-kilter illustrations, also did *Baloney Henry P.* (Viking, 2001) and *Math Curse* (Viking, 1995).

Sierra, Judy. 1999. *Tasty Baby Belly Buttons*, illustrated by Meilo So. New York: Knopf.

An ALA Notable Book based on the Japanese legends of the Oni, who devoured human belly buttons. Meilo So's watercolors dance across the pages. *The Gift of the Crocodile* (Simon & Schuster, 2000) and *The Beautiful Butterfly* (Clarion, 2000) also attest to her storyteller's ear for rollicking prose.

Ward, Helen. 2003. *The Rooster and the Fox*. Brookfield, IL: Millford.

Lively retelling with beautiful watercolor and pastel illustrations. Her version of *The Hare and the Tortoise: A Fable from Aesop* (Millbrook, 1999) was an ALA Notable Book.

Young, Ed. 2004. *The Sons of the Dragon King: A Chinese Legend.* New York: Atheneum.

A balance of ink, brush and more formal cut-paper inserts illustrate this story celebrating fatherly love and individual differences. Young received the Caldecott Medal for *Lon Po Po: A Red-Riding Hood Story from China* (Philomel, 1989).

Zelinsky, Paul O. Illustrator and reteller. In his retelling of *Rapunzel* (Dutton, 1997), Zelinsky describes the basis of his version and paints in the style of the old masters. Winner of the Caldecott Award.

Chapter 9

Rhymes and Poetry

EXPLORING POETRY

Poetry expresses thought and emotion by using words chosen to convey an impression of sound, often arranged in rhythmic patterns but also, at times, in abstract or free verse. Poetry expresses thought and feeling with succinct, descriptive, evocative, carefully chosen words. Rhymes (nursery or Mother Goose), greeting card verses, certain nonsense verses, and limericks are not considered poetry by some authorities. An opposing view sees poetry as a continuum balanced by doggerel at one end and lyrical poetry at the other end. There is agreement that nursery rhymes and nonsense verses prepare the child for the appreciation of poetry.

EXAMINING MOTHER GOOSE AND OTHER RHYMES

Mother Goose **rhymes** and jingles can serve as an introduction to the world of literature. Young children can hear rhyme, alliteration, and onomatopoeia in such verses. The sound patterns, simple stories with quick action, interesting characters, and humor are appealing to young children, while brevity lays the foundation for longer and more involved verse. Other forms that appeal to children include tongue twisters, counting rhymes, finger plays, and riddles.

Our traditional Mother Goose rhymes originated in the English-speaking world. In Great Britain they are known as nursery rhymes, which are not limited to English-speaking cultures. All cultures have developed rhymes and jingles appropriate for small children.

Spotlight 9.1:   Rhyming Is Good
Spotlight on Public Libraries
Reading-readiness programs based on recent brain research promote heavy use of rhyme with preschool children. Programs for adults and other caregivers result in increased demand for attractively illustrated brief poems and rhymes.
Spotlight on School Libraries
The above advice also applies to schools where preschool programs are offered by the school or an outside agency.

Criteria

As you survey Mother Goose rhymes, consider the following questions as you note coverage, illustrations, setting, characters, arrangement, and special features.

- Coverage

  - How many rhymes are included?
  - Will children find both well-known and newer rhymes?
  - Are the versions familiar ones?
  - Does the text read smoothly?
  - Are there different types of rhymes in the collection?
  - Do the rhymes pertain to one or more subjects or themes?
  - Will children find rhymes from different cultures?
  - Are the rhymes presented in both English and the original language?
  - Does the translation overcome the inherent difficulty of conveying the language and humor of rhymes?
  - Is information about symbolic poetry, such as political nursery rhymes, provided for adults?
  - Are there lists of further readings for adults?

- Illustrations

  - Has only one medium been used or several employed?
  - Is the medium appropriate for the mood of the collection?
  - Are the illustrations colorful?
  - Is the style of the artwork appropriate for the collection?
  - Do the illustrations complement or explain the text?
  - Do the illustrations capture the mood and humor of the rhymes?

- Does the design of the title page capture the mood and coverage of the collection?
- Do the cover and endpapers enhance the collection?

- Setting

  - Can children relate to the setting?
  - Is the setting appropriate for the rhymes?
  - Does the setting contribute to the collection?

- Characters

  - Do the characters include children and adults?
  - Do the characters represent various ethnic backgrounds accurately?
  - Does the personality of the character match the rhymes?
  - Are animals personified, or are they realistically portrayed?

- Arrangement

  - How are text and illustrations arranged on the page?
  - Is the text cluttered with several verses and related illustrations?
  - Are unifying illustrations used for related verses?
  - How can one distinguish a rhyme ending and the beginning of another?
  - Is each verse titled to help identify beginning and end?
  - Is there a common theme to the collection, or do the rhymes appear unrelated?

- Special Features

  - Is there a table of contents?
  - Does the index include entries for poet, title, first line, and subject?
  - Are the sources of the verses identified?
  - Is the book designed for use with one child or with a group of children?

STUDYING POETRY FOR CHILDREN

In learning about poetry, you will begin to distinguish the difference between trite and original works and between the creative and the superficial. The more successful poets provide the reader with new experiences and insights, including those of an emotional nature. The poet's use of descriptive and narrative language enhances the reader's or listener's imagination of a particular sight, sound, touch, taste, or smell.

There are two major types of poetry for children. **Narrative poems**, which they initially prefer, tell a story about a particular person or event, such as in a ballad. **Lyrical poems**, in which the poet describes emotions and thoughts rather than telling a story, also are enjoyable. Examples include haiku, limerick, and other short poems.

Narrative Poems: Ballad

The **ballad**, or **folkpoem**, one of the first forms of poetry, is derived from our oral tradition. The early ballads with no known author were transmitted by minstrels. Among these, children will recognize "John Henry" and "Yankee Doodle." Literary ballads share the characteristics of the traditional folk ballad, but the author is known.

Characteristics of the ballad:

- presents a simple narrative, usually relating a single episode
- can be adopted for singing or giving the effect of a song
- makes frequent use of dialogue
- has marked rhythm and rhyme
- uses a repeated refrain
- each stanza consists of four lines, with the second and fourth lines rhyming.

Lyric Poems

Haiku is of Japanese origin. Children are able to grasp the simplicity of the images and can create their own.

Characteristics of haiku:

- lyric, unrhymed poems
- not restricted by rhyme patterns
- poems of 17 syllables arranged in three lines of 5, 7, and 5 syllables
- single, simple word pictures designed to evoke a feeling relating to nature

The **limerick** form, with the rhythm and sound adding to the humor, is a popular form for children to imitate.

Characteristics of the limerick:

- is usually a narrative
- is light verse, often nonsensical (humorous), about people's actions, manners, and idiosyncrasies
- consists of one stanza with five lines: lines one, two, and five rhyme and are of the same length; lines three and four rhyme and are of the same length, but shorter than the other lines

EVALUATING ELEMENTS OF POETRY

Poets use the elements of rhythm and meter, sounds, imagery, and forms to communicate a message. Carefully chosen words are used. Poets tend to minimize the number of words employed to convey an idea or feeling. They opt for words with definite rhythm, sound, and meaning. Their arrangement of words influences the rhythm, sound, effect, and meaning of the poems.

Ralph Fletcher in *Poetry Matters: Writing a Poem from the Inside Out* (HarperCollins, 2002) demonstrates, with examples and through interviews with children's poets, how poets express emotions, images, and rhythm.

As you examine poetry for children, look for these elements. How do the poets use them? How does the poet speak to and establish rapport with the child? How and what do the elements contribute to the poem?

Rhythm and Meter

The **rhythm** of the poem, the beat or regular cadence of the poem, may be metered or spontaneous and implies movement and events. When formalized into **meter**, the poem's pattern of rhythm consists of beats and stresses. Each line is made up of a given number of accented and unaccented syllables that appear in a set order.

Sounds

The words in poetry tend to be arranged to create rhyme, combinations of sounds, and repetition of sound. When looking for the rhyme pattern, people tend to think immediately of **end rhyme**, where sounds at the end of the line agree; but poets may also arrange sound patterns with rhyming words within a line as well as the devices of assonance, alliteration, and consonance. **Assonance** is the pattern in which the same vowel sound is heard within a line or within a few lines. **Alliteration** is the repetition of the same consonant at the beginning of words, and **consonance** is the repetition of the final consonant sounds.

Sound patterns may be repeated sounds and combinations of sounds in the words. Poets choose words with auditory appeal for effectiveness. The poet's words may be real or imaginary. The term **onomatopoeia** refers to words that imitate the name of an object or action or illustrate the word's meaning. Examples of onomatopoeia include *buzz, hiss, clump, snuffle.*

Imagery

The words may have **connotative** meanings, ones of association for the reader, or **denotative**, that is, explicit, meanings. The poem provides the context for the meaning, and a variety of figures of speech convey the meanings.

Poetry is compact. Each word is carefully chosen; one term can convey many meanings. Poets use **figurative language** to achieve this compression. By comparing or contrasting two objects, ideas, or feelings—explicitly or implicitly—the connotation of one word or phrase gives meaning to another.

Poets also make extensive use of **metaphor** and **similes**, two forms of comparison. A simile is the more direct and specific form of comparison. When you see the words *like* or *as* in a poem, the author is using a simile to make the connection between the two words. If the poet uses a verb or noun without *like* or *as* to imply comparison, it is a metaphor. In this case the poet uses one idea or object as if it were another idea or object. A form of metaphor is **personification**. By giving human attributes to things, the poet brings them into the reader's life. **Hyperbole**, or extravagant exaggeration, appeals to children and also suggests meanings for the words.

Forms

Form refers to how the poem is structured and put together. Poems may have certain shapes created by writing a specified number of lines. Sound patterns can also shape a poem, for example, which lines rhyme.

Among the traditional poetry forms are poems with two or more verses divided by an empty space, stanzas with verses repeating the same pattern, and patterns of a regular meter and rhyme scheme. However, many poems defy these traditional patterns. In children's literature one finds various forms, including ballad, limerick, haiku, free verse, and concrete poetry. Paul B. Janeczko in *A Kick in the Head: An Everyday Guide to Poetic Forms* (Candlewick, 2005) includes examples of 29 forms, each of which is fully explained in notes at the end of the book. Colorful multimedia collages and brushwork by Chris Raschka, along with witty icons, enhance the examples.

Free verse does not have a particular meter, and it may lack rhyme. The line lengths are often irregular.

Characteristics of free verse:

- lacks regular rhyme and meter
- depends on rhythm or cadence for its poetic form
- may look different from a traditional poem on the printed page, but when read aloud sounds like traditional poetry
- represents reflective writing
- often treats abstract and philosophical subjects
- may use a printed arrangement that suggests a rhythmical unit or cadence

In **concrete** the meaning is carried out by the shape of the poem or the setting of the poem. For example, in a poem about a skyscraper, the type can be set so the words are in the shape of a skyscraper. A poem about a seal that looks like a seal is another example. In another type of example, the viewers' experiences affect their interpretations of the poems. If a variety of words appear on different parts of a mobile, two viewers may see different combinations and find different meanings.

A Poke in the I: A Collection of Concrete Poems by Paul Janeczko, illustrated by Chris Raschka (Candlewick, 2001), provides examples of how the placement of words, various type faces, and the use of space add meaning to the words.

Characteristics of concrete poetry:

- Merges visual, verbal, and auditory elements
- May be presented through arrangement of words, letters, and punctuation marks
- Is usually written and printed in a shape that portrays the subject

ESTABLISHING SELECTION CRITERIA

As you further study poetry, the distinctions between trite and original works and between the creative and the superficial will become apparent. The more successful poems introduce the reader to new experiences and insights, including emotional ones. The poet strives harmoniously to unite the words, ideas, moods, pictures, feelings, rhythm, and structure into a meaningful whole. The poem provides the context in which the rhythm, sound, and sense of the words interact to bring common experience to readers and listeners.

Poems are concerned with real or imaginary experiences and should be those to which the child can relate. A key question is always whether the poetry speaks to the child. Poetry about childhood is directed to nostalgic adults rather than to children. Anthologies may include poems written for a child or poems written for adults that the compiler thinks will appeal to children. When you read poetry aloud to children, their responses will give an awareness of the poem's impact. Note their body language, facial expressions, and attention span.

Read the poems aloud. Poetry comes from our oral tradition, and so the most effective test of a poem is an oral rendition. Using this technique helps you understand the poet's use of language and rhythm, know the timing of the poem, and appreciate the voice dynamics needed to interpret the poem.

Choose collections that include both contemporary and older poems. One example of such a collection is *A Family of Poems: My Favorite Poetry for Children*, selected by Caroline Kennedy with illustrations by Jon J. Muth (Hyperion Books for Children, 2005). This collection includes a variety of styles by poets from around the world who represent different generations. Some works may be familiar, others lesser known. The ten translated works in their original language appear at the end of the book. Kennedy shares her family's tradition of children creating a scrapbook of poems selected for their mother and grandparents in place of gifts. The range of subjects addressed reflects the range of interests of children with some humorous and serious entries. The collection is enriched with poems by children with whom Kennedy has shared poetry.

Stoplight 9.1:   Poems—What to Avoid
Avoid poems that: • patronize childhood or give a nostalgic view of childhood • are overly rhythmic, singsongy poems and those that are super-sentimental, saccharine, and use unnatural affects • are beyond the child's real or imagined experiences and understandings • are too difficult or too simple • use obsolete or difficult language • are cliché burdened, hackneyed, merely "cute," preachy, and didactic • are condescending or oversimplify • have long, descriptive passages • are pedantic or about a subject in which children have little interest

Single Poem, Criteria

- Is the poem unique?
- What is the purpose of the poem?
- Is the purpose appropriate for children?
- Does the poem appeal to children?
- How has the poet created the emotional intensity of the poem?

- Language

    - Does the rhythm reinforce and create meaning for the poem?
    - Is the rhyme natural sounding or contrived?
    - Does the sound add meaning to the poem?
    - Will a child understand the similes and metaphors?
    - Does the poem create sensory images of sight, touch, sound, smell, and taste?
    - What is the quality of the imagination in the poem?
    - Will the child see something in a new way?

- Shape

    - Does the shape of the poem contribute to the meaning of the poem?
    - Does the arrangement of the words contribute to the meaning of the poem?

Anthologies, Criteria

- Purpose
    - What is the purpose of the collection?

- Is the purpose stated in the introduction or an opening section of the book?
- Does the purpose fill a need in the collection?
- Does the selection of poems included meet the purpose of the collection?
- Who is the intended audience?
- Are the selections appropriate for that audience?
- Does the compiler have the background and qualifications to handle that purpose?

- Scope

  - Are the poems by a variety of authors, familiar and unknown, traditional and contemporary?
  - How many poems are included?
  - Do the poems duplicate ones you already have in other books?
  - Do the poems relate to one another?
  - Does the anthology include a variety of forms of poetry?

- Language

  - Is a variety of meter found in the poems?
  - Is there a variety of sound patterns?
  - Do the poems include uses of alliteration, onomatopoeia, or repetition?
  - Do the verse patterns enrich the content of the poems?
  - Is figurative language imaginative and appropriate?

- Subjects

  - Does the anthology focus on one subject?
  - Will there be sufficient use of poems on that subject to merit purchasing it?
  - Will the subject appeal to children?

- Organization

  - How are the poems arranged and organized?
  - Is there a table of contents?
  - Are there one or more indexes?
  - Can a reader locate poems by title, poet, first line, and subject?

- Illustrations

  - Do the illustrations enrich the effectiveness of the poetry?
  - Are they merely decorative?

- Are the illustrations placed appropriately?
- Do they distract from the poetry?

• Other Features

- Are there commentaries with background information about the poems?
- Is the source of each poem identified?
- Does the anthology include biographical information about each poet?
- Do the acknowledgments and copyright information sections provide more information about the poems?

• Physical Characteristics

- Is the paper of appropriate quality?
- Is the paper an appropriate color for the subject or mood of the poetry?
- Is the page layout uncluttered?
- Is the size of the book one a child can handle?
- Is the size of print appropriate for the intended audience?
- Do white spaces or frames set off individual poems?

Spotlight 9.2:   Using Anthologies
Spotlight on Public Libraries
A well-illustrated anthology of short poems arranged by topics that interest children and match preschool theme units will be used by parents and caregivers alike.

Box 9.1:   Using Award Books as Guides: Poetry
If you are not familiar with authors of children's poetry, you can begin with the works of poets who have received the National Council of Teachers of English (NCTE) Excellence in Poetry for Children Award. This award recognizes a poet's entire body of poetry written for children ages 3 through 13, not a particular poem or book of poetry. The award began in 1977, was awarded annually until 1982, and now is awarded every three years. See Figure 9.1 for a list of the NCTE Award winners.

Figure 9.1:	National Council of Teachers of English Excellence in Poetry for Children Award Recipients, 1977–2006
1977	David McCord
1978	Aileen Fisher
1979	Karla Kuskin
1980	Myra Cohn Livingston
1981	Eve Merriam
1982	John Ciardi
1985	Lillian Moore
1988	Arnold Adoff
1991	Valerie Worth
1994	Barbara Juster Esbensen
1997	Eloise Greenfield
2000	X. J. Kennedy
2003	Mary Ann Hoberman
2006	Nikki Grimes

Source: "NCTE Award for Poetry for Children." (September 3, 2006) Available: www.ncte.org/elem/awards/poetry?source=gs

SUMMARY

Poets express their ideas and feelings in a variety of forms, from traditional poems like the ballad to free verse or concrete poetry. The characteristics of the form and appearance of the poem in a single book or with others in an anthology leads to the criteria used in evaluating poetry.

REFERENCES

"IRA Lee Bennett Hopkins Promising Poet Awards." (August 27, 2006) Available: www.reading.org/association/awards/childrens_hopkins.html

"NCTE Award for Poetry for Children." (September 3, 2006) Available: www.ncte.org/elem/awards/poetry?source=gs

"NCTE Award for Poetry for Children." (August 27, 2006) Available: www.ncte.org/elem/awards/poetry/106862.htm

RESOURCES

Academy of American Poets, Sponsor of National Poetry Month since April 1994. (August 27, 2006) Available: www.poets.org/index.cfm; "National Poetry Month." (August 27, 2006) Available: www.poets.org/php/prmID/47

This event is observed by schools, libraries, and bookstores throughout the United States.

Chukovsky, Kornei. 1963. *From Two to Five.* Translated and edited by Miriam Morton. Berkeley, CA: University of California Press.

Classic work addresses poetry as the young child's natural language.

Fletcher, Ralph. 2002. *Poetry Matters: Writing a Poem from the Inside Out.* New York: HarperCollins.

Fletcher provides a guide for students and teachers with an emphasis on expressing emotions, images, and rhythm rather than focusing on form. Includes interviews with Kristine O'Connell George, Janet S. Wong, and J. Patrick Lewis.

Hopkins, Lee Bennett. 1998. *Pass the Poetry, Please!* 3rd ed. New York: HarperCollins.

Describes activities for bringing children and poetry together. Explains how to read poetry aloud. Introduces 24 poets through a biographical sketch and their poetry.

Janeczko, Paul B. 1999. *How to Write Poetry.* Scholastic Guide series. New York: Scholastic.

Offers practical suggestions and encouragement for aspiring poets individually or in groups. Includes illustrative poems, bibliographies, and a glossary.

Janeczko, Paul B. 2005. *A Kick in the Head: An Everyday Guide to Poetic Forms*, illustrated by Chris Raschka. Cambridge, MA: Candlewick.

Carefully selected accessible poems are identified by Raschka's colorful multimedia collages and brushwork, similar to Zen calligraphy, and a witty icon. Each of the 29 forms is described and later more fully explained in notes at the end of the book.

Prelutsky, Jack, sel. 2005. *Read a Rhyme, Write a Rhyme*, illustrated by Meilo So. New York: Knopf.

Provides a starting point for writing poems on various subjects. Each of a double-page spread includes three poems and a "poemstart." The latter provides the first three lines of a poem, followed by suggestions for what one might write. Other ideas include possible rhyming words and ideas for different approaches.

RECOMMENDED POETS AND COMPILERS

Florian, Douglas. Author and illustrator known for his nonsense verse and humorous illustrations (watercolor and colored pencil). Florian's *Autumnlings: Poems and Paintings* (Greenwillow, 2003) is accessible to newly independent readers because he continues to invent words, offers descriptive spellings, and uses simple rhyme schemes. *Autumnlings* is a companion to *Winter Eyes* (Greenwillow, 1999) and *Summersaults* (Greenwillow, 2002). Enjoyable for young readers and for adults to share aloud. To introduce children to different animal groupings, try his *Bow Wow, Meow Meow: It's Rhyming Cats and*

Dogs (Harcourt, 2003) or *Lizards, Frogs, and Polliwogs: Poems and Paintings* (Harcourt, 2001), in which children can sort fact from fantasy.

Grimes, Nikki. Author and poet, on the subjects of friendship, coming of age, and community. Grimes is the 2006 Winner of the NCTE Award for Poetry for Children. In *What Is Goodbye?* (Hyperion, 2005), through the alternating words of a sister, Jerilyn, and her brother, Jesse, Grimes captures the confusion, grief, and silences that a family face in the death of an older brother. The work closes with a poem for two voices as the family learns to smile again. Raul Colon's muted colored paintings create a realistic and emotional dreamlike quality.

A return of one of Grimes's favorite protagonists is *Danitra Brown, Class Clown* (Amistad, 2005), who is described by her classmate Zuri as a true friend in all types of situations faced by preadolescent girls. E. B. Lewis's illustrations visually express the spirit and energy of the friendship. In *At Jerusalem's Gate: Poems of Easter* (Erdmans, 2005) Grimes's reflections of the first Easter are enhanced by colorful woodcuts by David Frampton. *Tai Chi Morning: Snapshots of China*, illustrated by Ed Young (Cricket Books, 2004) is a travelogue, sketchbook, and collection of poems recalling Grimes's travels to China in 1988. She compares what she sees with what is happening in the entire world. Young's pen-and-ink drawings visually show the culture of China and the spirit of Grimes's impressions. Grimes's Web site is found at: www.nikkigrimes.com (August 26, 2006).

Hopkins, Lee Bennett. A widely acclaimed author, poet, and compiler whose collections cover a range of topics, many with a curriculum-related focus. Evident in all his work is his mission to recognize quality in children's poetry and to engage teachers, librarians, and children in the dialogue. Examples include *Wonderful Words: Poems about Reading, Writing, Speaking, and Listening* (Simon & Schuster, 2004), illustrated by Karen Barbour and *Alphathoughts: Alphabet Poems* (Wordsong, 2003), illustrated by Marian Baggetta. Each poem defines or describes an object or concept beginning with the letter.

Other titles have themes, such as *Home to Me: Poems Across America* (Orchard Books, 2002), with colorful and appealing illustrations by Stephen Alcorn. This is a collection of commissioned poets to describe the diverse geographical settings in the United States. From around the world (in terms of old and new poets plus subject orientation) is *Days to Celebrate: A Full Year of Poetry, People, Holidays, History, Fascinating Facts, and More* (Greenwillow, 2005), illustrated by Stephen Alcorn with a calendar listing events as an introduction to each chapter. Hopkins's anthologies are also found in the An I Can Read Book series, including *A Pet for Me: Poems*, illustrated by Jane Manning (HarperCollins, 2003), and *Christmas Presents: Holiday Poetry*, illustrated by Melanie Hall (HarperCollins, 2004).

Janeczko, Paul. Poet, anthologist, and author who is committed to sharing his enthusiasm for poetry, children, and young adults. He is editor of many award-winning anthologies. A lively and colorful collection is *A Poke in the I: A Col-*

lection of Concrete Poems, illustrated by Chris Raschka (Candlewick, 2001). The poems range from a single word (the way the type is placed on the page) to words arranged in a particular shape. The word and/or page arrangement, the typefaces, and the use of space add meaning to the poems. Some extend over a double-page spread. Even the table of contents uses the techniques of space, variety of typefaces, and decoration. This team also did *A Kick in the Head: An Everyday Guide to Poetic Forms* (Candlewick Press, 2005).

Kuskin, Karla. Poet, author, and illustrator whose nimble verses can be read aloud. She is known for her strength of rhythm, internal and end rhymes, and play with language. For an example of her effective image-creating metaphors see *Toots the Cat* (Holt, 2005), illustrated by Lisze Bechtold—a delight for cat lovers. Told from a different angle is *So What's It Like to Be a Cat?* (Atheneum, 2005), in which a feline with personality is interviewed by a boy. Betsy Lewin's watercolor cartoons are a match with the expressive responses of the cat.

A fresh perspective on an old story is *The Animals and the Ark* (Atheneum, 2002), with Michael Grejniec's watercolor illustrations capturing the humor of the animals' boredom. A four-page spread of the unrest leads to "At precisely that moment the sun broke through," with bright colors capturing a new beginning. *Moon, Have You Met My Mother? The Collected Poems of Karla Kuskin* (Laura Geringer, 2003) opens with a poem as Kuskin reminisces about writing poetry since childhood. The poems are arranged thematically and cover a wide range of subjects. Another for the read-aloud list.

Lewis, J. Patrick. Poet and picture book author whose works often have a direct curriculum connection. For example, one could almost classify as nonfiction his *Swan Song: Poems of Extinction* (Creative Editions, 2003), with carefully crafted woodcuts by Christopher Wormell and the provision of scientific names, date of extinction, last known location, and a time line of world events affecting the environment. Endnotes provide further information. An outstanding combination of poetry, art, and science.

A World of Wonders: Georgraphic Travels in Verse and Rhyme (Dial, 2002), with pictures by Alison Jay, offers lighthearted ways for children to remember geographical terms, such as the differences between stala**c**tite (from **c**eiling) and stala**g**mite (from the **g**round). Another lighthearted title is *Scien-Trickery: Riddles in Sciences* (Harcourt, 2004), illustrated by Frank Remkiewicz. Answers are provided with each riddle, plus Notes add further explanations. The pleasure of reading is explored in *Please Bury Me in the Library* (Harcourt, 2005), illustrated by Kyle M. Stone. Lewis's Web site is found at: www.jpatricklewis.com (August 26, 2006).

Nye, Naomi Shihab. Poet, essayist, author, and anthologist known for her elegant, uncommon language that stimulates private thoughts and group discussions. The latter is particularly descriptive of *19 Varieties of Gazelle: Poems of the Middle East* (Greenwillow, 2002), which explores questions of family, people, conflict, and hope. Her *A Maze Me: Poems for Girls*, illustrated by Terre Maher (Greenwillow, 2005), has a potential audience far beyond girls (around 12 years old), since as the poems range from observations in daily life to exploring abstract ideas. For many of the poems a detailed image is related to its application in daily life. There's humor too, such as "Baby-sitting should not be called/ sitting. Because it is chasing, bending/picking up, and major play." For younger children, *Baby Radar* (Greenwillow, 2003), illustrated by Nancy Carpenter, presents a toddler's view as she goes for a ride in her stroller. Nancy Carpenter's realistic pen-and-water illustrations capture the humor and exuberance for life in the simple adventures.

Prelutsky, Jack. Poet, anthologist, and translator known for his irreverent style, technical versatility, and awareness of children's preferences combining nonsensical with the macabre. His humor and inventive wordplay are evident in *Scranimals* (Greenwillow, 2002), illustrated by Peter Sis—a work that allows both artists (the poet and the animator) to use their imagination as they did in *The Dragons Are Singing Tonight* (Greenwillow, 1999), *Monday's Troll* (Greenwillow, 1996), and *The Gargoyle on the Roof* (Greenwillow, 1993). Realism and imagination are combined in *The Frog Wore Red Suspenders* (Greenwillow, 2002), enhanced with watercolor illustrations by Petra Mathers. A number of the poems play with American place names, providing a geographical connection to the classroom.

Another example of Prelutsky's talents is *If Not for the Cat: Haiku* (Greenwillow, 2004), illustrated by Ted Rand, with its mix of sumi brush drawings in India ink, traditional watercolors, chalk, spatter, and printmaking technique that capture the spirit of the poems. The index is by "Who Is Who." Prelutsky's interest in inspiring children to write poetry is found in *Read a Rhyme, Write a Rhyme* (Knopf, 2005), illustrated by Meilo So (see annotation in the recommended resources in this chapter). For biographical information, see www.poets.org/poet.php/prmPID/68 (August 27, 2006).

Singer, Marilyn. Poet and author whose works include nonfiction, novels, short stories, and picture books. An earth science link is found in *How to Cross a Pond: Poems about Water* (Knopf, 2003), with a range of poetic forms accompanied by swirling illustrations in blue ink and watercolor by Meilo So. Companion volumes by these two are *Footprints on the Roof: Poems about the Earth* (Knopf, 2002) and *Central Heating: Poems about Fire and Warmth* (Knopf, 2004). Also science related is *Fireflies at Midnight* (Atheneum, 2003), which is strikingly illustrated by Ken Robbins's photographs and has a focus on how animals spend their days in summer. In *Creature Carnival* (Hyperion, 2004) the world of creatures from myths, legends, and popular culture provide the imaginative base. The creatures are identified at the end of the book. Look for Singer at www.marilynsinger.net (August 27, 2006).

Stevenson, James. Illustrator, poet, and author known for his humor and understanding of what is important and meaningful to children. Continuing his series that started with *Sweet Corn: Poems* (Greenwillow, 1995) Stevenson's *Corn-Fed* (Greenwillow, 2002) and *Corn Chowder* (Greenwillow, 2003) present humorous and poignant poems of everyday life from both a child's perspective and a grandparent's, making this a natural for multigenerational sharing. The watercolor sketches and the text layouts, with a variety of fonts, different sizes, and varying arrangements, enhance the appeal of the book and help readers see everyday things in a fresh and funny way.

Wong, Janet S. Poet and author of picture books. In her earlier works she drew on her Korean, Chinese, and American background and observed the differences among these countries' customs and cultures. Her recent titles represent the diversity of our country. For would-be writers, see *You Have to Write* (McElderry, 2002), illustrated by Teresa Flavin, with its reassuring advice about everyone having something unique to say. *Knock on Wood: Poems about Superstitions*, illustrated by Julie Paschkis (McElderry, 2003), covers familiar and lesser-known superstitions on a wide range of topics with humor and haunting images, both verbally and visually, in watercolor scenes and matching frames. Includes notes about the superstitions and the author's personal experiences. This team also did *Night Garden: Poems from the World of Dreams* (M. K. McElderry, 2000). Check out Wong at www.janetwong.com (August 27, 2006).

PART III

SPECIAL SELECTION CRITERIA FOR SPECIFIC SUBJECTS

Chapter 10

Information and Reference Books

EXPLORING INFORMATION BOOKS

Information books are written to inform, to lead the child from a fact or facts to a concept or a principle. The author's attitude (tone) toward both the subject and the reader affects the reception of fact and concept. Children's lack of experience poses a challenge. The task is to arouse their curiosity without suggesting that the facts are miraculous or beyond their comprehension. The ultimate goal is to lead children to a process of discovery that may extend into their adult lives.

Information seekers represent a wide range of ages, possibly preschoolers through adults. Alphabet books, counting books, and simple concept books often found in the "Easy" section of public and school libraries can provide information for the younger children. Older children doing research reports will seek books that document the author's sources.

Just as the range of ages is wide, so are the topics. They may be natural science identification books or explorations of such complex subjects as democracy. Topics commonly reflect the wide ranges of subjects in children's schoolwork and in their personal interests.

To set the stage for thinking about criteria for selection of information books, consider commonly accepted desirable characteristics of **expository writing** with helpful graphics and logically developed information. Authors show respect for their readers by identifying their point of view, sharing their interest in the subject, and encouraging questioning attitudes on the reader's part.

Expository writing includes these characteristics:

- Explains or sets forth information; reports events, actions, and behaviors
- Seeks to inform
- Uses illustrations to clarify or explain
- Is written in the present tense
- Is usually written in third person
- Is organized by description, sequence, comparison/contrast, cause and effect, and problem solving
- Uses information-giving words
- Uses headings and titles
- Employs technical vocabulary
- Employs a terse writing style
- Explains abstract concepts
- Reader assumes information is accurate and attends to the organization of the information
- Reader uses flexible, slower reading rate

In addition to the general criteria described in this chapter, there are characteristics unique to various subjects. The next chapter will discuss those characteristics and identify appropriate questions to consider in selecting such books.

Award Books as Guides: The Orbis Pictus Award and Sibert (ALSC) Award

Examples of well-written information books are those that have received the National Council of Teachers of English's *Orbis Pictus* Award for Outstanding Nonfiction. Established in 1989, the award is to recognize and promote excellence in nonfiction writing for children. The committee's decision is based on accuracy, content, style, organization, illustration, and format.

Box 10.1: *Orbis Pictus*
Orbis Pictus by Amos Comenius, published in 1657, is recognized as the first known information book for children. Woodcuts illustrate everyday objects.

Figure 10.1:	*Orbis Pictus* Award for Outstanding Nonfiction Recipients, 1999–2005		
Year	**Title**	**Author**	**Publisher**
1999	*Shipwreck at the Bottom of the World: The Extraordinary True Story of Shackleton and the Endurance*	Jennifer Armstrong	Crown 1998
2000	*Through My Eyes*	Ruby Brides, Margo Lundell	Scholastic 1999
2001	*Hurry Freedom: African Americans in Gold Rush California*	Jerry Stanley	Crown 2000
2002	*Black Potatoes: The Story of the Great Irish Famine, 1845-1850*	Susan Campbell Bartoletti	Houghton Mifflin 2001
2003	*When Marian Sang: The True Recital of Marian Anderson: The Voice of a Century*	Pam Munoz Ryan	Scholastic 2002
2004	*An American Plague: The True and Terrifying Story of the Yellow Fever Epidemic of 1793*	Jim Murphy	Clarion Books 2003
2005	*York's Adventures with Lewis and Clark: An African-American's Part in the Great Expedition*	Rhoda Blumberg	HarperCollins 2004

Source: National Council of Teachers of English. (September 3, 2006) Available: www.ncte.org/elem/awards/orbispictus

A similar award is the Robert F. Sibert Informational Book Medal established by the Association for Library Service to Children in 2001, which "is awarded annually to the author of the most distinguished informational book published in English during the preceding year." (Association for Library Service to Children, January 27, 2007. Available: www.ala.org/ala/alsc/awardsscholarships/literaryawds/sibertmedal/Sibert_Medal.htm)

The committee's criteria include clarity and accuracy in both text and illustrations, documentation, stimulating presentation, engaging writing, appropriateness of style for reader, and respect for the reader.

Box 10.2:   Robert F. Sibert
Sibert was President of Bound to Stay Bound Books, Inc. of Jacksonville, Illinois. The company sponsors the award, which is administered by the Association for Library Service to Children.

	Figure 10.2: Robert F. Sibert Informational Book Medal Recipients, 2001–2007		
Year	**Title**	**Author**	**Publisher, Year**
2001	*Sir Walter Ralegh and the Quest for El Dorado*	Marc Aronson	Clarion Books 2000
2002	*Black Potatoes: The Story of the Great Irish Famine, 1845–1850*	Susan Campbell Bartoletti	Houghton Mifflin 2001
2003	*The Life and Death of Adoph Hitler*	James Cross Giblin	Clarion Books 2002
2004	*An American Plague: The True Terrifying Story of the Yellow Fever Epidemic of 1793*	Jim Murphy	Clarion Books 2003
2005	*The Voice That Challenged a Nation: Marian Anderson and the Struggle for Equal Rights*	Russell Freedman	Clarion Books 2004
2006	*Secrets of a Civil War Submarine: Solving the Mysteries of the H. L. Hunley*	Sally M. Walker	Carolrhoda Books 2005
2007	*Team Moon: How 400,000 People Landed Apollo 11 on the Moon*	Catherine Thimmesh	Houghton, 2006
Source: Association for Library Service to Children. (January 27, 2007) Available: www.ala.org/ala/alsc/awardsscholarships/literaryawds/sibertmedal/ Sibert_Medal.htm			

Components of Information Books

Authors work with elements of intellectual content when writing information books. They determine the scope of the book, do research for accuracy of information, and decide how they want to treat their subject. One of the important decisions they make is how they will organize the information. In information books special features such as indexes, glossaries, and appendices may be prime sources of information. Like other good writers, authors of information books are cognizant of our diverse society and the ability levels of young readers.

Criteria and Guidelines for Specific Components of Information Books

A challenge for writers of informational books is how to focus and when to quit. The writer must choose a key idea, relate it to facts and concepts that are familiar to the child, clarify the concept, and then lead the child to becoming a future problem solver.

- Scope

Questions to consider regarding scope include:

- Are all significant facts included?
- Is there sufficient content to make the book informative?
- Does the book provide enough information to merit its selection?
- In books for young readers, is the author able to limit the scope of the subject while retaining important facts and presenting them logically?

Information is always changing regardless of the subject. Recent discoveries, for instance, have revealed new information about planets. In the field of technology, changes occur rapidly. Political boundaries change and countries are renamed. The author is challenged to provide up-to-date information, current spelling of words, and clear explanations of theories while identifying opinions and biases.

- Accuracy

Questions that address accuracy:

- Are facts, theories, and opinions clearly distinguished?
- Is the copyright date recent? If this version of the book is a revision, has material been updated where needed?
- Does the author document the original source of the information or illustrations where appropriate? Citations can be found in footnotes, source notes for photographs and other graphic materials, an author's note, a bibliography, or in a section entitled "Acknowledgments."
- Does the author note the help of a subject specialist in checking the book for accuracy?
- Do the facts differ from ones found in other books or sources?
- In historical or biographical works does the interpretation of persons and events reflect current scholarship?
- Is the setting accurate in terms of time period, geographic location, social and political order, speech patterns, and costume?

Traditionally, books classified with a Dewey decimal number and shelved in the section of the library labeled "Nonfiction" were considered the information books: those written to present and discuss facts. Today, students will also find **blended** books, those containing fictional and factual writing. Well-known examples are David Macaulay's *Cathedral* (Houghton Mifflin, 1973) and Joanna Cole's Magic School Bus series [Examples: *The Magic School Bus in the Time of Dinosaurs* (Scholastic, 1995) and *The Magic School Bus Plays Ball: A Book about Forces* (Scholastic, 1998)].

Fictionalized biographies provide another example of mixing facts and fiction. To select these books, one must apply criteria used for the more traditional nonfiction works as well as the criteria for fiction. The emphasis in this chapter will be on criteria for the informational aspects of these books.

In writing either nonfiction or blended books, authors need to go beyond the minimal presentation of facts. They should help the child ask questions while stimulating his or her imagination and interest. Writers can alert readers to potential for new discoveries by using phrases such as *scientists believe, so far as we know, perhaps,* and *may have.* They can also point out that the young reader may have an opportunity to expand this knowledge in the future.

Writers can broaden a child's perspective by putting the topic in a broader context and pointing out relationships instead of limiting the discussion to bare facts. For example, an event can be described in the context of the historical period. Relationships can be drawn between the event and its integration into the arts, architecture, myths, folklore, botany, biography, music, science, technology, or crafts of that time period. A writer of biographical works can create a social history by creating a sense of the people and the times.

- Treatment of material

Questions to consider regarding treatment:

- Is the level of knowledge needed to use or understand the material in the book appropriate for the intended audience?
- In historical works are important preceding and subsequent events presented?
- Does the author create dramatic moments without resorting to clichés?
- Are statistics used judiciously without bombarding the reader?
- Are facts presented in a context meaningful to the child?
- When the author states a personal opinion or offers an interpretation, is there evidence to support the author's statement?
- Does the book include different viewpoints on a subject?
- Does the book encourage the reader to inquire further about the subject?
- Does the book show how the context relates to the topic?
- Is there a discussion of the broader picture such as social issues?
- Does the author use problem-solving situations that include open-ended questions, models for observation, and suggestions for further exploration?
- Do the illustrations and text encourage the child to reflect on a topic?
- If social life and customs are being discussed, does the author demonstrate respect for ethnicity and plurality?

- Organization

The method by which the author organizes and presents information can help or hinder the reader's use of a book. Organizational patterns include:

- Alphabetical
- Order of interest to the author or reader
- Description
- Sequence
- Chronological
- Place and spatial relations
- Cause and effect
- Comparison and contrast
- Discovery or invention
- Degree of familiarity
- Broad to narrow

Each pattern has advantages and disadvantages for the reader. In an alphabetical arrangement the reader must use the same term as the author. The "order of interest," an attention getter, may be of low information value. An example of a book arranged by order of interest could be a book about geology that opens with a volcano erupting.

In the description approach, the author presents details about the characteristics of the person, place, thing, or idea. The author may use the sequence approach, presenting the information in the order of occurrence. This technique is also used in books giving directions, such as craft books or cooking books. This is similar to the time order used in narratives. The author may use numbers to indicate the order or terms, such as *then, next, last, before, after,* and *finally*.

The chronological approach is appropriate for a) history of a country, a culture, or a region, b) history of a family or a person, or c) life cycles of animals; however, young readers may lack the sense of time needed to understand chronological relationships. The author may use a time line to help the reader see the relationships. A chronology can be used in the context of a journal for one day or a specific time period, as in *My Tour of Europe by Teddy Roosevelt, Age 10,* edited by Ellen Jackson, illustrated by Catherine Brighton (Millbrook Press, 2003).

Place and spatial relations are commonly used in geographic information. The presence of maps, diagrams, or other visual guides can expand or clarify the text. The cause-and-effect approach may be too complex for a young child's ability, although the author may want the reader to discover the connection. Terms that alert the reader include *if, so, so that, because of, as a result of,* and *since*.

Comparisons are commonly found in dictionaries with the groupings of synonyms and antonyms of a word. Other examples of comparisons include the similarities and differences of wild and tame animals or comparing traditional and contemporary social practices. The author will alert the reader by using terms such as *same as, alike, similar to, resembles, compared to, different from, unlike, but,* and *yet*.

Basing a biography on a single discovery or invention may tend to shove the scientific problems and facts around and create a one-sided picture of the subject. Books for younger children may move from the familiar to the unknown with the emphasis on the facts as separate pieces of information. An example of the broad-to-narrow subject approach is moving from the topic of weather to types of storms, such as thunderstorms, hailstorms, and snowstorms.

Other books may combine some of the above patterns or use a nonlinear approach with distinct units of information outside of the main text. They can be highlighted by the use of arrows, color, lines, shapes, or different fonts.

Questions to consider regarding organization:

- Is the information presented in a logical order?
- Is the system of organization appropriate for the subject and purpose of the book as well as the intended audience?
- Do headings and subheadings help to access a topic?
- Do changes in fonts or size of lettering direct the reader's eye?
- Are graphics used to direct the viewer's eye?

- Literary Quality

Like writers of other genres, the authors of information books are concerned with style or how they use language. Here are some desirable characteristics.

- Simple and effective comparisons using metaphors and similes
- Variety in sentence length and construction
- Use of imagery and figurative language
- Combinations of narrative techniques, such as poetry and prose
- Use of attention grabbers at the beginning of new sections
- Use of writer's passionate voice about the subject, sharing his or her interest in the subject
- Use of vivid details

Questions to consider relating to literary quality:

- Is the book clearly written?
- Are ideas logically developed?
- Will the text catch and hold the interest of the reader?
- Will the book be a good "read aloud"?
- Is there a central issue or problem?
- Is there a theme or main idea?
- Is there a sequence of events or an account of accurate and current factual evidence that clarifies or offers solutions to a problem?
- Is there a point of view or narrative voice?
- Does the writing have a distinctive tone?
- Does the writer respect the child?

- Special Features

Access to information is another critical factor. Tables of contents, indexes, and the change of type size for different sections can help the reader locate specific information. In fact, a 64-page book can benefit from an index owing to the large number of facts that are frequently found even in this size book.
Questions to consider regarding special features:

- Does the book provide access to the information through a table of contents; lists of tables, charts, and illustrations; the use of headings and subheadings within the text; indexes; or a glossary with guides to pronunciation?
- Does the index have cross-references?
- Does the book lead the reader to further information through appendices, bibliographies for further reading, or suggested activities?

- Illustration

Information may be presented solely through text; through a combination of text and illustrations, as in **photoessays**, where both play important roles; or through illustrations that provide information not repeated in the text. Each approach calls for appropriate assessment. Visual learners, English-as-a-Second-Language (ESL) children, and reluctant readers obtain information from graphics. Visual materials should be evaluated for that potential use.

Questions to consider regarding illustrative material:

- Do the illustrations clarify the text?
- Are illustrative materials captioned?
- Are diagrams, drawings, and maps clearly labeled?
- Is distortion avoided in charts and graphs?
- Are relative sizes shown?
- Are drawings, photographs, and other visual images sharp and clear?
- Are enlargements or other magnifications labeled?
- Are the illustrations positioned close to the appropriate text?
- Do the illustrations add aesthetic appeal to the book?
- Are the sources cited?
- In activity books are children pictured doing age-appropriate activities?
- Does the **legend**, or the explanation accompanying photographs or other illustrative material, repeat information from the text or provide additional information? Look at Jim Murphy's *The Great Fire* (Scholastic, 1995) to see how legends supplement and support the text. Notice, too, how the map is used throughout the book to illustrate the spreading of the fire. You also will find source notes acknowledging the original source of the illustrations.
- What role do illustrations play in the presentation of information?
- Are different type fonts used to indicate new subjects or different levels of information?

- Multicultural Aspects

Remember to consider the multicultural aspects of informational books. Questions to consider regarding multiculturality:

- Are males and females represented in text and illustrations?
- Is the text gender neutral?
- Is stereotyping avoided?
- Do the illustrations include minority group members, senior citizens, and people with disabilities?
- Are the examples or experiments relevant to a wide number of settings (rural, urban) and to children from a range of economic levels?

- Are the materials recommended for experiments or recipes ones that children will find in their homes?
- Are controversial subjects treated in a balanced manner? Will the child learn about differing viewpoints?

ASSESSING SERIES

A large number of nonfiction series exist. One example is the British-based Dorling Kindersley Eyewitness Books, which have close-up photographs on white paper with clear labels and eye-catching designs. These books are physically appealing. As you consider them, think about the amount of information provided. Do the visuals present sufficient information to help your students? Does the text also provide information? Do they complement other sources of information on the subject?

Series to avoid are those with pedantic writing, use of unfamiliar terms and concepts, limited information, and unappealing format or size of print. These are often formula books with a format that may not permit full inclusion of appropriate information.

Stoplight 10.1: Smart Buying Approaches
Although it is comforting to children to have a whole book on their assigned topic, avoid spending the majority of your budget duplicating skinny country, state, and animal books on similar subjects. The same sparse information may be repeated in each, rather than one book complementing another and adding to a child's knowledge.

Criteria

As with series in other genres, there are questions one should consider before selecting these titles.

- Are there inconsistencies within a series?
- Are there inconsistencies among different series published by the same company?
- If the series originally was published in another country, will U.S. children understand the language and concepts used in the presentation?
- Is there sufficient information to make the book worth purchasing?
- Are the research, enthusiasm for the subject, and depth of coverage equal to that found in other titles?

Stoplight 10.2: Information and Reference Books—Buyer Beware!

Avoid these undesirable elements:

- condescension (talking down to the reader)
- oversimplification (simplifying information so it is distorted)
- anthropomorphism (assigning human behavior to animals)
- didacticism (preaching)
- propaganda (generalizations without factual support)
- confusing information
- sloppy writing
- inaccuracy
- lack of respect for the subject

EVALUATING REFERENCE BOOKS

Each year we use fewer print reference sources. In some cases, this is because the print version no longer exists. Electronic sources are updated more frequently, and search capabilities are generally superior. When making a decision as to which format to select, consider the child user's developmental level and the child's access to a computer.

There are still resources that are more accessible in the print form; atlases come immediately to mind. If computer time is limited or group study of a resource will aid learning, both forms may be needed. The enticing content of a book like *Guinness World Records* (Bantam Books, 2000–) motivates children to learn how to find one fact in a thick book. Handling a print encyclopedia teaches them to navigate a multivolume resource. Animal encyclopedias are commonly found in reference sections for children.

Local histories may be available only in a print format. They may be acquired from the local public library or museum, a local history club, or the state library or museum. The local chamber of commerce is another source for this type of information.

Online catalog searching readily identifies circulating material on particular subjects. Many reference questions can be answered in this way. As both children's ability to search and database designers' recognition of the child user increase, the proportion of print versus electronic reference material can be adjusted.

Criteria

In addition to the general questions for information books, other questions you will want to consider include:

- Authority

    - What are the credentials of the editors?
    - Who decides what information will be included and the format of the book?
    - Are the qualifications of the authors, consultants, and contributors listed in the introduction or preface?
    - Are their qualifications appropriate for the subjects covered?

- Scope

    - Is the purpose of the work stated in the title, the introduction, or the preface?
    - Does that purpose meet instructional or personal needs of users?
    - Does the work fulfill its purpose?
    - Does the work provide an overview or an in-depth coverage of the topic?
    - What are the stated limitations?

- Accuracy

    - When you compare dates, facts, illustrative materials, and statistics with other sources, do you find the information to be accurate and up-to-date?
    - Are items in the bibliographies recent?

- Treatment of Material

    - Are both sides of controversial issues presented?
    - Are facts distinguished from opinions?
    - Are subjects of equal importance given equal space?
    - Are instructions for how to use the book clearly written?
    - Have foreign names been translated into English?

- Arrangement

    - Is the arrangement clear and appropriate for the purpose of the reference work?
    - Is the information easy to access?

- Special Features

    - Are the subject headings appropriate for both the child and adult user?
    - Is there a pronunciation guide?
    - Are there author, illustrator, title, series, subject, and other appropriate indexes?

- Does the index identify the exact map, latitude, longitude, and grid information needed to locate a specific place on a map?

- Format

  - Is the binding strong enough for the size and weight of the volume and for use by children?
  - Can children handle the weight, shape, and size of the book?
  - Can you open a volume so the pages are flat and a two-page spread is not lost in the binding?
  - Is a variety of type sizes and spacing used to set off different sections?
  - Are the contents clearly indicated on the outside of the volume?
  - Is the paper opaque enough so that the type does not show through?
  - Are distinctive headings and subheadings within a page used to isolate or highlight information, making it easier to find?

- Aesthetic Qualities

  - Are illustrations informative and appealing?
  - Are colors used to provide information and appeal?
  - Will the graphic design appeal to and be appropriate for the intended audience?

- Comparison

  - Does the reference work offer features not found in similar books?
  - Is the price appropriate for the book's anticipated use and quality?

SUMMARY

The components of information books (scope, accuracy, treatment, organization of information, literary merit, special features, illustrative materials, and multicultural aspects) serve as points on which criteria can be established for judging individual titles. Books in series and reference books raise additional questions to consider when making selection decisions.

REFERENCES

Association for Library Service to Children. "Robert F. Sibert Informational Book Medal." (January 27, 2007) Available: www.ala.org/ala/alsc/awardsscholarships/literaryawds/sibertmedal/Sibert_Medal.htm

Kristo, Janice V., and Rosemary A. Bamford. 2002. "Science Nonfiction." In *Adventuring with Books: A Booklist for Pre-K–Grade 6* edited by Amy A. McClure and Janice V. Kristo. 13th ed. Urbana, IL: National Council of Teachers of English, 1–24.

Moss, Barbara. 2003. *Exploring the Literature of Fact: Children's Nonfiction Trade Books in the Elementary Classroom.* New York: Guilford Press.

National Council of Teachers of English. "Orbis Pictus Nonfiction Award." (September 3, 2006) Available: www.ncte.org/elem/awards/orbispictus

RESOURCES

Moss, Barbara. 2003. *Exploring the Literature of Fact: Children's Nonfiction Trade Books in the Elementary Classroom.* New York: Guilford Press.
Offers teachers a guide for selecting and using nonfiction trade books in their classroom with an emphasis on reading skills. Includes students' responses to the literature.

RECOMMENDED REFERENCE BOOKS

Guinness World Records. 2000–. New York: Bantam.
This is such a popular general information handbook that some libraries keep the most recent edition in the reference collection and circulate older editions.

McGraw-Hill Children's Dictionary. 2003. New York: McGraw-Hill.
For children in elementary and middle schools, featuring easy-to-read entries. Photographs and drawings illustrate some definitions, adding to the appeal of the book.

Merriam-Webster's Primary Dictionary. 2005. Springfield, MA: Merriam-Webster.
Recommended for kindergarten up, this accessible dictionary, with its jokes and puns, has entries for concepts, plus the usual nouns and verbs.

Porter, Malcolm. 2005. *Children's Atlas of the World.* Strongville, OH: Gareth Stevens.
Provides basic data with easy-to-read maps. Fact boxes provide information about individual countries and their flags.

Reader's Digest Children's Atlas of the World. 3rd ed. 2003. Chappaqua, NY: Reader's Digest.
An introductory atlas with pictures and symbols used to communicate information. Does include pronunciation guides.

World Almanac and Book of Facts. 2005. New York: Pharos Books.
A standard "ready reference" combines traditional coverage (statistics, award winners, sports information, nature and science facts) with contemporary topics. Some colored illustrations.

World Book Encyclopedia. 1931–. Chicago, IL: World Book.
This is an accessible resource for children with its extensive number of cross-references so that information can be located without using the index. Numerous illustrations with many in color take up about one-third of the total space of the encyclopedia.

Chapter 11

Additional Subjects

In addition to criteria identified in earlier chapters, there are unique characteristics pertaining to books on particular subjects that call for additional considerations. This chapter includes alphabet books, concept books, and the following subjects: biography, "how-to-do-it," mathematics, music, science and technology, social studies, and visual arts. Some of the questions used in this chapter reflect the curriculum standards adopted by various professional organizations identified in the "References" at the end of the chapter.

EVALUATING ALPHABET BOOKS

Alphabet books have different purposes and uses. A common purpose is to teach the name and shape of letters to young children through a word and picture; sometimes there is a narrative. More advanced presentations involve the use of riddles or puzzles and engage the child in hunting for hidden pictures, locating obscure objects, and noting the positioning of letters. Other characteristics that add appeal are the use of alliteration and a rhyming text. For alphabet books that use unfamiliar objects, such as birds, or herbs, a glossary is helpful.

The alphabet also may be used to organize information about a subject or theme. Such titles are often shelved with other nonfiction titles.

Spotlight 11.1:   Choose Carefully
Spotlight on Public Libraries
Some alphabet books are showcases for artwork rather than vehicles for accurate teaching of the alphabet.

Criteria

Questions to consider for books designed to teach the name and shape of letters:

- What is the real purpose of the book?
- Who is the intended audience?
- Are objects or animals clearly presented?
- Will the child recognize the objects or animals?
- Does the author or illustrator avoid using an object that may be known by several names?
- Are upper- and lowercase letters used appropriately?
- Where is the letter placed in relation to the object or animal that illustrates it?
- Is each letter fully formed?
- Is the style of print appropriate for the audience?
- Are the words used appropriate for the audience?
- Do the organization and development of the material create a unified book?
- Is the book primarily a showcase for the artist's work?

JUDGING CONCEPT BOOKS

Concept books are designed to introduce young children to shapes, colors, sizes, a class of objects, or an abstract idea. The information may consist of photographs or other illustrations with no words or labeled images of the object. Tana Hoban's *Cubes, Cones, Cylinders, and Spheres* (Greenwillow, 2000) is an example of how a skilled photographer can present information. Concept books usually do not have story lines.

Criteria

Questions to consider in evaluating concept books:

- Is a provocative concept introduced?
- Does the book help the child see similarities and differences?
- Does it help the child see relationships?
- Does the book help a child develop a vocabulary?
- Is the object or the class of objects clear?
- Are the functions of the objects clear?
- Does the information move from familiar to unfamiliar?
- Does it move from simple to complex?

Spotlight 11.2:   Selecting for the Youngest Readers
Spotlight on Public Libraries Books for babies and toddlers provide a way for adults to introduce letters, vocabulary, and concepts. Illustrations or photographs of children of different backgrounds who are engaged in various activities should appear in your collection.

SCRUTINIZING BIOGRAPHY

Biography is a history of a person's life written by someone else based on the author's research and reading about the individual in order to portray his or her life accurately and interestingly. A person writes an **autobiography** about his or her own life. A well-written biography is a social history. Like historical fiction, it should reflect values and attitudes consistent with the time period covered.

Common elements in a biography are facts, an overriding concept or theme, and the writer's interest in and enthusiasm for the subject. Characteristics of a well-written biography are realistic, believable dialogue and accurate information. Teachers use biographies to teach about other times, provide role models, and demonstrate examples of setting personal goals.

As you think about biographies, consider a cautionary note from Betsy Harvey Kraft, author of *Mother Jones: One Woman's Fight for Labor*, who reminds us that "with any historic figure, it is often hard to separate fact from fiction" (Kraft, 1995: 3).

Biographies for children, like those for adults, include a variety of types, ranging from authentic to fictionalized biography. The writer of **authentic biographies** follows the same rules as those used in scholarly works for adults. The author provides documentation for sources of information, such as letters, diaries, videotape recordings, and eyewitness accounts. Conversations are limited to known statements by the individuals. Russell Freedman's works fall into this category.

Authors of **fictionalized biographies** also base their telling on careful research. In this type of biography, the author personalizes the subject and creates dramatic episodes through the use of imagined conversations or through expression of the character's thoughts.

Biographies vary in coverage of their subject. The most comprehensive ones, called **complete biographies**, cover the subject's life from birth to death, such as Russell Freedman's *Babe Didrikson Zaharias: The Making of a Champion* (Clarion, 1999). **Partial biographies** focus on one period, one event, or a characteristic of the subject.

In **picture book biographies** illustrations play a dominant role in presenting the information. Diane Stanley's illustrations capture the historical period, the society in which the subject lived, and the artwork of the period.

Collective biographies usually present brief sketches of several individuals. The biographies may share a common theme, be about people in similar situations, or be about individuals unrelated to one another.

Criteria

Selection of biographical works may involve applying the criteria for fiction (see Chapter 6), picture book as format (see Chapter 5), or information works (see Chapter 10). In addition, consider the following questions:

- For the biography of an individual, can the reader access a particular period of importance in the subject's life?
- Is the subject's life distorted by significant omissions?
- Is the setting authentic?
- Does the person have believable values?
- Does the person face a believable problem or goal?
- Is there a sequence of factual events that leads to an achievement or contribution or, on the other hand, to trials and tribulations?
- Does the narrative have a theme or universal truth?
- Does the writer express or imply why the subject was chosen?
- Does the author use a suitable tone with an appropriate style?
- Does the use of quotations or dialogue bring the subject to life without disrupting the flow of the text?
- Does the author create a believable person, one with strengths and weaknesses?
- Does the author avoid manipulating facts to make a more interesting story?
- Does the author avoid didactic writing and stressing particular values and attitudes?
- Does the author avoid overly glamorizing the individual?
- Does the subject's life offer interest and meaning for today's child?
- In a collective biography, if there is a common theme, how effectively is the author able to maintain that theme?
- In a collective biography, does the author indicate the criteria used to select entries? Does each subject meet the criteria?
- In a fictionalized biography, does the author inform the reader about which statements, dates, places, and names are true and which are not?
- In a fictionalized biography is the narrator's point of view appropriate, and does it enhance the story?
- Is there evidence of research on the part of the author or illustrator?
- Do photographs, drawings, maps, and other illustrative materials support or enhance the text?

> ## Spotlight 11.3: Nonfiction for Youngsters
>
> **Spotlight on Public Libraries**
>
> Even before children are assigned nonfiction books, they are curious about their world. Provide slim illustrated books about contemporary and historical figures. Parents and caregivers can then read these aloud to children.
>
> **Spotlight on School Libraries**
>
> A reminder that schools with Individualized Reading Programs (IRPs) or serving only primary grades will need nonfiction works at the beginning-to-read and early chapter book levels.

ASSESSING "HOW-TO-DO-IT" BOOKS (CRAFTS, ART, SEWING, COOKING, SPORTS)

Activity books, or those designed to inform children about how to make or do something, call for special criteria. Books dealing with magic, chemistry, and cooking should warn about hazards. The activities should rely on common and safe household ingredients. Children should be able to follow the directions and carry out the activity without adult supervision or assistance. Adults may need to gather the materials and prepare for the activity.

Criteria

Questions to consider:

- Are the directions complete and clearly written?
- Will the child be able to transfer the skills or strategies learned in the activity to another situation?
- Are there sufficient examples for the child to learn the skill or strategy?
- Is the activity worthwhile?
- Does the intended audience have the appropriate skills to perform the activities suggested?
- Is there a list of all materials and equipment that will be needed?
- Are these materials accessible to children using this book?
- Do instructions include safety rules and precautions?
- Do illustrations show each step in the process?
- Do illustrations show children doing age-appropriate procedures and adults performing more dangerous procedures?
- Do the projects encourage creativity?

- Is the finished product worth making?
- Does a cookbook provide nutritional information?
- Does the cookbook offer information about healthy eating plans?
- Are statistics used judiciously without bombarding the reader?

EXAMINING MATHEMATICS

Principles and Standards for School Mathematics (2000), from the National Council of Teachers of Mathematics(NCTM), calls for the use of children's books and for providing guides to how they can be used in teaching mathematics. For example, books can promote talking and writing about mathematics.

Remember that mathematical concepts can be found in folklore, fiction, and, yes, even poetry.

Criteria

- Does the book relate the use of mathematics to everyday life?
- Will the child learn about mathematics as a way of thinking?
- Does the book deal with numbers and operations, algebra, geometry, measurement, data analysis, and probability?
- Does the book engage the child in the processes of problem solving, reasoning and proof, and communicating?
- Is the information presented with mathematical accuracy?
- Do visual and verbal statements tell the reader what is to be counted or manipulated?
- Are the directions clear and organized in logical steps?
- Do the text and illustrations match?
- In counting books is there an open space around the numerals and objects?
- How are sets or groupings differentiated?
- In a narrative how does the author avoid losing the number concept or manipulation in the text?
- Do the illustrations give meaning to abstract mathematical principles?
- Does the content encourage interactive readers?
- How well does the book fulfill the criteria listed earlier in this chapter for how-to-do-it books?
- Does the book appeal to multiple ages?

STUDYING MUSIC

As with other subjects, one needs to consider not only books classified as music, but also biographies, picture books, poetry, and other sources of information related to music and musicians. For books about how to play an instrument, don't forget the criteria for how-to-do-it books. In the case of a collection of songs, add consideration of the organization, points of access (index, table of contents), themes, information about the background of the songs, and illustrations that capture the spirit of the songs. Consult with music teachers and musicians in evaluating these books.

Criteria

Questions to consider:

- Does the book explain the relationship between music and the other arts?
- Does the book demonstrate the relation of the music to history and culture?
- If musical scores are included, are the selections appropriate to the child's level of performance?
- Do the selections have child appeal?
- Are the type and arrangement clearly presented so the reader understands the musical notations?
- Will the child be exposed to current as well as classical musicians?
- Will the child be exposed to different styles of music?
- Will the child be exposed to music from various cultures?
- Will the book help the child learn how to evaluate music?

Spotlight 11.4: Selecting Music Books
Spotlight on Public Libraries Purchase songbooks in collections and in single illustrated versions for family use. Music shared is a popular cross-generation and cross-cultural activity. **Spotlight on School Libraries** Music teachers can help in identifying and selecting books about music and musicians.

ANALYZING SCIENCE AND TECHNOLOGY

Science books help children improve reading skills while they are learning about scientific principles. Children learn to sort through, analyze, and evaluate information. They gain understanding of the world and the relationship of science to daily living. In addition, the books can provide for individual differences when matched with a given child's learning patterns and areas of interest.

Keeping current in the fields of science and technology is a constant challenge; however, without knowledge of the field, it is hard to know if the information in the books one is selecting is accurate. A helpful source is the American Association for the Advancement of Science's *Science Books and Films* (American Association for the Advancement of Science, 1975–), which offers reviews by subject specialists. The National Science Teachers Association and Children's Book Council's annual "Outstanding Science Trade Books for Children" is another useful source for recommended titles.

Not only are developments within the field changing, but also social concerns add to the need for accurate and up-to-date information. In addressing the impact of the application of technology to the reproductive process and the real dangers of AIDS, Melissa Gross maintains,

> Children need information about homosexuality, sexual abuse, sexually transmitted disease, and contraception. . . . The need for timely information cannot be overstressed. Even very current books about AIDS have been found to give the mistaken impression that it is primarily a homosexual problem. Such misinformation can be deadly (Gross, 1995: 214).

Gross also stresses the need for books to be objective and action oriented, to make the reader aware of peer pressure, and to explain how to say No.

In the area of natural sciences there are some concepts that should be avoided:

- **Oversimplification**—concepts should not be confused with facts.
- Anthropomorphism—presenting animals as though they have human characteristics. Such personification may be appropriate for poetry and fiction but is not for science.
- **Teleology**—ascribing purpose to something in the natural environment.
- **Animism**—attributing conscious life and spirit to natural forms such as plants and rocks.

Criteria

- Is the information accurate?
- Are the depth and coverage of the information appropriate for the intended audience?
- Is terminology accurate, avoiding slang or euphemism?

- Does the author present the social and political issues involved?
- Does the author explain that science is a process, one to which the reader may contribute in the future?
- Does the book provide information about the author's background, qualifications, and other appropriate credentials?
- "What bias or perspective does the author bring to the writing?" (Kristo and Bamford, 2002: 5)
- Do books about experiments use the discovery method? Do they stress observation of scientific method, keeping records, and drawing inferences from conclusions?
- Is symbolic language interpreted?
- Are scientific abbreviations explained?
- Are directions completely and clearly written?
- Is safety stressed?
- Does the author warn about poisons or human toxicities and suggest antidotes?
- Are the ingredients recommended for use in experiments and their antidotes commonly found at home?
- Are opinion and fact clearly differentiated?
- Does the author explain the relationship among steps in an experiment?
- Is the book designed to teach or only to entertain?
- Do the visuals provide information about scientific laws and principles?
- Are correct anatomical terms used?
- Are topics such as the physical and psychological aspects of puberty treated in an objective and unemotional way?
- Does the author present different attitudes about topics such as contraception?
- Will children have an opportunity to read or consult books offering different viewpoints and values?
- Does the book provide access features (for example, index, glossary, table of contents, appended materials)?

SELECTING SOCIAL STUDIES

The area of social studies includes anthropology, archaeology, economics, geography, history, law, philosophy, political science, psychology, religion, and sociology. Children's books help build vocabulary, provide new experiences, make connections among subjects within the curriculum, provide problem-solving situations, have children engage in research, and help them develop an appreciation for informational literature. As one example, Linda K. Rogers and Karen Bromley write about the value of using children's books to develop geographic literacy. They suggest that "Teachers identify the settings of stories (e.g., location, place, and/or regions), show students where the story takes place in relation to their own location, and explain the unique characteristics of a place and/or region" (Rogers and Bromley, 1995: 1).

The National Council for the Social Studies and Children's Book Council's "Notable Social Studies Trade Books for Young People" is a helpful annual list of recommended titles.

Criteria

Questions to consider:

- Does the book address concepts of likeness and difference?
- Does it explore the relationships of time, continuity, and change?
- Does the book discuss the interplay of environment, people, and places?
- Does it explore the development of personal identity and what influences it?
- Does the book describe how institutions are formed and changed, how they influence individuals, and the potential for conflict among them?
- Does the book look at how people create and change structures of power, authority, and governance?
- Is there a glossary and pronunciation guide of terms and places?
- Do maps and other visual materials extend the text?
- Does the book describe how people organize for the production, distribution, and consumption of goods and services?
- Does it explore the relationships among science, technology, and society?
- Does the book address global connections and interdependence?
- Does it identify the ideals, principles, and practices of citizenship in a democracy?

CONSIDERING VISUAL ARTS

Art books typically focus on one of the following: 1) basic art elements or books about visual perception; 2) art history; or 3) a single topic, such as the biography of an artist, information about a specific genre, or works from an art movement. Again, each focus needs to be evaluated in terms of how effectively it fulfills its purpose for the intended audience.

Criteria

Questions to consider:

- Does the book explain the techniques and processes?
- Does it explore the relationship of the visual arts to history and cultures?

- Does the book identify the relationship between the visual arts and other disciplines?
- What is the quality of the reproductions?
- Is the format of the book manageable?
- Is the book organized chronologically, thematically, or by subject?
- Are males and females of diverse cultures included?
- How skillful is the author in involving the reader in looking, learning, and appreciating?
- Does the text offer more than brief facts?
- Does the book provide information about the present location of art originals?

Spotlight 11.5:   Selecting Art Books

Spotlight on Public Libraries

The cartoon/drawing sections may be the most frequent nonacademic requests by elementary-age children. Be prepared to supply beginning and intermediate art instruction books.

Spotlight on School Libraries

Art teachers can be a key resource in identifying, selecting, and encouraging classroom teachers to use art books.

Spotlight 11.6:   Thinking Nationally

Spotlight on School Libraries

Changes in nationally adopted curriculum guidelines and standards influence the characteristics teachers and school librarians seek in books on a particular subject.

SUMMARY

Accuracy is a basic criterion for all nonfiction books. The unique characteristics of some individual subjects call for additional considerations in their selection. For example, safety features or warnings may be critical.

REFERENCES

ArtsEdge. 1992. *National Standards for Arts Education.* (August 27. 2006) Available: http://artsedge.kennedy-center.org/teach/standards/

Gross, Melissa. 1995. "Sex Education Books for Kids, Grades K–6." *Journal of Youth Services in Libraries* 8, no. 2 (Winter): 213–216.

International Reading Association. (August 26, 2006) Available: www.ira.org

Kristo, Janice V., and Rosemary A. Bamford. 2002. "Science Nonfiction." In *Adventuring with Books: A Booklist for Pre-K–Grade 6.* 13th ed. Urbana, IL: National Council of Teachers of English.

National Council for the Social Studies and Children's Book Council. "Notable Trade Books for Young People." (August 26, 2006) Available: www.ncss.org/resources/notable

National Council of Teachers of English. 1996. *Standards for English Language Arts.* Urbana, IL: National Council of Teachers of English. (August 26, 2006) Available: www.ncte.org/standards

National Council of Teachers of Mathematics. 2000. *Principles and Standards for School Mathematics.* Reston, VA: NCTM.

National Science Teachers Association and Children's Book Council. "Outstanding Science Books for Students K-12." (August 26, 2006) Available: www.nsta.org/publications/ostb/

Rogers, Linda K., and Karen Bromley. 1995. "Developing Geographic Literacy: An Annotated List of Children's Literature." *Social Studies and the Young Learners* 8, no. 2 (November/December): 1–3.

Whitin, Phyllis, and David Whittin. 2002. "Mathematics in Our World." In *Adventuring with Books: A Booklist for Pre-K–Grade 6* edited by Amy A. McClure and Janice V. Kristo. 13th ed. Urbana, IL: National Council of Teachers of English, 176–194.

RESOURCES

California Department of Education. "Literature for Science and Mathematics: Overview." (August 27, 2006) Available: www.cde.ca.gov/ci/sc/ll/litscimathoverview.asp

Identifies over 1,400 titles considered outstanding for use with California Standards. Include titles in Spanish.

Kraft, Betsy Harvey. 1995. *Mother Jones: One Woman's Fight for Labor.* New York: Clarion.

Matthew, Kathryn I., and Joy L. Lowe. 2002. *Neal-Schuman Guide to Recommended Children's Books and Media for Use with Every Elementary Subject.* New York: Neal-Schuman.

Describes books, videos, software, CDs, cassettes, and Internet sites recommended for integrating children's literature for mathematics, science, language arts, social studies, physical education, health, art, and music. Suggests ways to use them with children. Appendix lists resources (journals, professional organizations, and Internet sites) for teachers and librarians.

Whitin, David Jackman and Phyllis. 2004. *New Visions for Linking Literature and Mathematics.* Urbana, IL and Reston, VA: National Council of Teachers of English and National Council of Teachers of Mathematics.

Provides their criteria linking them with the jointly developed standards from NCTE and IRA (International Reading Association) and those of NCTM. Evaluates individual titles and describes how they can be used in the classroom.

RECOMMENDED ALPHABET BOOKS

Cline-Ransome, Lesa. 2001. *Quilt Alphabet,* illustrated by James E. Ransome. New York: Holiday House.

The object of the uppercase letter is described in a four-line rhyming riddle and illustrated in realistic acrylic paintings. Both provide clues for the word. Letters with their words are found in the back of the book.

Demarest, Chris L. 2000. *Firefighters A to Z.* New York: Simon & Schuster.

Opening with a drawing of a firefighter in full gear, each page of pastel drawings captures the daily life of firefighters. The author's note offers additional explanations. A natural by a volunteer firefighter for the "community helpers" unit and for National Fire Prevention Month (October).

Ernst, Lisa Campbell. 2004. *The Turn-Around, Upside Down, Alphabet Book.* New York: Simon & Schuster.

Black borders frame the colored block capital letter, while the text moves around the page matching the changing object as perceptions change. An introduction to how things are perceived.

Fleming, Denise. 2002. *Alphabet under Construction.* Austin, TX: Holt.

In bold colored letters stenciled on handmade paper and with lots of action, Mouse creates the letters, as in the case of "kinks the K." Mouse obviously is having fun as he works.

Grobler, Piet. 2005. *Little Bird's ABC.* Birmingham, UK: Front Street.

Impish humorous watercolor illustrations and sounds like "Grrrr!" or sound effects like the "Plop" of a chicken's egg. The South African illustrator includes both upper- and lowercase letters on white space in a lively work that invites participation.

Hobbie, Holly. 2000. *Toot and Puddle: Puddle's ABC.* London: Little, Brown.

Puddle the pig teaches Toot the turtle the alphabet and how to print his name. Entertaining story with descriptive phrases for the letters that will help children review them. Colorful watercolor illustrations create the story and the lively actions that illustrate the letters. Letters are in upper- and lowercase. Fun to read and fun for learning.

MacDonald, Ross. 2003. *Achoo! Bang! Crash! The Noisy Alphabet*. New York: Roaring Brook Press.

Boisterous sounds accompany the comic book–style illustrations of cause-and-effect events. MacDonald uses different sizes of 19th-century wood typefaces that add to the energy on the pages. "A Note on the Type" challenges viewers to identify the one time the author used the same typeface twice.

Metropolitan Museum of Art. 2002. *Museum ABC*. London: Little, Brown.

Each letter is shown in uppercase starting a sentence and using a word beginning with that letter. On the facing page are four examples found in art. Quality reproductions with attention to the detail needed to identify each object. Book closes with a listing of all of the pictures. Provides an opportunity for older children to compare how different artists present the same subject.

Moxley, Shelia. 2001. *ABCD: An Alphabet Book of Cats and Dogs*. London: Little, Brown.

Combining photographs and paintings, each animal's activity is described in words and sounds that aid in remembering the letters, which are in upper- and lowercase. For example, Tabitha taps her tambourine with perfect timing. The book closes with the uppercase letter under the picture, providing an opportunity for children to recall the appropriate verse and alliteration.

Rose, Deborah Lee. 2000. *Into the A, B, Sea: An Ocean Alphabet*. With pictures by Steve Jenkins. New York: Scholastic.

Science writer Rose's accurate and lively descriptions of sea creatures, as they "leap" or "grab," are brightly illuminated by Jenkins's paper collage capturing the textures of the animals and plants. A brief note about each creature is found at the end of the book, along with a pronunciation guide.

Schnur, Steven. 2001. *Summer: An Alphabet Acrostic*, illustrated by Leslie Evans. New York: Clarion Books.

Companion to *Autumn: An Alphabet Acrostic* and *Spring: An Alphabet Acrostic*. Boldly colored linoleum prints provide the setting for each poetic game that describes an activity of the season. Can inspire creative writing for children from second grade up.

Seeger, Laura Vaccaro. 2003. *The Hidden Alphabet*. New York: Roaring Brook Press.

Black windows frame each letter formed by the object identified on the frame. Bold colors, inviting format, and flaps call for participation by viewers.

RECOMMENDED CONCEPT BOOKS

Blackstone, Stella. 2006. *Cleo's Color Book*, illustrated by Caroline Mockford. Cambridge, MA: Barefoot Books.

Language that involves the child, first introducing each color and then asking the child to mix them. The illustrations are large and vivid with true colors.

Catalanotto, Peter. 2005. *Kitten: Red, Yellow, Blue* New York: Altheneum.

Children learn basic colors plus a few unusual ones in this whimsical introduction to both colors and community workers.

Dahl, Micale. 2004. *One Big Building: A Counting Book about Construction*, illustrated by Todd Ouren. Mankato, MN: Picture Window Books.
Bright, appealing illustrations highlight construction equipment, workers, and aspects of the completed skyscraper. Each number appears with its name, its numeral, and its number of dots. Readers are invited to discover a hidden numeral from 1 to 12 in each picture. A glossary, an index, Fun Facts, and a Web reference with activities are included.

Doherty, Gillian. 1998. *1001 Things to Spot on the Farm*, illustrated by Teri Gower. London: Usborne.
Children can develop their vocabulary and observational skills while they practice counting people, objects, and animals across the world. Bilingual students could use the picture clues to learn English words.

Greene, Rhonda Gowler. 1997. *When a Line Bends—A Shape Becomes*, illustrated by James Kaczman. Boston, MA: Houghton Mifflin.
Watercolor and ink illustrations expand the text, inviting viewers to see ten different shapes in the world around them. This beautifully designed book and its rhymes teach with humor.

Hoban, Tana. 1986. *Shapes, Shapes, Shapes*. New York: Greenwillow.
Vivid photographs full of different shapes for children to discover. The book begins with a legend identifying each shape.

Kalan, Robert. 1979. *Blue Sea*. Illustrated by Donald Crews. New York: Mulberry.
Luminous paintings show comparative size, while repeating text emphasizes that biggest is not always the best.

Lewin, Betsy. 2003. *Cat Count*. Austin, TX: Holt.
Lively text and pictures with just enough information to entice the reader/listener to turn the page and enjoy the next rhyme and number. Enriching vocabulary and humor throughout.

Metropolitan Museum of Art. 2005. *Museum Shapes*. London: Little, Brown.
In order to find the shape on the left-hand page, a child studies a work of art on the right. The following page presents four more opportunities to find that shape. Isolating and naming the shape on the next page further reinforce the learning. Older readers will appreciate the captions at the end of the book. Each gives details of the featured artwork.

Schaefer, Carole Lexa. 2003. *One Wheel Wobbles*, illustrated by Pierr Morgan. Cambridge, MA: Candlewick Press.
Follow this eccentric family using from one to ten wheels to reach the biggest wheel of all.

Shaw, Charles G. 1947. *It Looked Like Spilt Milk*. New York: HarperCollins.
White shapes of familiar objects on a striking blue background challenge children to muse about perception versus reality. A classic.

RECOMMENDED AUTHORS AND ILLUSTRATORS

Armstrong, Jennifer. Writer of informational books and historical fiction. *Audubon* illustrated by Joseph A. Smith (Abrams, 2003). This picture-biography focuses on events in Audubon's life between 1804 and 1812. Using Audubon's personal diaries, the author acknowledges some changes to create more drama, while the illustrator identifies sources for his predominately watercolor works. Add to your read-aloud list. An earlier work, Spirit *of Endurance: The True Story of the Shackleton Expedition to the Antarctic*, illustrated by William Maughan (Crown, 2000), offers a more in-depth look at the subject. *Magnus at the Fire* (Simon & Schuster, 2005), illustrated by Owen Smith, is an example of her historical fiction accounts for young readers. *Magnus,* with its action-filled illustrations and text, appeals to horse lovers as well as those wanting to learn about earlier times.

Arnosky, Jim. Realistic illustrator and naturalist who has been recognized for his contributions to science literature (Eva L. Gordon Award) and his ability to share his enthusiasm for nature with children. *Wild and Swampy: Exploring with Jim Arnosky* (HarperCollins, 2000) received the 2001 *Orbis Pictus* Award. Through an inviting personalized text, pen-and-ink sketches, and full-color acrylic illustrations, readers learn about swamps and their inhabitants. Includes sketches from his travel journal to demonstrate how he quickly constructs subjects and scenes.

In his One Whole Day series published by the National Geographic Society (examples: *Wild Ponies,* 2002; *Wolves,* 2001) Arnosky uses acrylic wash with pencil illustrations and simple text in large print. He encourages children to observe and participate in nature through works such as *Beachcombing: Exploring the Seashore* (Dutton, 2004); *Hook, Line, and Seeker: A Beginner's Guide to Fishing, Boating, and Watching Water Wildlife* (Scholastic, 2005)—great color photographs plus his drawings—and *Field Trips: Bug Hunting, Animal Tracking, Bird-Watching, and Shore Walking with Jim Arnosky* (HarperCollins, 2002), with its usual black-and-white drawings and sketches having enough detail to get one started. Check out Arnosky at www.jimarnosky.com (August 26, 2006).

Biesty, Stephen. Illustrator and creator of the Cross-Sections Series. In *Egypt in Spectacular Cross-Section* with text by Stewart Ross (Scholastic, 2005) Biesty uses the technique of following a boy on a journey down the Nile with the illustrations showing the terrain and providing three-dimensional glimpses into the structures and the activities taking place. The text and an Egyptian calendar provide points of context for the drawings. A glossary, a list of kings and queens, and a list of the deities provide additional information. Similar works include *Rome* (Scholastic, 2003) and *Coolest Cross-Sections Ever!* (Dorling Kindersley, 2001). The latter covers a wide range of subjects from earlier times to the human body with figures active within the body creating action such as flaring the nostrils. Minimal text is characteristic of this series.

Blumberg, Rhoda. Writer of acclaimed histories and the recipient of the *Orbis Pictus* Award and the Golden Kite Award, who captures the social, cultural, and personal aspects of her subjects with appealing narrative accounts while noting what is factual and what is to be explored in the future. She provides background and contextual information for the reader, including bibliographies, sources of quotations and illustrations, location of statues, field trip sites, and Web sites. In *York's Adventures with Lewis and Clark: An African-American's Part in the Great Expedition* (HarperCollins, 2004), the focus is on York's contributions and his likely perceptions. *Shipwrecked! The True Adventure of a Japanese Boy* (HarperCollins, 2001) is an exciting journey of a young boy into the world of whaling and the contrasts of two cultures. Befriended by an American captain, Manjiro (Americanized to John Mung) proves to be a brilliant student both academically and as a sea navigator. Manjiro's background leads him to a role in the opening of Japan to American trade. The book is enhanced with quotes and drawings by Manjiro.

Freedman, Russell. Award-winning (Newbery, and so forth) nonfiction writer of science, American history, and biography. The 1998 recipient of the Laura Ingalls Wilder Award, he identifies his sources of information and photographs, uses direct quotations, provides bibliographies, identifies places to visit, and provides Web sites for readers to learn more about the subject. He includes an index of people, places, and subjects. His *In the Days of the Vaqueros: American's First True Cowboys* (Clarion, 2001) includes lines from ballads (Mexican, Chilean). In *Children of the Great Depression* (Clarion, 2005), text and photographs portray their lives. *Confucius: The Golden Rule* (Scholastic, 2002) is based on translations of *The Analects of Confucius* and is enhanced with illustrations by Frederic Clement and "sayings" by Confucius.

Gibbons, Gail. Illustrator and author whose vibrant watercolor illustrations with captions and labels, plus clear text, make information accessible to young children. Terms are explained in the text and in the glossary. Her works cover a wide range of topics. In *Dinosaur Discoveries* (Holiday House, 2005), the end pages show the locations of fossil findings around the world. The colorful illustrations (including a time line) and text provide information, comparisons with today's animals and birds, definitions, and pronunciation guides. Includes author's note and index. In *Mummies, Pyramids, and Pharaohs: A Book about Ancient Egypt* (Little, Brown, 2004), colorful watercolor illustrations, with her typical labels, present everyday life and the burial of a pharaoh in a pyramid. A description of "Ancient Egypt Discoveries" closes the book.

Giblin, James Cross. An author known for taking ordinary subjects and turning them into fascinating histories that cut across cultures. Source notes, bibliographies, and extensive indexes add to the informative nature of his works and reflect his research efforts. *The Amazing Life of Benjamin Franklin*, illustrated by Michael Dooling (Scholastic, 2000), has an accurate and inviting text. The book is enhanced with full-page oil paintings, other illustrative matter, a list of important dates in Franklin's life, descriptions of his inventions, "Sayings from

Poor Richard's Almanack," historic sites, a bibliography, an artist's note, and an index. Add this to the read-aloud list. Giblin's *Secret of the Sphinx* (Scholastic, 2004), illustrated by Bagram Ibatoulline, tells of Egypt's history and describes the roles of ancient craftsmen (men and women) and modern-day geologists.

Greenberg, Jan, and Sandra Jordan. An award-winning (Sibert, and so forth) team that covers the world of art and artists. *Action Jackson*, illustrated by Robert Andrew Parker (Roaring Brook Press, 2002), is a fictionalized account of Jackson Pollock's life in summer 1950, based on documented firsthand reports. Parker's acquaintance with Jackson is reflected in the illustrations. Includes reproductions of Pollock's works, a biographical sketch, identification of sources, biography notes, and a bibliography.

Lasky, Kathryn. Author known for clear, inviting, and carefully researched text. *Interrupted Journey: Saving Endangered Sea Turtles* has clear, detailed, and close-up photographs by her husband, Christopher G. Knight (Candlewick, 2001). Describes the role of volunteers and members of the New England Aquarium in saving this endangered species.

Man Who Made Time Travel, with illustrations by Kevin Hawkes (Farrar, Straus & Giroux, 2003), is a picture-biography paying tribute to John Harrison's life dedicated to the development and refinement of a timekeeper that could measure longitude, a tool important to sailors. Four of the five instruments are on display at the National Maritime Museum in Greenwich, England. Both author and illustrator provide bibliographies. *A Voice of Her Own: The Story of Phillis Wheatley, Slave Poet* (Candlewick Press, 2003), illustrated by Paul Lee, is a story about voice, identity, and freedom as seen in the life and poems of the first black woman published in America. An author's note, an illustrator's note, and a facsimile of Wheatley's first published book enhance the text.

Macaulay, David. An award-winning author (Newbery, and so forth) and illustrator of picture storybooks and informational books. Look for how he encourages readers/viewers to question why things look the way they do. As in the classic *Cathedral* (Houghton Mifflin, 1973), in *Mosque* (Houghton Mifflin, 2003) Macaulay uses fictional characters and information about construction details and the range of workers involved based on actual structures from the Ottoman Empire. Terms are explained in the text and by detailed drawings. Glossary. In *Angelo* (Houghton Mifflin, 2002) detailed color illustrations show the work of a master plasterer as he restores the facade of an old Roman church and establishes a friendship with a wounded pigeon.

Markle, Sandra. A writer whose clarity of text and clearly captioned and colorful photographs make her work accessible to children. Her series include Animal Predators (Carolrhoda Books), BIGGEST! LITTLEST! for younger children (Boyd Mills Press), Outside and Inside (Walker & Company), and Growing Up Wild. Her *Growing Up Wild: Penguins* (Atheneum, 2002) is typical, with its close-up shots, clear text, and glossary/index with pronunciation guide about the birth, care, growth, and education of baby Adelle penguins. From the Animal Predators series is *Killer Whales* (Carolrhoda, 2004), with typical illustrations and clear text. Markle offers clear directions and practical tips in *Family Science: Activities, Projects, and Games That Get Everyone Excited about Science!* (Wiley, 2005). Easy access is provided by the subject-organized table of contents and the extensive index. Children's books are identified in annotated bibliographies. Involves adults in the activities. Glossary of science terms.

Murphy, Jim. A recognized and respected author who portrays the feelings of the people involved in an event. He effectively uses and cites sources of illustrations (maps, photographs, and other documents) from the historical period, which help tell the story and its context. Two examples incorporating his typical enhancing features and a sense of "You are there" for the reader are *Inside the Alamo* (Delacorte, 2003) and *The American Plague: The True and Terrifying Story of The Yellow Fever Epidemic of 1793* (Clarion, 2003).

Pringle, Laurence. Author and editor on biological and environmental subjects and about people who work in those fields. He writes in an objective manner, provides glossaries, identifies agencies and organizations a reader may want to consult, lists Web sites, provides an index, and offers bibliographies including works for children. More recent titles include additional illustrations and text in the margins. *Scholastic Encyclopedia of Animals*, with color photographs by Norbert Wu (Scholastic Reference, 2001), is typical, with its pronunciation guides, descriptions of animals' characteristics and behavior, and discussion of their relationship to other living things.

A Dragon in the Sky: The Story of a Green Darner Dragonfly, illustrated by Bob Marstall (Scholastic, 2001), uses the life cycle approach, and even covers how to take care of dragonfly nymphs. A read-aloud candidate. *Dog of Discovery: A Newfoundland's Adventures with Lewis and Clark*, illustrated by Meryl Henderson (Boyd Mills, 2002), recounts in diary form, the role that Seaman played in obtaining food, protecting the camp, and making friends along the way. *Snakes: Strange and Wonderful*, illustrated by Meryl Henderson (Boyd Mills Press, 2004), is typical, with its colorful, detailed illustrations and lively text that explains unfamiliar terms.

APPENDICES

SELECTION SUPPORT TOOLS

Appendix I

Selection Terms Glossary

Accuracy: correctness of the information

Acrylic paint: water-soluble paint that dries and becomes water resistant

Action patterns in narratives: *See* cliff-hangers, sensationalism, suspense, fore-shadowing, and climax

Adapter: author who modifies traditional stories to make them accessible to contemporary readers

Alliteration: repetition of the same consonant at the beginning of words

Animal story: story in which animals behave like human beings, animals behave as animals but can talk, or animals behave as animals

Animal tale: story in which animals behave like human beings with exaggerated human characterization in order to teach a lesson

Animism: attribution of conscious life and spirit to natural forms, such as plants and rocks

Anthropomorphism: assignment of human behavior or feelings to animals

Assonance: pattern in which the same vowel sound is heard within a line or within a few lines

Asymmetrical: parts of the illustration are arranged so the shapes, patterns, and colors on either half of a central boundary are not identical

Authentic biographies: biography in which author provides documentation for sources of information and limits conversations to known statements by the individuals

Authority: refers to the qualifications of the people who created the book

Autobiography: a person writes about his or her own life

Backdrop setting: like the scenery in a drama, it sets a place for the action but doesn't take a role in the story

Balance: relationship of shapes, patterns, and colors in an illustration

Ballad: presents a simple narrative, usually relating a single episode derived from our oral tradition

Big books: oversize paperback books designed for use with large groups of children reading together

Binding: refers to how a book is encased

Biography: history of a person's life written by someone else based on his or her research and reading about the person in order to portray the individual's life accurately and interestingly

Blended books: contain fictional and factual writing

Board books: books with sturdy cardboard covers and pages

Book jackets: protective covers for a book; also provide information about a book

Chapter books: have more words and fewer pictures than the easy-to-read books and are divided into chapters

Character: a person, personified animal, or inanimate object whose actions and personal qualities are limited by that character's role in the story

Characterization: the method a writer uses to describe and reveal the characters

Chronological: time of day or days in the week are the same for all characters

Classic: a book with permanence, one that remains a favorite for more than one generation of children

Cliff-hanger: using suspense at the end of the chapter to set the stage for the next chapter

Climax: if the author does not relieve the suspense, the story

Closed ending: when the twists and turns of the story have been unraveled and the reader finds a satisfactory ending

Color: characterized by hue, intensity, and value

Complete biographies: cover the subject's life from birth to death

Concept book: term used to describe the category of books in which basic information is presented, usually for the young child

Concrete poetry: meaning is carried out by the shape of the poem or the setting of the poem

Conflict: the main character (protagonist) may face a conflict against self (internal conflict of feelings within the protagonist); nature (as seen in survival stories); a person (the antagonist); or society (the rules at one's school can represent society)

Connotation: the associations, images, or impressions that a word brings to a reader, not the literal meaning of the word

Connotative: meaning derived from the reader's association with the words

Consonance: repetition of the same consonant at the beginning of words

Contemporary realism: refers to stories about people, animals, or objects set in current times

Creation myths: stories people have told to explain creation

Cross-over books: a marketing term for books of interest to both young readers and adults

Cycle format: one book is linked to another through characters, settings, or both

Denotative: meaning of words is explicit

Denouement: point where the reader knows how the story is going to end

Diction: the writer's word choice that gives the flavor of the time, place, and events

Didacticism: instruction, often in a preachy tone

Display faces: typefaces used on title pages and for chapter headings

Double-page spread: illustration that extends over both sides of pages that face each other

Dynamic character: character who changes as a result of the impact of events

Easy readers: or beginning readers; designed for independent use by new readers and often appear in series

Edge: use of a contrasting color to distinguish the shape from the background or another object

End rhyme: where sounds at the end of the line agree

Endpapers: the first and last spreads inside the front and back covers

Episodic structure: there is a conflict and resolution in each character linked to the other chapters by characters or theme

Etching: process in which the drawings are reproduced from a metal plate on which acid has been used to create the lines

Etiological: animal tales that explain the why of natural phenomena, basing the explanation of animal traits or characteristics and customs of people

Explicit theme: theme stated by a character or flatly stated in the narrative

Expository writing: explains or sets forth information; reports events, actions, and behaviors

Fable: a brief, didactic tale in which an animal or inanimate object speaks in human language and represents different aspects of human nature

Fairy tales: imaginary tales that involve enchantment, supernatural elements, or magical powers

Fantasy: refers to authors' imaginative stories about people, animals, and objects in settings outside of our daily lives

Fantasy stories: stories that are realistic in most details but require readers who are willing to suspend their disbelief about a character, theme, or setting

Fiction: a narrative product of the writer's imagination whose purpose is to amuse, entertain, or stimulate our understanding of the human condition

Fictionalized biographies: author personalizes the subject and creates dramatic episodes through the use of imagined conversations or through expression of the character's thoughts

Figurative language: use of figures of speech to create comparison or associations; use of words in the nonliteral sense

Flat character: character is not fully developed

Folk literature: refers to stories with uncertain origins that were handed down orally from one storyteller to another

Folk poem: presents a simple narrative, usually relating a single episode derived from our oral tradition

Folklore: refers to the beliefs, manners, customs, observations, superstitions, tales, ballads, proverbs, music, and art of an earlier time

Folktales: have common tripartite structure—construction (introduction), struggle (development of the story), and major climax (the conclusion)

Foreshadowing: author provides clues to what will happen later on, providing a pattern of predictability

Form: refers to how the poem is structured and put together

Formula series: one character who appears in several volumes

Fractured fairy tales: modern humorous tales in which the reteller uses the features of the original tale while making a spoof of it

Free verse: verse that does not have a particular meter, and it may lack rhyme

Front matter: pages between the front endpapers and the first page of text; may also be illustrated

Genre: refers to a type of literature sharing common characteristics

Gouache: opaque watercolors made by mixing water directly into a powdered pigment

Graphic novel: a format for nonfiction titles as well as for novels. A graphic novel is a story told through a combination of pictures and text, usually in comic format.

Gutter: place where the two pages come together

Haiku: poems of 17 syllables arranged in three lines of 5, 7, and 5 syllables

Hero myths: a story in which the hero, who accepts a dangerous assignment, may be assisted or hindered by the gods but remains the focus of the story

High fantasy: a subcategory of fantasy; the focus is on the conflict between good and evil

Historical fiction: stories told by a contemporary about people, animals, or objects set in an earlier time period

Hue: refers to the six pure colors: red, orange, yellow, green, blue, and violet

Humorous tales: tales that revolve around a character who makes funny mistakes; also called drolls, noodleheads, sillies, and numbskulls tales

Hyperbole: exaggeration or overstatement meant to create humor or emphasis, not to be taken literally

Illustrated book: one that has occasional illustrations serving a decorative purpose rather than extending the text

Imagery: an appeal to the senses (taste, smell, hearing, touch, sight) and to the reader's emotions

Implied themes: themes that are revealed through the characters' actions and reactions

Information books: books written to inform, to lead the child from a fact or facts to a concept or a principle

Integral setting: setting that plays a role in the story and may clarify conflict or explain a character's action

Intensity: refers to the brightness or dullness (the strength) of a color, which can be made duller by adding the color opposite it on the color wheel

Interactive book: book that involves a child by asking a question, for example, or by inviting a child to repeat words or clap to the rhythm of the words

Interactive fiction: reader selects from several choices to determine the progress of the story

International literature: books originally published in countries outside the United States

ISBN: International Standard Book Number

Jobber: a company that sells books from many publishers

Leading: the white space between lines

Legend: explanation accompanying photographs or other illustrative material

Legends: tales about a specific historical event, person, or place presented as fact

Limerick: light verse, often nonsensical (humorous), about people's actions, manners, and idiosyncrasies; limericks consist of one stanza with five lines: lines one, two, and five rhyme and are of the same length; lines three and four rhyme and are of the same length but shorter than the other lines.

Line: defines an object and gives substance, shape, and mass

Linoleum block print: impression created by cutting into a linoleum block, removing pieces, and creating a raised surface (in relief); when inked, this surface pressed against the paper creates a reversed impression of the design or image.

Literary fairy tales: written by known authors

Literary merit: in narratives (fiction works), refers to how the author deals with the literary components (theme, plot, setting, character, and style)

Literary series: character is a rounded, three-dimensional person who grows and develops in the story

Lyrical poems: poet describes emotions and thoughts rather than telling a story

Manga: a type of graphic novel generally associated with Japan

Metaphor: implied comparison of dissimilar things without using *like* or *as*; one idea or object is spoken of as if it were another idea or object

Meter: formalized pattern of rhythm consisting of beats and stresses

Motif: the smallest part of a tale that exists independently, often reoccurs three or seven times in a story, although four times is characteristic of Native American tales

Multicultural literature: refers to books depicting characters from many backgrounds

Mystery stories: suspense comes from unexplained events and actions, with an explanation or resolution by the end of the story

Myths: story told as if factual but representing beliefs about supernatural forces, and told with dignity and simplicity

Narrative poems: tells a story about a particular person or event, such as in a ballad

Narrative structures: arrangement of the actions in a story: chronological order and progressive or episodical plot(s)

Nature myths: story that explains natural phenomena such as changes in seasons, characteristics of animals, earth formations, astronomy

Oil paints: mix of color pigments into an oil base

Onomatopoeia: words that imitate the name of an object or action or illustrate the word's meaning

Open ending: leaves the conclusion up to the reader

Organization: affects how easily a reader can locate information

Oversimplification: simplification that distorts the information

Page layout: refers to where the type and illustrations are placed on the page

Paperback edition: a book with a paper binding

Parable: characteristics of fable, but the main character is a human being

Partial biographies: focus on one period, one event, or a characteristic of the subject

Pastels: a soft, chalky drawing material similar to charcoal and available in a wide range of colors

Personification: assigning human attributes to things

Perspective: artist's use of lines and patterns to lead the viewer's eye to what the viewer is supposed to see

Photoessays: information through a combination of text and illustrations where both play important roles

Pictorial elements: shape, line, space, edge, color, proportion, and detail used to tell the story

Picture book: book that is usually 32 pages in length (these books may also be 48 or 64 pages) consisting primarily of illustrations

Picture book biographies: illustrations play a dominant role in presenting the information

Picture storybook: genre in which pictures and text play equal roles in telling the narrative

Plot: involves the action (what happens in the story), the story line (the sequence of events), and how the writer chooses these to present and resolve the conflict

Poetry: expresses thought and emotion by using words chosen to convey an impression of sound, often arranged in rhythmic patterns but also, at times, in abstract or free verse

Point of view: refers to the teller of the story, who may be the author or one of the characters

Poster paint: a form of tempera

Pourquoi: animal tales that explain the why of natural phenomena, basing the explanation on animal traits or characteristics and customs of people

Prebound book: a book with a reinforced binding put on prior to its being sold

Printmaking: drawn item is reversed when printed on another surface

Progressive plots: rendition of the event is dictated by dramatic structure

Proportions: the relationship of the size of one object with another, may be realistic or highly exaggerated

Protagonist: the main character

Proximity: refers to the location of various objects in relationship to one another

Realistic fiction: refers to stories with believable characters existing in realistic settings and facing problems appropriate for that time and setting

Retellers: author who modifies traditional stories to make them accessible to contemporary readers

Rhyme: a short poem for young children

Rhythm in illustration: movement expressed by repeating colors, shapes, lines, or textures

Rhythm of poetry: beat or regular cadence of the poem, which may be metered or spontaneous

Rounded character: character is three-dimensional with contradictions and realistic complexities

Science fiction: subcategory of fantasy in which scientific laws and technological inventions play a key influence in the conflict and resolution

Scope: refers to the author's goal or the purpose of the book and the breadth and depth of coverage

Scratchboard: artist scratches a picture into the surface of a two-layer board, which results in a high contrast between the remaining and scratched away areas

Selection aids: bibliographies that recommend specific titles. Also known as selection tools

Selection tools: See *Selection aids*

Sensational: story where the author does not relieve the suspense

Sentimentality: results of a writer's creating a tear-jerking situation that plays excessively on the reader's sentiments

Series books: one character who appears in several volumes

Setting: refers to when and where the story takes place and the descriptive details about the place of action

Shapes: forms created by lines, colors, and value; shapes can be flat and two-dimensional or fully rounded and three-dimensional

Silk screen: stencil created by blocking out parts of the silk, squeezing the ink through the open mesh of the silk on the paper, and creating an image that is not reversed

Simile: comparison using the words *like* or *as*; subcategory of metaphor

Source notes: notes provided by the adapter, reteller, or editor to describe the origin of the story and the changes made

Space: used by artist to create negative areas (empty) or positive (enclosed) areas

Special features: maps, tables, graphs, photographs, and other illustrative materials; additional text in the margins; glossaries, appendixes, indexes, bibliographies, and recommended reading lists—can be used independently of the main content

Static character: character who does not change

Stereotype: when a character has only a few traits and these are generally attributed to the social or racial group of which the character is a member

Stock character: character who has a specific personality trait that is often used in other stories or has a specific role in society

Style: refers to how the book is written, how the author uses words to communicate ideas, establish moods, and anticipate understanding

Suspense: raises anticipations and expectations about what will happen, when it will happen, why it happened, the solution of the problem, the outcome of events, and the well-being of the character

Symmetrical: parts of the illustration are arranged so the shapes, patterns, and colors are identical on either side of a central boundary

Tall tales: highly exaggerated accounts of exploits

Teleology: ascribing purpose to something in the natural environment

Tempura: formed by mixing colored pigment with a binder and water

Textbooks: designed for instruction in a classroom

Theme: central idea of the story, what the story means

Tone: in literature, tells us how the author feels about his or her subject, characters, and readers

Trade books: designed for library and home use

Trade edition: a hardback book, such as you find in bookstores

Transitional books: greater number of words per line, fewer illustrations, justified right margins, and longer chapters than easy readers

Translations: books translated from their original language into English

Treatment: refers to how the author presents the material

Trickster stories: feature one character that is a trickster in animal shapes

Typeface: size and style of the letters and characters of the text; the typeface affects the appearance and accessibility of the book

Unity: the result of the artist's technique in relating various parts of an illustration to one another to create an integrated whole

Value: refers to the lightness or darkness of a color and can be changed by adding white or black

Variants: versions of the same story with shared common elements, such as the plot or character, but possibly different settings or motifs

Verso: back of a page, the left-hand page

Watercolor: a powder color that mixes with water

Woodblock print: impression created by cutting into a wood block, removing pieces, and creating a raised surface (in relief); when inked, this surface pressed against the paper creates a reversed impression of the design or image.

Wordless: the story line is told entirely with pictures or with a minimum of words

Appendix 2

Master List of Resources

This bibliography supplements abbreviated versions of the Resources listings at the end of earlier chapters (noted by chapter number at the end of annotation, for example, Chapter 3) with additional entries.

The audience for all Resources is college of education and library science students, librarians (public and school), teachers, parents, caregivers, and in some cases children.

The criteria used for selecting each Resources entry include:

- Will it aid the adult in selecting and using books with children?
- Will it add to the adult's knowledge of children's literature?
- Will it help the adult gain knowledge of the child's needs?
- Will it provide inspiration or humor for the adult?
- Do resources provide sources of help and what type? (bibliographies, activities, and so forth)
- Does the handbook present information directly relating to the child's reading experience? Books promoting reading through craft activities are outside the scope.
- Does the book focus on activities that promote a child's seeking books for information, pleasure, reading development, and literacy skills?
- Is the why behind the writer's selections or position clearly stated or implied, without being theoretical?

The list includes:

- bibliographies: a key source for identifying books on various subjects, for specific audiences or specific uses
- collections of essays with descriptive and/or evaluative discussions

- reference works, such as dictionaries and encyclopedias
- children's literature surveys/texts typically covering criteria; classroom use; recommended titles (sometimes on a disc); appendices with lists of award winners, reviewing sources, Web sites, and other resources for adults
- resources identified in professional books, such as surveys of children's literature that are used as textbooks. If you're lucky, you may be able to pick up a used copy, with the database disc not opened, in the used-book section of a college bookstore.

Backes, Laura. 2001. *Best Books for Kids Who Think They Hate to Read: 125 Books That Will Turn Any Child into a Lifelong Reader*. Roseville, CA: Prima. Advice for parents and others encouraging reluctant readers ages 7–14. Especially useful are the author's "Eight Characteristics That Give Books Reader Appeal." Each book entry includes a cover photo, an excerpt, a synopsis, appeal, and suggested reading level. Provides bibliographic and genre information.

Baharona Center for the Study of Books in Spanish for Children and Adolescents. "Recommended Books." San Marcos, CA: California State University San Marcos. Available: www.csusm.edu/csb (accessed August 7, 2006).

Banta, Gratia J. 2004. "Reading Pictures: Searching for Excellence in Picture Books." *Children & Libraries* 2, no. 3 (Winter): 30–34.
Also available in *The Newbery and Caldecott Awards: A Guide to the Medal and Honor Books*, Chicago: ALA Editions, 2004. Identifies elements of design, describes how adults can increase their understanding of cultural context, and identifies ways to develop visual literacy. (Chap. 5)

Brown, David K. "Children's Literature Web Guide." Calgary, Alberta: Doucette Library of Teaching Resources University of Calgary. Available: www.ucalgary.ca/~dkbrown/index.html (accessed August 10, 2006).
Provides extensive links to information about awards, lists, authors, illustrators, publishers, booksellers, associations, conferences, events, journals, and resources for parents, teachers, storytellers, writers, and illustrators (Chapter 2).

Bruchac, Joseph. 2003. *Our Stories Remember: American Indian History, Culture, and Values through Storytelling*. Golden, CO: Fulcrum.
Commentary and recommended readings to understand the many stories from different native groups. Each chapter begins with a poem, song, or quote. Story sources, other versions of the stories, and an index are included (Chapter 3).

Campbell, Laura Ann. 1999. *Storybooks for Tough Times*. Golden, CO: Fulcrum.
Organized by themes such as "Adoption" and "Fears"; describes picture books that may help children understand the issues they are facing. Index of authors and titles (Chapter 7).

Canadian Children's Book Center. 2000. *The Storymakers: Writing Children's Books: 83 Authors Talk about Their Work*. Markham, Ontario: Pembroke.
Provides biographical information, including awards received and descriptions

of how they work. Companion volume to *The Storymakers: Illustrating Children's Books* (1999) (Chapter 2).

Carle, Eric. 1996. *The Art of Eric Carle*. New York: Philomel.
Includes his autobiography, essays about his work, a step-by-step photo essay on his collage techniques and examples of his illustrations (Chapter 5).

Christelow, Eileen. 1995. *What Do Authors Do?* New York: Clarion.
Written for children; follows an author and an illustrator from the time they get a creative idea to the publication of each book (Chapter 2).

Chukovsky, Kornei. 1963. *From Two to Five*. Translated and edited by Miriam Morton. Berkeley, CA: University of California Press.
Classic work addresses poetry as the young child's natural language (Chapter 9).

Circle of Inclusion Project. "Nine Ways to Evaluate Children's Books That Address Disability as Part of Diversity." Lawrence, KS: University of Kansas. Available: www.circleofinclusion.org/english/books/section1/a.html (accessed August 27, 2006).

Codell, Esme Raji. 2003. *How to Get Your Child to Love Reading: For Ravenous and Reluctant Readers Alike: Activities, Ideas, and Inspiration for Exploring Everything in the World through Books*. Chapel Hill, NC: Algonquin Books.
Codell is an enthusiastic, knowledgeable, and resourceful advocate for children, books, literature-based education, and making connections between authors and readers. She offers many practical suggestions, sketches of authors and illustrators, and identification of a wealth of resources. Supplemented through her Web site: PlanetEsme.com.

Coon, Cheryl. 2004. *Books to Grow With: A Guide to Using the Best Children's Fiction for Everyday Issues and Tough Challenges*. Portland, OR: Lutra Press.
Recommends for parents books of 100 pages or less in length that deal with a wide range of children's experiences, such as going to the doctor, knowing someone with Alzheimer's disease, potty training, and nuclear war.

Cullian, Bernice E., and Diane G. Person, eds. 2003. *Continuum Encyclopedia of Children's Literature*. New York: Continuum.
Articles about all aspects of children's literature, including biographical sketches of authors and illustrators, with some photographs (Chapter 2).

Day, Frances Ann. 2000. *Lesbian and Gay Voices: An Annotated Bibliography and Guide to Literature for Children and Young Adults*. Westport, CT: Greenwood Press.
Includes detailed descriptions of 275 recommended titles. Suggests guidelines for evaluating books with lesbian and gay content (Chapter 3).

Deeds, Sharon, and Catherine Chastain, eds., for the Association for Library Service to Children. 2001. *New Books Kids Like*. Chicago, IL: American Library Association.
Provides recommendations from ALSC; members arranged by type of literature, such as fractured fairy tales.

Fletcher, Ralph. 2002. *Poetry Matters: Writing a Poem from the Inside Out*. New York: HarperCollins.

Offers a guide for students and teachers to expressing emotions, images, and rhythm rather than focusing on form. Includes interviews with Kristine O'Connell George, Janet S. Wong, and J. Patrick Lewis (Chapter 9).

Fry, Edward. 2000. *How to Teach Reading: For Teachers, Parents, and Tutors.* Rev. ed. Westminster, CA: Teachers Created Resources.
This practical manual includes his Readability Graph and many handy tips, with an emphasis on the use of better literature for content and writing.

Galda, Lee, and Bernice E. Cullian. 2002. *Literature and the Child.* 5th ed. With CD-ROM database. Belmont, CA: Wadsworth.
Typical of surveys addressing teachers and students using books in the classroom setting.

Gebers, Jane L. 2003. *Books Are for Talking Too!* 3rd ed. Austin, TX: PRO-ED.
A speech-language pathologist offers teachers and parents suggestions for using low-text children's books to promote emergent literacy, communication skills, and literacy achievement.

Glazer, Joan I., and Cyndi Giorgis. 2005. *Literature for Young Children.* 5th ed. Upper Saddle River, NJ: Pearson.
For those working with children in preschool through third grade; the focus is on the child's development: language, intellect, personality, social, moral, aesthetic, and creative.

Hansen-Krening, Nancy, Elaine M. Aoki, and Donald T. Mizokawa, eds. 2003. *Kaleidoscope: A Multicultural Booklist for Grades K–8.* 4th ed. Urbana, IL: National Council of Teachers of English.
Provides criteria for the annotated recommendations of books "published from 1999–2001 featuring protagonists who are Native American, African American, Asian American, or Latino American," including bilingual and multilingual literature (Chapter 3).

Hepler, Susan, and Maria Salvadore. 2003. *Books Your Kids Will Talk About!* Washington, DC: National Education Association.
Aimed at teachers and parents. Hepler and Salvadore discuss themes and recommend uses for each annotated title. Enhanced with quotes from children, parents, and teachers.

Hopkins, Lee Bennett. 1998. *Pass the Poetry.* 3rd ed. New York: HarperCollins.
Describes activities for bringing children and poetry together. Explains how to read poetry aloud. Introduces 24 poets through a biographical sketch and their poetry (Chapter 9).

Horn Book and the Association for Library Service to Children. *The Newbery and Caldecott Medal Books: 1986–2000.* Chicago, IL: American Library Association.
Opens with essays on the medal winners, followed by reviews from *Horn Book* and *Booklist* with the medalist's acceptance speech (Chapter 1).

Huck, Charlotte et al. 2004. *Children's Literature in the Elementary School.* 8th ed. Revised by Barbara Z. Kiefer. Includes CD-ROM database. New York: McGraw-Hill.

Of the surveys for classroom teachers, this has maintained strong tie-ins to use in curriculum and discussion of individual titles and authors.

Immroth, Barbara, and Kathleen de la Pena McCook. 2000. *Library Services to Youth of Hispanic Heritage*. Jefferson, NC: McFarland.
Essays describing a variety of services to youth of Hispanic heritage. Part III covers collections, addresses Spanish-language selection issues, and identifies a selected list of distributors (Chapter 3).

"Internet Public Library." School of Information, University of Michigan. Available: www.ipl.org (accessed August 7, 2006).
Provides information for teachers and parents on a wide range of topics including authors (Chapter 2).

Jacobs, Joseph. 1993. *English Fairy Tales*. Illustrated by John Batten. New York: Knopf.
One of several volumes of world tales written in language ready for oral storytelling. Source notes (Chapter 8).

Janeczko, Paul B. 2005. *A Kick in the Head: An Everyday Guide to Poetic Forms*. Illustrated by Chris Raschka. Cambridge, MA: Candlewick.
Carefully selected accessible poems, representing 29 forms, are identified by Raschka's colorful multimedia collages and brushwork, similar to Zen calligraphy, and a witty icon. Each form is fully explained in notes at the end of the book (Chapter 9).

Janeczko, Paul B. 1999. *How to Write Poetry*. New York: Scholastic.
Offers practical suggestions and encouragement for aspiring poets, individually or in groups. Includes illustrative poems, bibliographies, and a glossary (Chapter 9).

Janson, H. W., and Anthony F. Janson. 2003. *History of Art for Young People*. New York: Abrams.
Or the authors' 1995 *History of Art*, 5th ed. (Abrams), which has 1,266 illustrations. Comprehensive in coverage, providing additional information through maps and a glossary (Chapter 5).

"Kay E. Vandergrift's Special Interest Page." New Brunswick, NJ: School of Communication, Information and Library Studies, Rutgers University. Available: www.scils.rutgers.edu/~kvander (accessed August 10, 2006).
Provides information, discussion groups, and links to authors and illustrators. An extensive resource for discussions about children's literatures and of links to sites for authors and illustrators (Chapter 2).

Knowles, Elizabeth, and Martha Smith. 2005. *Boys and Literacy*. Westport, CT: Libraries Unlimited.
Arranged by genre, including a chapter on graphic novels. Provides discussion questions and annotations of books and journal articles; and identifies bibliographies. Author and title indexes.

Kuharets, Olga R., ed. 2001. *Ventures into Cultures: A Resource Book of Multicultural Materials and Programs*. 2nd ed. Chicago, IL: American Library Association.

Various authors discuss cultures, with recommendations of fiction and nonfiction materials, including grade levels, program ideas, Web sites, and a resource list (Chapter 3).

Latrobe, Kathy H., Carolyn S. Brodie, and Maureen White. 2003. *Children's Literature Dictionary: Definitions, Resources, and Learning Activities*. New York: Neal-Schuman.

Focuses on artistic, literary, and production terms, with suggestions for related activities.

Leedy, Loreen. 2004. *Look at My Book: How Kids Can Write and Illustrate Terrific Books*. New York: Holiday House.

Written for children. Presents instructions, from getting an idea to several ways of creating the physical book. Identifies magazines that publish children's works (Chapter 2).

Leonard, Marcia. 2005. "The Start of Something Big: How an Unusual Exhibit Revolutionized the Way We View Picture-Book Art." *School Library Journal* 51, no. 9 (September): 50–55.

Describes the beginnings of the annual "The Original Art" exhibition sponsored by Society of Illustrators in New York City. Identifies locations of original artworks (Chapter 5).

Lima, Carolyn W., and John A. Lima. 2005. *A to Zoo: Subject Access to Children's Picture Books*. 7th ed. Westport, CT: Libraries Unlimited.

Index to over 27,000 titles (fiction and nonfiction) for preschoolers through 2nd graders, including 4,000 published since 2001. Access is by subject, title, author, and illustrator (Chapter 7).

"Linda Lucas Walling Collection: Materials for and/or about Children with Disabilities." BEST Center, South Carolina State Library. Available: www.libsci.sc.edu/facts/walling/bestfolder.htm (accessed September 6, 2006).

In addition to describing this collection for and about children with disabilities, the Web site provides evaluative criteria specific to categories of disability (Chapter 3).

Lindsay, Nina. 2003. "I Still Isn't for Indian." *School Library Journal* 45, no. 11 (November): 42–43.

Recommends reading several reviews for a title, seeking the advice of native people, and striving to improve the accuracy and quality of future books (Chapter 3).

Lipson, Eden Ross. 2000. *The New York Times Parent's Guide to the Best Books for Children*. 3rd ed. New York: Three Rivers Press.

Identifies 1,001 books, from wordless and early reading to those for young adults. The selections are "for adults who understand that reading is the key to the future—indeed, to the preservation of civilization—but who also read for their own entertainment and hope their children will, too" (p. xi).

Lowe, Joy L., and Matthew, Kathryn I. 2004. *Discoveries and Inventions in Literature for Youth*. Lanham, MD: Scarecrow Press.

Descriptive annotations cover a wide range of books, from picture books to young adult literature and professional resources.

Lukens, Rebecca J. 2005. *A Critical Handbook of Children's Literature*. 7th ed. Boston, MA: Allyn & Bacon.

Of the survey titles, Lukens focuses on literary qualities with her analysis and discussion of E. B. White's *Charlotte's Web*.

Lynch-Brown, Carol, and Carl M. Tomlinson. 2005. *Essentials of Children's Literature*. 5th ed. Boston, MA: Pearson.

Of the survey books focusing on classroom use of literature, this is the only one that discusses and offers criteria for selecting plays. Another unique feature is the authors' attention to international literature.

Lynn, Ruth Nadelman. 2005. *Fantasy Literature for Children and Young Adults: A Comprehensive Guide*. 5th ed. Westport, CT: Libraries Unlimited.

Author, illustrator, title, series, and subject access to annotations arranged in categories (for example, animal fantasy, high fantasy). The over 7,600 novels and story collections listed were published in English in the United States (Chapter 7).

Macaulay, David. 1999. *Building the Book Cathedral*. Boston, MA: Houghton Mifflin.

In honor of the 25th anniversary of *Cathedral*, Macaulay describes through words and illustrations the development of an idea into a book with the changes that took place (Chapter 2).

Macdonald, Margaret Read, and Brian W. Sturm. 2001. *The Storyteller's Sourcebook: A Subject, Title, and Motif Index to Folklore Collections for Children 1983–1999*. Farmington Hills, MI: Thomson Gale.

Access points include geographic or ethnic origin. Provides plots and identifies which collections contain the tale (Chapter 8).

Marantz, Sylvia, and Ken Marantz. 2005. *Multicultural Picturebooks: Art for Illuminating Our World: 1997–2004*. 2nd ed. Lanham, MD: Scarecrow Press.

Describes selected titles organized geographically. Provides a chapter on multicultural and cross-cultural experiences. Indexes by author, illustrator, title, and subject (Chapter 3).

Matthew, Kathryn I., and Joy L. Lowe. 2002. *Neal-Schuman Guide to Recommended Children's Books and Media for Use with Every Elementary Subject*. New York: Neal-Schuman.

Describes books, videos, software, CDs, cassettes, and Internet sites recommended for integrating children's literature for mathematics, science, language arts, social studies, physical education, health, art, and music. Suggests ways to use them with children. Lists resources (journals, professional organizations, and Internet sites) for teachers and librarians (Chapter 11).

McClure, Amy A., and Janice V. Kristo, eds. 2002. *Adventuring with Books: Books for Pre-K–Grade 6*. 13 ed. Urbana, IL: National Council of Teachers of English.

This outstanding bibliography covers fiction and nonfiction on many subjects, with consideration of our diverse society. The books were child tested, and the evaluative annotations are enhanced by the children's opinions. (All chapters)

Moss, Barbara. 2003. *Exploring the Literature of Fact: Children's Nonfiction Trade Books in the Elementary Classroom*. New York: Guilford Press.

Offers teachers a guide for selecting and using nonfiction trade books in their classroom, with an emphasis on reading skills. Includes students' responses to the literature (Chapter 10).

Multicultural Review: Dedicated to a Better Understanding of Ethnic, Racial, and Religious Diversity. 1992. Westport, CT: Greenwood.

Articles and reviews of multicultural materials. December issue includes cumulative index for that year. Subscription information available at www.mcreview.com (accessed August 26, 2006) (Chapter 3).

Nash, Jennie. 2003. *Raising a Reader: A Mother's Tale of Desperation and Delight*. New York: St. Martin's Press.

Nash recalls her experiences, expectations, and concerns over her attempts to have her daughters become readers who will share her enthusiasm. Offers ways to encourage reading and lists of resources for parents.

Odean, Kathleen. 2003. *Great Books for Babies and Toddlers: More than 500 Recommended Books for Your Child's First Three Years*. New York: Ballantine Books.

Aimed at parents, with suggestions for reading aloud and other activities with one or more children. Her earlier bibliographies include *Great Books about Things Kids Love: More than 750 Books for Children 3 to 14* (Ballantine, 2001); *Great Books for Girls: More than 600 Recommended Books for Girls Ages 3–13* (rev. ed., Ballantine, 2002); and *Great Books for Boys: More than 600 Books for Boys 2 to 14* (Ballantine, 1998).

Park, Linda Sue. 2005. *Project Mulberry*. New York: Clarion.

Two stories in one. Alternating chapters, with one telling a contemporary growing-up story and the other a dialogue between one of the characters and the author, providing insight into the creative writing process (Chapter 2).

Prelutsky, Jack. 2005. *Read a Rhyme, Write a Rhyme*. Illustrated by Meilo So. New York: Knopf.

Provides a starting point for writing poems on various subjects. Suggests what one might write for some poems and offers ideas on possible rhyming words and for different approaches for the same beginnings of a poem (Chapter 9).

Reading Is Fundamental. 2005. *The Art of Reading: Forty Illustrators Celebrate RIF's 40th Anniversary*. With a foreword by Leonard S. Marcus. New York: Dutton.

Illustrators describe a children's book that influenced them and offer their illustration for that work. Enhanced by photographs of the illustrators and of books they knew as a child (Chapter 5).

Rockman, Connie C., ed. 2004. *Ninth Book of Junior Authors and Illustrators*. New York: H. W. Wilson.

Includes statement by each author and illustrator, biographical information, bibliography of representative works, list of suggested readings, and Web sites. The index covers this edition and others in the Junior Book of Authors series since the second edition in 1951 (Chapter 2).

Schon, Isabel. 2003. *The Best of Latino Heritage, 1996–2002: A Guide to the Best Juvenile Books about Latin People and Cultures*. Lanham, MD: Scarecrow Press.
Arranged by country. Evaluative annotations suggest grade level. Indexed by subject, title, author, grade level, and series (Chapter 3).

Scieszka, Jon. 1998. "Design Matters." *Horn Book Magazine* 74, no. 2 (March/ April): 196–208.
Through text and illustrations describes the role and the influence of the designer in creating a picture book (Chapter 2).

Seale, Doris, and Beverly Slapin, eds. 2005. *A Broken Flute: The Native Experience in Books for Children*. Walnut Creek: Altamira Press; Berkeley, CA: Oyate.
A collection of essays, poems, reviews, and criteria for evaluating children's books depicting native life. Both recommended and nonrecommended titles are critiqued for authenticity and accuracy. Over 400 children's and teen titles are examined (Chapter 3).

Shulevitz, Uri. 1997. *Writing with Pictures: How to Write and Illustrate Children's Books*. New York: Watson-Guptill.
An excellent resource based on his works and teaching (Chapter 5).

Silvey, Anita. 2002. *The Essential Guide to Children's Books and Their Creators*. Boston, MA: Houghton Mifflin.
Focuses on contemporary American authors and illustrators, with updates of information on these individuals from her earlier work, *Children's Books and Their Creators* (Houghton Mifflin, 1995). Both works include essays by some of the creators (Chapter 2).

Smith, Henrietta. 2004. *The Coretta Scott King Awards: 1970–2004*. Chicago, IL: American Library Association.
Traces the history of the awards. Provides biographical information about the African American authors and illustrators receiving the awards (Chapter 3).

Stan, S., ed. 2002. *The World through Children's Books*. Lanham, MD: Scarecrow Press.
Companion work to *Children's Books from Other Countries*, edited by Carl M. Tomlinson (1998). The earlier book covered works published from 1950 to 1996; the newer one covers 1996 to 2000 publications. Provides an overview of international children's literature and descriptive annotations for recommended titles; identifies other resources: children's book awards, organizations, publishers, and distributors of foreign-language and bilingual books. Indexes include those for author, illustrator, title, translator, and subject (Chapter 3).

Steiner, Stanley F. 2001. *Promoting a Global Community through Multicultural Children's Literature*. Englewood, CO: Libraries Unlimited.
Annotated bibliography, arranged by subject, includes picture books, fiction,

and nonfiction. Suggests activities. Provides information on publishers of multicultural materials and resources for infusing literature into content areas (Chapter 3).

Temple, Charles, et al. 2002. *Children's Books in Children's Hands*. 2nd ed. Includes CD-ROM database. Boston, MA: Allyn & Bacon.
Focuses on classroom use, with discussions of "literature circles." Includes interviews with authors, illustrators, and editors.

The Newbery and Caldecott Awards: A Guide to the Medal and Honor Books, 2006 Edition. Chicago, IL: American Library Association.
Includes Sue McCleaf Nespeca's essay "Sharing Picture Books with Children to Promote Art Appreciation." Descriptive annotations for each book. Lists media used in the Caldecott books (Chapter 1).

The Stories of Hans Christian Andersen. 2003. Translated by Diane Crone Frank and Jeffrey Frank. Boston, MA: Houghton Mifflin.
Notes follow each story. Translators intend to restore the essentially Danish colloquial voices of the tales. Includes the original illustrations by Vilhelm Pedersen and Lorenz Frolich (Chapter 8).

Tomlinson, Carl M., ed. 1998. *Children's Books from Other Countries*. Lanham, MD: Scarecrow. Sponsored by the United States Board on Books for Young People.

Tomlinson, Carl M., and International Children's Books on Literature Committee. 2002. "International Children's Books on Literature" in *Adventuring with Books: A Booklist for Pre-K–Grade 6*. 13th ed. Edited by Amy A. McClure and Janice V. Kristo. Urbana, IL: National Council of Teachers of English.

Trevino, Rose Zertuche. 2006. *The Pura Belpre Awards: Celebrating Latino Authors and Illustrators*. With DVD. Chicago, IL: American Library Association.
Provides a history of the award and the work of Pura Belpre, describes the award winners, includes biographical sketches, and suggests booktalks and activities. Identifies other resources (Chapter 3).

VandeKieft, Lynette. "Historical Fiction in the Elementary School Classroom." Master of Arts in Literacy Instruction Program. East Lansing, MI: Michigan State University.
Includes several links to aid selection. Available: www.msu.edu/~vandeki3 (accessed September 6, 2006) (Chapter 7).

Ward, Marilyn. 2002. *Voices from the Margins: An Annotated Bibliography of Fiction on Disabilities and Differences for Young People*. Westport, CT: Greenwood.
Evaluative descriptions of 200 books for children (K–12) published between 1990 and 2001. Access by title, author, age level, and subject (Chapter 3).

Webber, Desiree, and Sandy Shropshire. 2001. *The Kids' Book Club: Lively Reading and Activities for Grades 1–3*. Westport, CT: Libraries Unlimited.
Provides procedures for handling activities based on 15 titles, including information about the author and/or illustrator, suggested discussion questions, and a list of related titles.

Whitin, David Jackman, and Phyllis Whitin. 2004. *New Visions for Linking Literature and Mathematics*. Urbana, IL: National Council of Teachers of English; Reston, VA: National Council of Teachers of Mathematics.

Provides criteria linking the recommended titles with the jointly developed standards from NCTE and IRA (International Reading Association) and those of NCTM. Evaluates individual titles and describes how they can be used in the classroom (Chapter 11).

York, Sherry. 2002. *Children's and Young Adult Literature by Latino Writers: A Guide for Librarians, Teachers, Parents and Students*. Worthington, OH: Linworth Publishing.

Nonevaluative listing with bibliographic information, ordering information, number of chapters, summary, subjects, genre/form, setting, interest level, reading level, test coverage, where reviewed, awards, and inclusion on lists (Chapter 3).

Zipes, Jack, ed. 2000. *Oxford Companion to Fairy Tales: The Western Fairy Tale Tradition from Medieval to Modern*. Oxford: Oxford University Press.

Entries arranged in dictionary style provide access to illustrators, authors, subjects, and countries (Chapter 8).

Appendix 3

Organizations That Support Children's Books

Many organizations are interested in children's books; their creation and use. This listing is only a beginning. Be sure to check out other groups, including

- local public library
- state library and state department of education or public instruction
- professional association at the state, national, and international level
- publishers' Web sites, which often have information about their authors and illustrators
- bookstores and Internet-based sellers

Academy of American Poets
584 Broadway, Suite 604
New York, NY 10012
212–274–0343
Fax: 212–274–9427
E-mail academy@poets.org
www.poets.org (accessed August 7, 2006)
 Academy of American Poets, Sponsor of National Poetry Month since April 1994. "National Poetry Month": www.poets.org/php/prmID/41 (accessed August 7, 2006)
 "Poetry Month FAQ": www.poets.org/php/prmID/47 (accessed August 7, 2006) This event is observed by schools, libraries, and bookstores throughout the United States (Chapter 9).

American Association for the Advancement of Science, AAAS

1200 New York Avenue NW
Washington, DC 20005
202–326–6400
webmaster@aaas.org
www.aaas.org (accessed August 7, 2006)
   Publishes *Science Books & Films* (ISSN 0098–324X, five issues per year). American Association for the Advancement of Science, 1975–. Best Lists available: www.sbfonline.com (accessed August 7, 2006) (Chapter 11).

American Homeschool Association

Box 3142
Palmer, AK 99645
800–236–3278
www.americanhomeschoolassociation.org (accessed August 7, 2006)
   Publishes *Home Education Magazine* (ISSN 0888–4633, six issues per year), available online at www.homeedmag.com/blogs/resources/ (accessed August 7, 2006).

American Library Association, ALA

50 East Huron Street
Chicago, IL 60611
800–545–2433
Fax: 312–440–9374
ala@ala.org
www.ala.org (accessed August 27, 2006)
   Journals: for example, *Booklist: Includes Reference Books Bulletin; Book Links; Children & Libraries.*

ArtsEdge

John F. Kennedy Center for the Performing Arts
2700 F Street, NW
Washington, DC 20566
aoi@artsedge.kennedy-center.org
http://artsedge.kennedy-center.org/ (accessed August 7, 2006)
   National Standards for Arts Education, available online at: www. artsedge. kennedy-center.org/teach/standards (accessed August 7, 2006) (Chapter 11).

Association for Library Service to Children, ALSC

American Library Association
50 East Huron Street
Chicago, IL 60611
800–545–2433 ext. 2163
Fax: 312–280–5271

alsc@ala.org

www.ala.org/ala/alsc/alsc.htm (accessed August 7, 2006)

Batchelder Award: "The Mildred L. Batchelder Award." www.ala.org/ala/alsc/
awardsscholarships/literaryawds/batchelderaward/batchelderaward.htm (accessed
September 6, 2006) (Chapter 3).

Belpre Award: "The Pura Belpre Award." www.ala.org/Template.cfm?Section=
bookmediaawards&template=/ContentManagement/ContentDisplay.
cfm&ContentID=147610 (accessed September 6, 2006) (Chapter 3).

Caldecott Medal: "Welcome to the Caldecott Medal Home Page!" Chicago:
Association for Library Service to Children. www.org/ala/alsc/awardssholarships/
literaryawds/caldecottmedal (accessed January 27, 2007). Provides information
about the award and honor books (Chapter 5).

Newbery Medal: "Newbery Medal & Honor Books, 1922—Present."
www.ala.org/alsc/awardsscholarships/literalawds/newberymedal/newberyhonors/
newberymedal.htm (accessed January 27, 2007) (Chapter 1).

"Notable Children's Books" by Notable Children's Book Committee of the Association for Library Service to Children (ALSC), a division of the American Library Association, is published in the March issue of *School Library Journal*.
www.ala.org/ala/alsc/awardsscholarships/childrensnotable/notablecbooklist/current
notable.htm (accessed January 27, 2007) (Chapter 4).

"Robert F. Sibert Informational Book Medal." www.ala.org/ala/alsc/
awardsscholarships/literaryawds/sibertmedal/Sibert_Medal.htm (accessed January
27, 2007) (Chapter 10).

Wilder Award: "The Laura Ingalls Wilder Award." www.ala.org/ala/alsc/
awardsscholarships/literaryawds/wildermedeal/wildermedal/htm (accessed September 6, 2006) (Chapter 2).

Canadian Children's Book Centre, CCBC

Suite 101, 40 Orchard View Blvd.

Toronto, Ontario M4R 1B9

416–605–0010

Fax: 416–975–8970

info@bookcentre.ca

www.bookcentre.ca (accessed August 7, 2006)

Promotes writing and illustrating for children, offers publications in print and
online, provides reviews, maintains a reference library, and for its members offers research services. Provides guides to children's books and information about
Canadian children's authors, illustrators, and the book trade (Chapter 2).

Children's Book Council, CBC

12 West 37th St., 2nd Floor

New York, NY 10018

212–966–1990

Fax: 888–807–9355

www.cbcbooks.org (accessed August 7, 2006)

Provides information about children's trade books, publishers, authors, illustrators, as well as a directory of sites for authors and illustrators.

"Choices Booklists: Children's Choices." The 2005 annotated list appeared in the October issue of *The Reading Teacher*. www.reading.org/resources/tools/choices_childrens.html (accessed August 10, 2006) (Chapter 2).

"Notable Trade Books for Young People," by a Book Review Committee of the National Council for the Social Studies in cooperation with the Children's Book Council. The list is published in the April/May issue of *Social Education*. www.socialstudies.org/resources/notable (accessed August 7, 2006) (Chapter 11).

"Outstanding Science Trade Books for Students K–12." A cooperative effort of the National Science Teachers Association and the Children's Book Council. The list is published in the March issue of *Science & Children*. www.nsta.org/ostb (accessed August 10, 2006) (Chapter 11).

Cooperative Children's Book Center, CCBC

School of Education
University of Wisconsin-Madison
600 North Park Street, Room 4290
Madison, WI 53706
608–263–3720
Fax 608–262–4933
www.education.wisc.edu/ccbc/ (accessed August 7, 2006)

"Fifty Multicultural Books Every Child Should Know" plus lists and links to multicultural award Web sites. The Alternative Press Collection, listed in the center's MADCAT, contains over 1,700 books from 325 small presses (Chapter 3).

Eric Carle Museum of Picture Book Art

125 West Bay Road
Amherst, MA 01002
413–658–1100
Fax: 413–658–1139
info@picturebookart.org
www.picturebookart.org (accessed August 7, 2006)

Provides information about the museum and features illustrators (Chapter 5).

International Board on Books for Young People, IBBY

Nonnenweg 12, Postfach
CH–4003 Basel, Switzerland
(1011) 272–2917
Fax: (1011) 272–2757
ibby@ibby.org
www.ibby.org (accessed August 7, 2006)

Publishes *Bookbird: The Journal of International Children's Literature* (Chapter 3). Sponsors "Hans Christian Andersen Awards." www.ibby.org/index.php?id=273 (accessed August 7, 2006). Provides link to USBBY, the United States section.

International Reading Association, IRA
800 Barksdale Road
Box 8139
Newark, DE 19714
800–336–7323
Fax: 302–731–1057
pubinfo@reading.org
www.reading.org (accessed August 7, 2006)

Sponsors an annual list of 25 "Notable Books for a Global Society" (fiction, nonfiction, and poetry for K–12). Criteria for the inclusion is given on the Web site. The list is published in the fall issue of *Dragon Lode.*

Also sponsors "Choices Booklists: Children's Choices." The 2005 annotated list appeared in the October issue of *The Reading Teacher.* www.reading.org/resources/tools/choices_childrens.html (accessed August 10, 2006)

Includes "IRA Children's Book Awards," "Focus on Beginning Readers: IRA Programs and Resources" (Chapter 11).

Library of Congress
101 Independence Ave, SE
Washington, DC 20540
202–707–5000
www.loc.gov (accessed August 10, 2006)

Also see the American Folklife Center at www.loc.gov/folklife, which provides title, subject, geographical, and distributor access to information on the world's cultures. Entries, such as "Asian American" provide "Teacher's Guide to Folklife Resources," lesson plans, and titles for further study (Chapter 8).

National Art Education Association, NAEA
1916 Association Drive
Reston, VA 20191
703–860–8000
Fax: 703–860–2960
jfleming@naea-reston.org
www.naea-reston.org (accessed August 26, 2006)
Publishes *Journal of Art Education.* (Chapter 11).

National Association for the Education of Young Children, NAEYC
1313 L Street, NW, Suite 500
Washington, DC 20005
800–424–2460, or 202–232–8777

Fax: 202–328–1846
webmaster@naeyc.org
www.naeyc.org (accessed August 26, 2006)
Publishes *YC: Young Children,* covering birth through age 8.

National Book Foundation
95 Madison Avenue, Suite 709
New York, NY 10016
212–685–0261
Fax: 212–213–6570
www.nationalbook.org (accessed August 26, 2006)
　Sponsors the National Book Awards.

National Council for the Social Studies, NCSS
8555 Sixteenth Street, Suite 500
Silver Springs, MD 20910
301–588–2049
Fax: 301–588–2049
information@ncss.org
www.ncss.org (accessed August 26, 2006)
　Carter G. Woodson Book Award and Honor Book Recipients. www.socialstudies.org/awards/woodson (accessed August 26, 2006)
　Expectations of Excellence: Curriculum Standards for the Social Studies. Online. Washington, DC: National Council for the Social Studies. www.ncss.org/standards (accessed August 26, 2006) (Chapter 11).
　"Notable Trade Books for Young People" by a Book Review Committee of the National Council for the Social Studies in cooperation with the Children's Book Council. The list is published in the April/May issue of *Social Education.* www.socialstudies.org/resources/notable (accessed August 26, 2006) (Chapters 4, 11).
　Publishes *Social Studies and the Young Learner* (Chapter 11).

National Council of Teachers of English, NCTE
1111 W. Kenyon Road
Urbana, IL 61801
217–328–3870 or 877–369–6283
Fax: 217–328–9645
www.ncte.org (accessed August 26, 2006)
　National Council of Teachers of English (NCTE) and the International Reading Association (IRA). *Standards for English Language Arts* (Chapter 11).
　"Orbis Pictus Nonfiction Award." www.ncte.org/elem/awards/orbispictus (accessed August 26, 2006) (Chapter 5).

National Council of Teachers of Mathematics, NCTM
1906 Association Drive
Reston, VA 20191
703–620–9840
Fax: 703–476–2970
webmaster@nctm.org
www.nctm.org (accessed August 26, 2006)
   Publishes *Teaching Children Mathematics, Principles and Standards for School Mathematics* (Chapter 11).

National Research Council
National Academy of Sciences
500 Fifth Street NW
Washington, DC 20001
www.nationalacademies.org/nrc/ (accessed August 26, 2006)
   National Research Council. 1996. *National Science Education Standards.* Online at: http://books.nap.edu/catalog.php?record_id=4962 (accessed August 26, 2006) (Chapter 11).

National Science Teachers Association, NSTA
1840 Wilson Boulevard
Arlington, VA 22201
730–243–7100
www.nsta.org (accessed August 26, 2006)
   Publishes *Science and Children.* National Science Teachers Association and Children's Book Council. "Outstanding Science Books for Children." "Outstanding Science Trade Books for Students K–12" is a cooperative effort of the National Science Teachers Association and the Children's Book Council. The 2005 list was published in the March issue of *Science & Children.* www.nsta.org/publications/ostb (accessed August 26, 2006) (Chapters 4, 11).

Oyate
2702 Mathews St.
Berkeley, CA 94702
510–848–6700
Fax: 510–848–4815
oyate@oyate.org
www.oyate.org (accessed August 26, 2006)
   "Oyate is a native organization working to see that our lives and histories are portrayed honestly, and so that all people will know our stories belong to us." Oyate evaluates and distributes materials, conducts workshops, and manages a small resource center (Chapter 3).

Society of Illustrators
Museum of Illustration
128 East 63rd Street
New York, NY 10021
212–838–2560
Fax: 212–838–2561
info@societyillustrators.org
www.societyillustrators.org (accessed August 26, 2006)
    Provides biographical information about its members and honorees (Chapter 5).
USBBY (see International Board on Books for Young People, IBBY).

Appendix 4

Selection Policy Statements and Resources

Collection development statements and selection policy statements help guide our selection decisions, whether we work in a public or school library. Our environment influences the weight or emphasis we give to each selection criterion. Both institutions may look for books reflecting the ethnic diversity of the community and the need of children to become familiar with other ethnic groups and cultures, but they may not emphasize certain criteria at that level.

Public libraries tend to focus on criteria relating to content, artistic merit, and development of literacy skills of books for recreational and informational use. In relating the Association for Library Service to Children's core competencies to practice, Rosanne Cerny, Penny Markey, and Amanda Williams describe a children's collection as one that "promotes an appreciation of art and literature and introduces other cultures, times, and lifestyles." Collections

> hold materials that young customers *want* [original in italics] to read. This does not mean, however, that the library provides only popular materials or bestsellers. Philosophically it means that libraries encourage children's imaginations, their interests, and their curiosity. It implies that we have more wide-range collections than a school library, for example, which primarily contains curriculum support (Cerny, Markey, and Williams, 2006: 35, 42).

This emphasis on literary and artistic merit is in contrast to a school with a learner-centered collection. Sandra Hughes-Hassell and Jacqueline C. Mancall point out that the same basic selection criteria apply; however, the emphasis in all selection decisions is on whether the resources match learner characteristics and address the teaching-learning context. This means that certain criteria, such as appropriateness, scope, treatment, and arrangement, become more central to the decision-making process, while other criteria, such as literary quality, reputation of the author or illustrator, aesthetic quality, and physical quality, may become less important. In other words, selection shifts from purchasing "the best" to purchasing the "most appropriate" (Hughes-Hassell and Mancall, 2005: 43).

As you read this sampling of statements, think about which criteria you would use to achieve your objectives. Lists of statements usually are preceded by phases such as "the materials should," "books will be selected that," or "library media materials should." Here are some selection phrases:

- Be accessible to students of varied abilities, and meet informational and interest needs of all students.
- Be relevant to today's world.
- Author has expertise in the subject matter.
- Material is current.
- Has the potential to be heavily used.
- Information is accurate.
- Treatment is balanced.
- Have appropriate access points, indexes, and cross-references.
- Have readable print.
- Experts would agree this is a good source.
- Have aesthetic, literary, or social value.
- Represents artistic, historic, and literacy qualities.
- Reflects the problems, aspirations, attitudes, and ideals of society.
- Contributes to the instructional program's objectives.
- Be appropriate for the age, ability level, and social and emotional development of the intended user.
- Be appropriate for the subject area.
- Meet quality standards in terms of content, format, and presentation.
- Physical format and appearance of materials shall be suitable for their intended use.

A common element in selection policies is the endorsement of intellectual freedom. This often includes a copy of "The Library Bill of Rights" and the identification of other documents issued by the Office for Intellectual Freedom of the American Library Association. Taking a position on intellectual freedom provides the basis for all selection decisions and also serves as a first line of defense when books are challenged.

RESOURCES

Arizona State Library, Archives and Public Records. "Collection Development Training for Arizona Public Libraries." Available: www.lib.az.us/cdt/index.htm (accessed August 28, 2006).

Aimed at small and rural public libraries, the training covers collection development including selection considerations and evaluation criteria for book selection.

Becker, Beverly C., and Susan M. Stan, for the Office of Intellectual Freedom of the American Library Association. 2002. *Hit List for Children 2: Frequently Challenged Books.* Chicago, IL: American Library Association.

Continues *Hit List: Frequently Challenged Books for Children,* by Donna Reidy Pistolis (American Library Association, 1996). Describes 20 titles or series in terms of content, quotes from reviews, and recognitions, such as "Best book of the year"; traces the challenges; lists where reviewed; identifies references about the author and/or illustrator; and cites other sources recommending the book or series.

Cerny, Rosanne, Penny Markey, and Amanda Williams. 2006. *Outstanding Library Service to Children: Putting the Core Competencies to Work.* Chicago, IL: American Library Association.

Relates competencies developed by the Association for Library Service to Children to practice. One example is "Demonstrates a knowledge and appreciation of children's literature, periodicals, audiovisual materials, Web sites, and other electronic media, and other materials that constitute a diverse, current, and relevant children's collection" (Cerny at al., 2006: 33).

Hughes-Hassell, Sandra, and Jacqueline C. Mancall. 2005. *Collection Management for Youth: Responding to the Needs of Learners.* Chicago, IL: American Library Association.

Describes the implications of using a learner-centered collection management approach in response to the vision of a learning environment that develops information literacy. This vision is the focus of the national guidelines *Information Power Building, Partnerships for Learning* (American Association of School Librarians and Association for Educational Communications and Technology, 1998). Covers policy elements and selection criteria (intellectual content, physical format, and other considerations).

Office of Intellectual Freedom (OIF) of the American Library Association home page. Available: www.ala.org/ala/oif (accessed September 6, 2006).

Provides links to the wealth of resources and documents available, including the "Library Bill of Rights." To view the various statements, see www.ala.org/ala/oif/statementspols/ (accessed September 6, 2006), "IFC Guidelines and Other Statements." Also includes materials designed for parents; see "For Children and Their Parents" at www.ala.org/ala/oif/foryoungpeople (accessed September 6, 2006). A key publication is the *Intellectual Freedom Manual* 7th ed. Chicago, IL: American Library Association, 2006. Includes the interpretations and history of documents relating to "The Library Bill of Rights," including "Access for Children and Young People to Nonprint Formats," "Access to Resources and Services in the School Library Media Program," and "Free Access to Libraries for Minors." Of particular interest is Theresa Chmara's essay "Minors' First Amendment Rights to Access Information." Describes the services and resources of OIF, including online ones and state contacts. Glossary.

"Resources for School Librarians." Available: www.sldirectory.com (accessed August 27, 2006).
Provides links to collection development policies and other sources dealing with selection and other aspects of school librarianship.

Van Orden, Phyllis J., Kay Bishop, and Patricia Pawelak-Kort. 2001. *The Collection Program in Schools: Concepts, Practices, and Information Sources*. 3rd ed. Englewood, CO: Libraries Unlimited.
Describes the development of a collection development policy, including a selection policy, and identifies selection criteria.

Wood, Richard J., and Frank Hoffman. 1996. *Library Collection Development Policies: A Reference and Writer's Handbook*. Lanham, MD: Scarecrow Press.
Includes policies from school and public libraries: Fairbanks North Star Borough (Alaska) Public Library, Haltom City (Texas) Public Library, Houston (Texas) Public Library, Mickey Reily (Corrigan, Texas) Public Library, Brazosport Independent School District (Freeport, Texas), Cypress-Fairbanks (Texas) Independent School District, and Jennings County (Indiana) Schools.

Author Index

Includes authors, compilers, editors, translators, poets, and organizations. Illustrators are listed in the illustrator index, but some also appear here. For lists of award-winning authors, please see pp. 11, 23, 68, 141, 151, and 153.

Illustrator Index

This index includes photographers, like Tana Hoban, and paper engineers, like Robert Sabuda. Illustrators, who are also authors, may be on this index and the author index. For a list of the Caldecott Award-winning illustrators, please see p. 68.

Title Index

Titles include books in italics with electronic sources and articles in quotation marks. For lists of award-winning titles, please see pp. 11, 23, 68, 141, 151, and 153.

Subject Index

About the Authors

Phyllis J. Van Orden's career includes experience as a school librarian, children's librarian, and library educator. Her Master of Arts in Library Science degree is from the University of Michigan, and her Doctorate in Education is from Wayne State University.

Van Orden's selection activities include service on the Newbery and Caldecott committees, editor of a number of editions of *Elementary School Library Collection*, and author of other publications. She served as President of the Association for Library Service for Children.

Sunny Strong selected children's books for Montgomery County Public Libraries in Maryland after earning her Master of Library Science degree at the University of Maryland. From 1985 to 1997, as Manager of Children's Services for Sno-Isle Libraries, she purchased materials for 19 locations.

The purpose of her teaching and writing is to identify quality, relevant books children will enjoy. Strong has taught at the University of Washington and Seattle Public University. Her present work includes recommending books to families at the public library, to those who work with children in child-care centers, and to children using the book loft at Imagine Children's Museum in Everett, Washington.